Generating Referring Expressions

ACL–MIT Press Series in Natural Language Processing
Aravind K. Joshi, Karen Sparck Jones, and Mark Y. Liberman, editors

Generating Referring Expressions
Constructing Descriptions in a Domain of Objects and Processes

Robert Dale

A Bradford Book
The MIT Press
Cambridge, Massachusetts
London, England

Set from electronic files provided by the author.
Printed and bound in the United States of America.

Library of Congress Cataloging-in-Publication Data

Dale, Robert, 1959–
  Generating referring expressions: constructing descriptions in a domain of objects and processes / Robert Dale.
      p.   cm.—(ACL-MIT Press series in natural language processing)
  "A Bradford book."
  Includes bibliographical references and index.
  ISBN 0-262-04128-6
  1. Reference (Linguistics)—Data processing. 2. EPICURE (Computer system).
3. Discourse analysis—Data processing. 4. Cookery—Data processing. I. Title.
II. Series.
P325.5.R44D35 1992
006.3'5—dc20   91-40780
                                                                              CIP

Contents

Preface

Any system for generating natural language has to have the ability to talk about things, and in order to talk about things it has to be able to construct referring expressions. This book describes EPICURE, a system that has the generation of referring expressions as its main aim. In the process of developing mechanisms appropriate to this task, the book also focuses on the underlying representation of complex entities and on the generation of structured discourses that talk about these entities. All this is done within the domain of cookery recipes—a choice that on first sight might appear to be a little lacking in seriousness but on closer inspection turns out to be characterized by a number of attributes found in more austere domains. In particular, the research reported ought to be of value in domains (such as those involving chemical and physical processes) where the entities to be represented and described are more complex than those found in airline reservation systems or simple blocks worlds, and in domains where the purpose of generating text is primarily instructional.

The book is based on my Ph.D. research at the University of Edinburgh's Centre for Cognitive Science in the period 1983–1988, updated to reflect a number of new ideas that have come to light since that work was completed. A great many people—in the old cliché, too many to mention here—have contributed, in one way or another, to the completion of the research, but I must pick out for special mention Judy Delin, Nick Haddock, Gerard Kempen, Ewan Klein, Jon Oberlander, Jeremy Olsen, Ehud Reiter, Graeme Ritchie, and Bonnie Webber. Alan Black's LaTeXing help and Paul Bethge's editing made all the difference to the production of the final text.

Notational Conventions

Example of Convention	Description of Convention
a linguistic example	Linguistic examples in the body of the text are in italics.
A displayed example	However, in displays, linguistic examples appear in roman text.
<u>This</u> is an example	In displayed examples, the particular item of interest (usually an anaphor or a noun phrase) appears underlined.
the block that is on <u>itself</u>	Wherever relevant in displayed examples, the antecedents of anaphors appear in italics.
Mike had dahl and Jo ϕ pakora	The symbol ϕ is used to indicate that an element is assumed to have been elided from a syntactic structure.
*The skunks is friendly	A sentence or phrase that is ungrammatical is denoted by a preceding '*'.
$\forall x F(x) = G(x)$	Italics are used for mathematical and logical symbols.
widget	Boldface is used to indicate that a technical term is being used for the first time.
SCRUMPY	Small capital letters are used to indicate the names of programs.
`foo(bar)`	A typewriter-like typeface is used to display program segments.
ako(blackeyebean, legume)	A sans serif font is used for terms in the knowledge representation language used.

Generating Referring Expressions

1 Introduction

1.1 What This Book Is About

This book describes EPICURE, a natural language generation system whose principal concern is the generation of **referring expressions** that pick out **complex entities** in connected **discourse**. Roughly speaking (the more precise intended meanings of these terms will become clearer later), by a referring expression we mean a linguistic form that is used to pick out an entity in some real or imaginary world; by complex entities we mean not only singular individuals such as the referents of simple noun phrases like *a cat* and *the mat*, but also what philosophers of language would call non-singular individuals (that is, entities which are described by mass and plural noun phrases such as *some cheese* and *a thousand sneezes*); and we take a discourse to be a coherent stretch of natural language larger than a single sentence or utterance. This last concept allows us to place particular emphasis on the generation of **anaphoric** referring expressions; informally, an anaphoric referring expression is an abbreviated linguistic form, where the entity picked out by that expression can be determined only by making use of contextual information, and not from the content of the linguistic form itself. So, anaphoric referring expressions are typically used to refer to entities that are in some way known to the hearer—usually because they have been referred to already, or because they are somehow present in the environment (either because their existence is already assumed or because they are physically present).

In order to support the generation of referring expressions, we also describe a language generation system that provides the appropriate infrastructure. EPICURE is designed to generate connected discourse from specifications of plans of action. In this book the particular plans considered are cookery recipes, although the general ideas worked out here should be straightforwardly applicable to plans constructed in other domains. By accessing a database of information that indicates which plans of action the hearer is assumed to know how to perform, EPICURE decides what level of description is required for the hearer to understand the actions in the plan. A description of each action then forms the basis of an utterance to be generated. For each entity to be mentioned in each such utterance, EPICURE generates an appropriate referring expression, taking into account the structure and the content of the discourse so far and also what the hearer can be assumed to know on the basis of information external to the discourse. Thus, by modifying the system's knowledge of the hearer's knowledge, different discourses may be generated.

1.2   The Phenomena Considered

Much has been written on the nature of anaphora, and there is little need for an extensive overview here.[1] We adopt the definition of anaphora suggested by Hirst (1981a: 4):

> **Anaphora** is the device of making in discourse an abbreviated reference to some entity (or entities) in the expectation that the perceiver of the discourse will be able to disabbreviate the reference and thereby determine the identity of the entity.

Our principal concern is the generation of three particular kinds of anaphora: **pronominal anaphora**, **definite noun phrase anaphora**, and **one-anaphora**, as exemplified by (1.1), (1.2), and (1.3), respectively.

(1.1)   a. *A cat* walked into the room.

        b. It was wearing a red collar.

(1.2)   a. *A cat* and a dog walked into the room.

        b. The cat was wearing a red collar.

(1.3)   a. A cat and a dog walked into the room.

        b. The cat was wearing *a red collar*, and the dog was wearing a blue one.

Natural language makes available a number of other anaphoric forms, but the generation of these three types constitutes the primary focus of the present work. In particular, we will examine the following practical

---

1. Hirst 1981a provides an excellent survey; a condensed version is available (Hirst 1981b). Other interesting and useful surveys of anaphora can be found in Halliday and Hasan 1976, Webber 1979 (chapter 2), and Carter 1987 (chapter 2).

decisions that must be made by any system that is to be considered sophisticated in this area:

- When can a pronoun be used to refer to an entity?
- When can a definite determiner be used in referring to an entity?
- How is the semantic content of a referring expression decided upon?
- When can *one*-anaphora be used to refer to an entity?

These questions, in turn, give rise to a more fundamental philosophical question: What kinds of things are "entities"? We will examine these questions within the context of generating discourses from plans.

Of course, many aspects of the generation of referring expressions are *not* touched upon in the present work. In particular, we will not attempt to cover spoken language, or deixis (i.e., language used to identify extralinguistic referents, perhaps in conjunction with implicit or explicit pointing); we will be concerned only with the written form, as befits machines that are not yet entirely comfortable either speaking or pointing. There are, of course, similarities between spoken and written language, and between deictic and nondeictic uses of language, and many of the ideas discussed here may have some bearing on these other forms of language use; however, the differences are sufficiently complex to warrant the more specific focus adopted here.[2] Finally, the book is concerned only with the resources available in English, although many of the issues discussed may be of relevance to other natural languages.

1.3   The Aims of the Work

The work described here has aims on two levels. The more general aims are of a methodological nature, and are best considered against the background provided by two observations on the current state of research in the generation of natural language.

First, there is a need for consolidation in the field. For a long time, research in natural language generation has been the "poor relative" of work in natural language understanding: many more researchers have

---

2. For some work that integrates language and gesture in the generation of referring expressions, see Kobsa et al. 1986, Reithinger 1987, and Wahlster et al. 1991.

been attracted to the problems posed by the latter than to those posed by the former. The situation is no longer as extreme as it was, and recent years have seen more widespread recognition of work on language generation: the most widely cited works in this area are those of Davey (1978), McDonald (1980a), McKeown (1982, 1985), and Appelt (1982, 1985). Still, it is very noticeable that, whereas there is now a well-grounded body of theory available for natural language understanding (for example, in the area of parsing techniques), there is no such comparable consolidation of results within the work on language generation. In fact, it is often not clear whether different systems are addressing the same questions.

Second, sufficient work has now been done in the field that the days when a text could be published describing yet another generation system are past; research in language generation must now become more oriented toward in-depth analysis of particular aspects of the generation task, building on what has gone before. Unfortunately, some of the necessary foundations have not yet been put in place. One major problem is the lack of agreement among researchers as to what the input to the generation process should be, and so each system makes its own assumptions and develops its own *ad hoc* techniques for solving the particular problems that arise from those assumptions.

Given these observations, this book attempts to consolidate and build upon the work already done on one particular problem in language generation: **referring**. The book extends considerably the ideas presented in the major works mentioned above, and also those of a number of other researchers. Apart from this desire to consolidate, the work described here is also driven by a desire to be generally useful. Given the current lack of agreement with regard to choices of formalism and representation, we will try to be explicit and objective about the assumptions that have been made. Some first steps are taken toward the development of a representation language that will support distinctions relevant to the purposes of generating the wide variety of referring expressions to be found in natural language.

Of course, the book also has aims of a more specific nature. At the level of the particular issues it addresses, the major aim is to provide computational solutions to the generation of the phenomena briefly described in the previous section; that is, to present a collection of algorithms and data structures for the generation of pronouns, anaphoric definite noun phrases, and *one*-anaphoric phrases.

In order to provide generation algorithms that are as generally appli cable as possible, we adopt and develop a more complex and principled underlying ontology than is generally used in such circumstances. This results in an approach to the representation of complex entities that permits the generation of a wider range of noun phrase structures than would otherwise be possible.

In addition, the system described makes explicit use of information about discourse structure in an explicit discourse model. Work on the notion of discourse modeling in language generation was identified as crucial in the 1982 ACL panel on text generation (Mann et al. 1982), and that need is taken to heart here. In so doing, we also make use of work on the structure of discourse by Grosz and Sidner (1985, 1986); we make some specific observations in this regard that contribute to the simplicity of the approach taken to pronominalization.

1.4   Starting Points

The work reported here adopts particular stances on certain issues, and takes particular themes as starting points. The most important of these are as follows.

1.4.1   Methodology

The work described here is, in the first instance, an exercise in compu tational linguistics. Unlike some other work in natural language gen eration (for example, McDonald 1980a, 1980b; Kempen and Hoenkamp 1987; De Smedt and Kempen 1987; De Smedt 1990), the present work does not make any claims for the psychological reality of the results ob tained; similarly, it does not claim to unearth any deep linguistic truths. However, it is informed by research in psychology and linguistics: it is necessary to have some psycholinguistically informed idea of the hearer's memory constraints, for example, in order to generate expressions that the hearer will understand; similarly, there are useful generalizations and observations to be gleaned from work in linguistics, without which the coverage of any system would be greatly impoverished. Thus, the overall aim is for an engineering solution to the problem of the generation of referring expressions that is sound from the point of view of linguistic theory and cognizant of the relevant data from psycholinguistics.

1.4.2   The domain of application

The richness and breadth of natural language means that any attempt at a computational treatment has to narrow its focus in various respects. Apart from concentrating on particular linguistic phenomena, it is usual to also concentrate on a particular domain of application.

In this book, the chosen domain can be most generally described as the description of plans of action; the particular focus is on the description of cookery recipes. Cookery recipes usually look something like that shown in figure 1.1.[3] The cookery recipe domain is an interesting domain for a number of reasons. It is fairly well defined, and yet it exhibits some remarkably complex phenomena; it comes as no surprise, then, that it has been chosen as a domain of investigation by a number of researchers. Lehrer (1969, 1972) has examined the vocabulary of cooking terms in depth, Hammond (1986) uses recipe construction as a domain for the investigation of planning techniques, Tsang (1986) discusses temporal aspects of planning in cookery recipes, and Karlin (1988) describes work on a natural language interface to a computer-generated animation system that operates in the domain of cooking.

From the point of view of the research described here, this domain has two interesting properties: it allows us to examine some of the issues that arise in generating discourses whose structure mirrors that of the plans that underlie them, and it permits us to make use of a sophisticated ontology that encompasses more than just simple entities. The results of the research should be applicable in many domains that have an instructional element or require a more complex underlying ontology than is normally found in work in computational linguistics.

1.4.3   What to say versus how to say it

There is a fairly standard distinction made in the generation literature between the decisions of *what to say* and *how to say it*.[4] The decisions involved in determining what to say are usually referred to as **conceptual** or **strategic**, and the decisions involved in determining how to say something are usually referred to as **linguistic** or **tactical**. In more

---

3. This recipe is from Rose Elliot's *Bean Book*.
4. The distinction was first discussed in detail by Thompson (1977), although the distinction itself is surely older.

CREAM OF BUTTER BEAN SOUP

4 oz butter beans
1 large onion
1 medium-sized potato
2 carrots
2 sticks celery
1 oz butter
$1\frac{1}{2}$ pints water or unsalted stock
$\frac{1}{2}$ pint milk
a bouquet garni: a couple of sprigs of parsley, a sprig of thyme and a
bayleaf, tied together
4–6 tablespoons of cream
sea salt
freshly ground black pepper
grated nutmeg

Soak the butter beans, then drain and rinse them. Peel and chop the
onion and potato; scrape and chop the carrots; slice the celery. Melt the
butter in a large saucepan and add the vegetables; saute them for 7–8
minutes, but don't let them brown, then add the butter beans, water or
stock, the milk and the bouquet garni. Simmer gently, with a lid half on
the saucepan, for about $1\frac{1}{4}$ hours, or until the butter beans are tender.
Remove the herbs, then liquidize the soup, stir in the cream and add
the sea salt, freshly ground black pepper and nutmeg to taste. Reheat
the soup, but don't let it boil. Serve each bowl sprinkled with croutons.

Figure 1.1
A recipe for butter bean soup.

recent work, these two phases of the generation task tend to be referred to as **text planning** and **linguistic realization** respectively.

Most well-known work in generation adopts the distinction; thus, MUMBLE (McDonald 1980a) is a tactical component that assumes the existence of a strategic component in the form of an "expert speaker" that provides some specification of what is to be said. On the other hand, TEXT (McKeown 1982, 1985) is a strategic component that produces utterance specifications that are passed to a separate tactical component for realization.

From the point of view of implementing a working computer model of language generation, the distinction is a very useful one, allowing as it does the modularization of the task into two distinct components. However, some argue that the modularity the distinction embodies is also of theoretical merit; to back up this view, there are a number of workers in cognitive psychology who propose models of the human language production process that consist of separate processing modules, Levelt (1989) being only the most recent (although his model is perhaps the most fully articulated). Levelt's notions of the **Conceptualizer** and the **Formulator** correspond to the text planner and the linguistic realization component, respectively.

Closer examination of the way particular researchers apportion tasks between the two components in what has become known as the **standard model** shows that all is not well. The general idea is that each of the two components makes use of different knowledge sources:

> Because the textual and the tactical components of a text planner[5] are concerned with different linguistic abstractions, they can be seen as implementing different strata of linguistic theories. As such, they should be kept separated. The textual component needs to do work to identify what needs to be expressed in semantic and textual (discourse) terms; the realizer makes decisions based on grammatical notions. Not all the factors affecting the two processes are shared. There are no reasons for the textual component to have to know all the tactical component knows and vice versa. The respec-

---

5. The terminology here is a little nonstandard—Paris' "text planner" corresponds to the generator in entirety, and the "textual component" corresponds to what we have called the text planner—but the passage expresses the general idea well.

> tive concerns of the two components ... define the boundary
> between them. (Paris 1988: 58)

Appelt (1982) was the first to explicitly reject the notion that the
text planner and the realization component could be separated in this
way; other detractors followed, most notably Danlos (1987). The intuition that underlies the uneasiness with the distinction has been well
articulated only in the last few years, however; Meteer (1990) and Rubinoff (1990) focus on this question, and Meteer names it the problem of
expressibility. A major reason for adopting the distinction was to enable the construction of modules that required access to some knowledge
sources but not others; but this is the distinction's undoing, since, in particular, removing access to linguistic knowledge from the domain of the
text planner introduces the possibility that the text planner might com-
pose a message that is not realizable. A number of proposed solutions
to this problem leave the distinction between text planner and realizer
in place. In particular, Meteer (1990) suggests the encoding within the
text planner of a level of representation called **text structure**, which
permits abstract characterization of linguistic resources; and Rubinoff
(1990) suggests abandoning the one-way flow of information between
text planner and realizer, and replacing this with a two-way communication channel by means of which the realizer can query the planner for
further information or alternative decisions when problems are encoun-
tered.

The psycholinguists also have an answer, which is almost a hybrid-
over-time of these two computational approaches:

> ... the mature speaker has learned what to encode when
> preparing a message for expression. ... It is no longer nec-
> essary for the Conceptualizer to ask the Formulator at each
> occasion what it likes as input. The language-specific re-
> quirements on semantic structure have become represented
> in the Conceptualizer's procedural knowledge base. (Levelt
> 1989: 105)

In this book, we take the view that "what to say" and "how to say it"
are two sides of the same question; thus, the generator may be given the
"what to say" goal of requesting the hearer to make chestnut soufflé, and
decide that "how to say it" requires describing a particular plan of action.

Each such step in the plan can then be viewed as a specification of what to say, for which the generator has to decide how to say it. This recursion continues until an utterance is produced. To put it another way: a decision that from the outside might be categorized as a "how to say it" decision might be best described from the inside as a "what to say" decision. Thus, choosing *how* a particular entity should be referred to involves choosing *what* semantic content the description should contain.

Note that, in a computational system, this approach does not preclude the use of distinct components for the different levels of the process, which simply call each other recursively. So, we can accept the arguments of those who say that the distinction (at least as originally stated) is suspect; at the same time, we can adopt the distinction as a useful conceptual viewpoint.

1.4.4 Planning and language generation

There are two ways in which the artificial intelligence notion of planning [6] connects with work in language generation. First, there are language generation systems whose purpose is to describe plans of action such as might be produced by a planning system; in such cases, the language generation program is basically a tactical component, assigned the task of determining how to say what the planner has specified has to be said. A good example of this approach can be found in Mellish 1988 and Mellish and Evans 1989.

The second relationship between language generation and planning is more fundamental, however; this is the view that language itself is planned behavior, and so can be modeled using the same tools and techniques developed for other kinds of planning. This view sees linguistic acts as being on a par with physical acts, and is founded on speech-act theory (see, for example, Austin 1962 and Searle 1969). Within computational linguistics, work in this area was first suggested by Bruce 1975a and further developed in a body of work by Allen, Perrault, Cohen, and Levesque (Cohen 1978; Allen and Perrault 1978; Cohen and Perrault 1979; Perrault and Allen 1980; Cohen and Levesque 1980; Cohen 1981; Allen 1983).

In a manner similar to Appelt's work, the present work is intended to integrate the two uses of planning, so that the behavior that the system

---

6. Tate (1985) provides a good overview of the issues that arise in planning.

plans is the linguistic description of plans of action.[7]

1.4.5 Discourse structure

Another important starting point adopted in the current work is a notion of **discourse structure** derived from the work of Grosz and Sidner (1985, 1986). Under this approach, a discourse can be viewed as consisting of distinct discourse segments bearing both hierarchical and ordering relations to each other. The structure of the discourse that results from these relations plays a role in the construction of anaphoric expressions, and is used here to provide a basis for the approach taken to discourse modeling.

A considerable number of recent research projects have used some kind of tree structure to represent the content of generated text: see, for example, Jullien and Marty 1989, Mellish 1988, Zukerman and Pearl 1986, and Weiner 1980. The most influential and promising of all this work is that based on Rhetorical Structure Theory (RST) (Mann and Thompson 1986, 1988); under this approach, the tree structure encodes the rhetorical dependencies between adjacent clauses and segments of text. Although RST underlies a number of current attempts at the generation of coherent text (for example, Hovy 1990), many important details remain to be fully worked out. The texts on which we focus in the current work are relatively impoverished from a rhetorical point of view, and so a simpler model of discourse structure is sufficient.

1.4.6 Ontology and levels of representation

A major element of the work presented here is the recognition that, in the real world, entities are considerably more complex than those found in toy domains such as those consisting of nothing more than blocks and pyramids. The chosen domain presents interesting problems with respect to the representation of objects that can be countable or mass, objects that can be decomposed, and objects that can be collected together to create objects that did not exist previously. The distinctions we model at this ontological level are then mirrored appropriately in the two intermediate levels of representation used in the generation process.

---

7. Unlike Appelt's work, however, the present work does *not* include a full-blown planning mechanism; only limited reasoning about action is carried out by the system itself, as will be made clear in chapter 3.

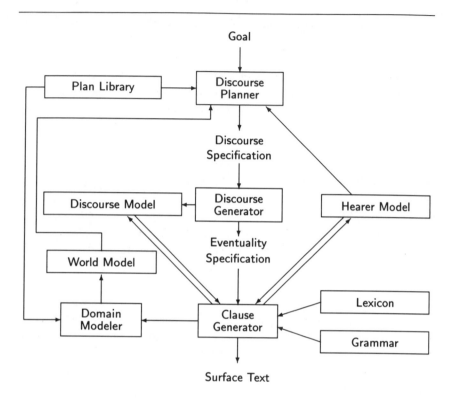

Figure 1.2
The overall structure of EPICURE.

1.5   An Overview of the System

The system described in the rest of this book is presented diagrammatically in figure 1.2, and operates as follows.[8]

EPICURE is presented with a top-level goal that is to be achieved. The **discourse planner** component uses its **plan library** in conjunction with its knowledge of what operations the hearer knows how to perform (as maintained in the **hearer model**) to produce a hierarchically struc-

---

8. In this diagram, data structures are represented by long flat boxes, whereas process modules are represented by the more squat boxes. An arrow pointing from box *A* to box *B* is intended to show that data flows from *A* to *B*.

tured **discourse specification** that specifies the actions that must be
requested of the hearer in order to achieve the goal state. As an example, if the system believes that the hearer understands what it means
to *sauté*, this concept can be used in an instruction; alternatively, the
operation may have to be decomposed into more detailed instructions,
such as *melt the butter*, *add the vegetables*, and *fry*.

Once a discourse specification has been constructed in this fashion, it
is passed on to the **discourse generator**, whose principal tasks are to
maintain the basic organization of the discourse model and to dispatch
the individual **eventuality specifications** to the **clause generator**
for realization. In general, an eventuality specification describes a single
action in the plan. The clause generator then uses information in the
discourse model, the hearer model, and the **world model** to decide
upon the semantic content of the corresponding utterance; this is then
unified with information stored in the system's **lexicon** and **grammar**
components to produce a surface string. The discourse model and the
hearer model are then updated appropriately. The **domain modeler**
ensures that the world model is updated with the effects of the action just
described, so that the state of each object in the domain is represented
correctly at any given time.

As an example, consider the recipe for butter bean soup in figure 1.1.
Various aspects of this recipe are not directly relevant to the issues discussed in this book, and are beyond the sophistication of EPICURE's
generation mechanisms. As will be described in detail in chapter 6, a
number of simplifications to the recipe permit us to focus on the particular phenomena that are of interest in the context of the present work.
Figure 1.3 shows the corresponding recipe as generated by EPICURE.
The various processes EPICURE goes through in order to construct this
text are described in chapter 6.

1.6 Structure of the Book

The remainder of this book is structured as follows.

In chapter 2 we ask: What kinds of things can be referred to? The
basic ideas used in the ontology we develop in answer to this question
have similarities to the approaches proposed by Link (1983) and Bach
(1986). The chapter specifies the representational formalism used to

1   four ounces of butter beans
2   a large onion
3   a medium potato
4   two carrots
5   two sticks of celery
6   one ounce of butter
7   1.5 pints of unsalted stock
8   0.5 pints of milk
9   four tablespoons of cream
10   some sea salt
11   some freshly ground black pepper
12   some grated nutmeg

13   Soak, drain and rinse the butter beans.
14   Peel and chop the onion.
15   Peel and chop the potato.
16   Scrape and chop the carrots.
17   Slice the celery.
18   Melt the butter.
19   Add the vegetables.
20   Saute them.
21   Add the butter beans, the stock and the milk.
22   Simmer.
23   Liquidize the soup.
24   Stir in the cream.
25   Add the seasonings.
26   Reheat.

Figure 1.3
EPICURE's version of the butter bean soup recipe.

describe the objects in the universe of discourse, which permits two basic kinds of entities: **generalized physical objects** and **eventualities**. We work out the consequences of using these notions, and also consider some of the limitations.

Chapters 3–5 describe the approach taken to natural language generation. Chapter 3 presents the generation framework adopted here. The mechanisms used to construct a discourse plan, and the construction and use of a discourse model, are described, and the two intermediate levels of representation used within the system are introduced.

In chapter 4 we examine the generation of referring expressions in detail. First, the interface used in EPICURE to mediate between the semantics of a noun phrase and its syntax are described; then, the processes used to determine the content of an initial reference to an entity are examined.

In chapter 5 we look at the problem of generating anaphoric references. We first consider the problem of deciding when it is safe to generate a pronominal reference to an entity. We then turn to definite noun phrase anaphora, and to the notion of **discriminatory power** as a tool for determining the required descriptive content of a referring expression. The chapter ends by describing the algorithms required for the generation of *one*-anaphora.

Chapter 6 presents a detailed worked example that demonstrates the mechanisms described in the previous chapters, summarizes the limitations of the present work, and suggests some possible extensions.

2 The Representation of Entities

2.1 Some Ontological Problems in Recipes

In this chapter, we focus our attention on the kinds of referents that occur in our chosen domain of cookery recipes. Our aim is to develop an ontology that encompasses at least the more common of the range of entities that can be referred to within that domain; our major concern is the representation of complex entities in such a way as to allow us to model their behavior and their change of state as the execution of a recipe proceeds, while at the same time making it straightforward to construct references to those entities.

We take the view that there are two kinds of entities in the world: informally, *things* and *events*. We are first and foremost concerned with the representation of things, although some use will be made of the parallels that can be drawn between things and events, and to that extent the representation of events will also be discussed.

From the point of view of representing the ingredients in a specific recipe, the first problem we have to face is that of deciding what constitutes an object.

2.1.1 The limitations of singular individuals

In most natural language systems, it is assumed that all the entities in the domain of discourse are singular individuals. Typically, each such entity is represented by a symbolic constant, which serves as a locus of information; the properties of the entity can then be represented by asserting propositions that predicate arbitrary properties of that entity. One of the most pervasive of the properties so expressed is what we might call **sortal class membership**, which is represented by the isa link found in most knowledge representation formalisms (although not always under that name). For example, if we have symbolic constants e_1 and e_2 that correspond to a table and a chair respectively, this information might be represented as

(2.1)   (#IS :E1 #TABLE)
         (#IS :E2 #CHAIR)

where the #IS concept is taken to mean something like "has as its basic description" (Winograd 1972: 118). Throughout the literature, a number of variations on this basic syntax are used to represent the same information; thus, in Appelt's system (Appelt 1985: 132), we have the simplified forms shown in (2.2).

(2.2)   (Table (E1))
         (Chair (E2))

In each case, the representation language embraces some finite set of object categories, and each object in the domain of discourse is said to be an instance of one of these categories.

However, as we consider more complex domains, such as recipes, we find that this simple notion is of limited value. Of course, we do find ingredients such as *a carrot*, and it would seem reasonable in such cases to represent this, analogously to the examples above, as something like

(2.3)   (isa x carrot)

where x is the internal symbol corresponding to the carrot in question. However, simple objects like these are the exception in the world of cooking. We find ingredients like *three carrots*; in such cases, we might take the view that we have a single noun phrase that specifies some plural number of singular individuals collected together. This is still possible within the representational framework used above: we could represent the set of objects in question using the conjunction of expressions

(2.4)   (isa x1 carrot) $\wedge$ (isa x2 carrot) $\wedge$ (isa x3 carrot)

and then invoke some mechanism to collect together these three objects in order to produce an appropriate referring expression. Plurality is then an issue for the generator, but not for the representation language.

This approach will work as long as we have an internal symbol for each individual that figures in the collection of individuals described. However, this is not always the case: we also find examples where the cardinality of the set described by the noun phrase is not specified, as in *three pounds of carrots*. In cases like this, the meaning of the noun phrase cannot be represented at all if we permit ourselves only singular individuals, since we do not know how many individual carrots the set in question comprises; intuitively, we want to be able to say that the noun phrase refers to a **set** of singular individuals, and so we need to be able to represent such an entity using our formalism.

Related problems are caused by other linguistic forms that make use of mass nouns rather than count nouns. The objects described are usually specified in terms of the substance of which they consist, in conjunction with some measure of quantity: for example, *3 tablespoons of water*. Here we have neither a set nor a singular individual, and so we must allow for a third kind of object that can be referred to by a noun phrase.

Of course, none of this is controversial from the point of view of linguistics: we know that nouns can be count or mass, and that noun phrases incorporating count nouns can be singular or plural. However, although semanticists have examined these problems at length (see, for example, Pelletier 1979 and Link 1983), and some work in knowledge representation within AI addresses related issues (see in particular Hayes 1974, 1978, 1985), no current work in computational linguistics works out the full ramifications of adopting a corresponding ontology.

2.1.2   The individuation of ingredients

A problem related to that just discussed is deciding exactly how many distinct objects one is dealing with in a given situation. Suppose we have the following list of ingredients:

(2.5)   one egg
         $\frac{1}{2}$ pint milk
         4 oz cheese
         salt

It seems reasonable to suggest that this list specifies four ingredients. However, suppose the list specifies two eggs rather than one:

(2.6)   two eggs
         $\frac{1}{2}$ pint milk
         4 oz cheese
         salt

Do we now have five ingredients in total, or are there still only four?

There are a number of possible approaches to this. We might take the view that the answer depends on the recipe itself. In (2.6), we might say that if the eggs are used together they constitute one ingredient, whereas if they are used separately they constitute two ingredients. Under this view, in (2.7a) they serve as one ingredient, but in (2.7b) the two eggs serve as distinct ingredients, and the fact that both are specified in the same item of the ingredients list can be attributed to some consideration of style or convenience (for example, listing them together makes it easier to determine what you might have to buy when you go shopping).

(2.7)   a. Beat the eggs ...

    b. Beat one of the eggs ...
       Use the white of the second egg to ...

However, this presumes a clear understanding of what it means to be "used together". Suppose we have an ingredients list containing the following items:

(2.8) $\frac{1}{2}$ pt milk
         $\frac{1}{2}$ pt vegetable stock

and the following instruction in the recipe:

(2.9)   Now add the milk and stock ...

There is a clear sense here in which the milk and the stock are being used together, and yet we would not want to say that they together constitute one ingredient.

Another approach would be to assume that each separate *orthographic* item in the ingredients list is a distinct ingredient. This too is problematic. In some cookery books, for example, salt and pepper appear in ingredients lists as separate items:

(2.10)   salt
         pepper

In others they are listed together as *salt and pepper*. Are we to say that in one case we have two ingredients but that in the other we have only one? It seems more plausible to say that different books follow different conventions for *structuring* the ingredients list. Thus, in some books we find

(2.11)   one onion
         two potatoes
         one carrot

but in others we find

(2.12)   one onion, two potatoes, and one carrot

This does not immediately help in deciding how many distinct ingredients we have; however, it is compatible with yet another approach: stipulating that each distinct noun phrase appearing in an ingredients list describes a distinct ingredient, even if that noun phrase is a conjunct within a larger noun phrase. To put this another way, if something warrants a distinct description then it ought to be considered a distinct object. Under this view, *two eggs* describes one ingredient, and *one onion, two potatoes, and one carrot* describes three ingredients. In the latter case, the way in which these ingredients are then collected together for description is the generator's responsibility: there is no symbol corresponding to the conjunction of the onion, the potatoes, and the carrot. By providing a parameter to control the style of output, either of the above orthographies could be generated.

However, what are we then to say of an ingredients list like that in (2.13)?

(2.13)   450 g mixed vegetables: carrot, cut into rings; potato, swede, diced; celery, leeks, sliced; cauliflower, broken into largish sprigs

The approach just suggested would require us to view this as a list of six ingredients (carrot, potato, swede, celery, leeks, and cauliflower). The difficulty here is that we know the weight of the six ingredients taken together, but not their separate weights, which presents us with a problem when it comes to representing the weight; ideally, we should provide the system with an additional symbol corresponding to the "higher level" ingredient, so that we have somewhere to attach the weight information.

In this book, we take the view that language itself is the best guide to ontology. As a result, we take each distinct noun phrase to correspond to an object, and we permit objects to contain other objects as constituents, so that the ingredients list input to the generator may already contain some prestructuring. Thus, in *salt and pepper* we have an object that has two objects (one a quantity of salt and the other a quantity of pepper) as constituents; and in

(2.14)   450 g mixed vegetables: carrot, cut into rings; potato, swede, diced; celery, leeks, sliced, cauliflower, broken into largish sprigs

we have an object (the *mixed vegetables*) that has six objects as constituents. On the other hand, in *two eggs* we have a single object. This does not preclude the possibility that subsequently in a recipe we might wish to decompose this object to produce two distinct objects which are referred to separately; however, we carry out such proliferation of objects only when this is necessary in order to be able to represent the required information.

2.2 A Survey of Objects in Recipes

Now that we have a better idea as to what we take to be an object within the cookery domain, we can go on to examine the wide variety of referring expressions to be found in recipes in more detail. In particular, consider the referring expressions that appear in the ingredients lists at the beginning of recipes.[1] A typical ingredients list might look like (2.15).

(2.15)   225 g roasted buckwheat
          300 ml water
          2 teaspoons yeast extract
          1 tablespoon tomato purée
          2 large onions, chopped
          2 sticks celery, diced
          1 tablespoon olive oil
          4 garlic cloves, crushed
          350 g dark, open mushrooms, washed and sliced
          salt, pepper, and tamari

Even within this relatively simple example, closer inspection reveals a great many complexities. In this section, we present a wide range of data in order to exemplify the variety of expressions that are to be found in real recipes. The representation language presented in the next section will not be able to represent the meanings underlying *all* the forms presented here, although it is capable of handling a considerable proportion of them, and all the more common ones.

We can view each ingredient listed at the beginning of a recipe as a specification of one object that plays a particular **role** in that recipe. The functional role of an ingredient within a recipe is its primary characteristic. Which particular substance or substances will be used to fulfil

---

1. The data that follow are drawn from two particular cookery books (*Beanfeast* by Rose Elliot, Fontana 1985, and *The Vegetarian Epicure* by Anna Thomas, Penguin 1973) but are representative of those found in many others.

this role is often relatively unimportant, and so an experienced cook can often replace the specified ingredient by substituting some other ingredient that is capable of performing the same role. Thus, when making a curry, if you have no ghee it is quite acceptable to replace the ghee by some other substance suitable as a base for frying, such as oil or butter; when making green lentil dahl, you could replace the green lentils themselves by some other kind of lentils without disastrous consequences (although it would then be inappropriate to call the end result "green lentil dahl").

There is much to be said for representing the ingredients in recipes in terms of their functional roles, as we shall discuss later; however, this is a considerable enterprise in its own right, and so in the current work we will continue to talk of ingredients solely in terms of their physical instantiations. Thus, each ingredient in an ingredients list is taken as specifying one preferred physical instantiation of the role to be filled by that ingredient.

As was suggested in the previous section, our first problems come with the view that objects in the domain can be treated as singular individuals.

2.2.1 Conjoined and disjoined specifications

If more than one ingredient performs a particular role in a recipe, these ingredients will typically be listed together in a conjoined noun phrase as a single entry in the ingredients list. Thus we have

(2.16)   a. salt and pepper

   b. chives and parsley, chopped

where in the first case the two ingredients together typically function in the role of "seasoning", and in the second case the two ingredients serve as a garnish. It is not only such "minor" ingredients that can be grouped together in this way; for example, in a recipe for a fruit-based dish, we find

(2.17)   2 apples, 2 pears, 1 orange, 1 banana

appearing as a single entry in the ingredients list. Notice that, in conjunctions of this sort, the descriptions applied to individual conjuncts take account of the context provided by the superordinate noun phrase:

(2.18)   4 whole eggs and 3 egg whites

This would sound a little odd as

(2.19)   4 eggs and 3 egg whites

Of course, context-sensitive description also occurs within the ingredients list as a whole, so we find forms like

(2.20)   a. extra olive oil or ghee for frying
         b. more fresh sliced pimiento

used when the recipe already lists these substances for other purposes.

The conjunction of ingredient specifications may also be achieved by quantifying across a number of separate ingredients, as in (2.21).

(2.21)   a. 10 each of allspice berries, juniper berries, and black peppercorns
         b. $\frac{1}{2}$ teaspoon each of allspice, cinnamon, and grated nutmeg

At the very least, phenomena such as these argue for the use of something more complex than a simple flat-structured list of ingredients in the representation of a recipe. As we have already seen, sometimes an item in the ingredients list will itself be a list of objects along with a top-level description:

(2.22)   a. 1 cup mixed vegetables: carrot, cabbage, celery, tomato
         b. raw vegetables: radishes, spring onions, carrot sticks, pieces of celery, and cauliflower florets

In such cases, the list need not be exhaustive, but may provide examples, as in (2.23).

(2.23)   a. 1 teaspoon dried herbs: peppermint, sage, or rosemary, for instance
         b. 1 tablespoon chopped fresh herbs, such as mint or coriander

The specification of an ingredient can also involve disjunction, offering alternative physical instantiations for a particular role within a recipe, as in (2.24).

(2.24)   a. 1 tablespoon rolled oats or 1 dessertspoon medium oatmeal

      b. 1 very large potato or 2 small potatoes

      c. 75 g chopped almonds or hazelnuts

Just as in the case of conjunctions, this list of alternatives can be provided with a higher-level description:

(2.25)   550 ml fruit juice: pineapple, apple, orange, or grape

Note that disjunctions and conjunctions can be combined within the same ingredient specification:

(2.26)   2 small pots yogurt and 0.25 pint water or 0.75 pint buttermilk

The mechanisms used in this book are adequate for the generation of most conjoined specifications. However, we will not attempt to generate disjunctive specifications, despite the fact that these are surprisingly common in recipes. The problems associated with disjunctive specifications of ingredients are discussed further at the end of this chapter.

2.2.2   Ingredient taxonomies and object packaging

We saw above that it is not sufficient to posit straightforward correspondences between object instances and "types" such as *carrot*. However, even before we deal with the problems arising from allowing mass and plural objects, there are other difficulties connected with the allocation of objects to categories. Not all ingredients have simple names such as *carrot* and *potato*; often, names are compound: *garlic clove*, *alfalfa sprouts*, *eating apple*, *avocado skin*. Note that there are various ways in which these names can be derived: a garlic clove is a clove-shaped *package* of garlic-matter, whereas an alfalfa sprout is a particular *kind* of sprout. In this respect, an eating apple is analogous to an alfalfa sprout; an avocado skin, however, is *part of* an avocado. The representation language to be presented later in this chapter is capable of making these distinctions.

This is particularly important from the point of view of subsequent reference. For example, a garlic clove is more likely to be subsequently referred to as *the garlic* than as *the clove*, whereas an eating apple can be subsequently referred to as *the apple* but not as *the eating*. This suggests that the generation of subsequent descriptions depends on the *semantic* issue of what substance is described, rather than the *syntactic* issue of what the head of the antecedent noun phrase was; we will pursue this point in more detail in chapter 5. Note, however, that any subsequent references to an *avocado skin* are likely to be of the form *the skin*. This suggests that, in the case of objects that are parts of other objects, the part name is the important element from the point of view of subsequent reference.

2.2.3   Quantities

In general, the description of an ingredient consists of a specification of two things: its substance and its quantity. The quantity of an ingredient can be specified in several ways. As we saw above, sets of singular individuals can be specified in terms of the cardinality of the set, as in *three carrots*. Quantities of mass substances, on the other hand, are specified by means of volume or weight, as in *three pints of milk* and *two pounds of rice*. Sets of individuals can also be specified by weight, as in *three pounds of carrots*.

Apart from the standard metrics for solids and liquids, quantities can also be specified using measuring devices such as *teaspoons* and *cups*, as in *1 cup of olives*; these sorts of measurements may also be qualified, as in *1 heaped tablespoon tahini*.

Quantities can be specified to varying degrees of exactness: a measurement can be approximate (*about 1.5 lb unbleached, hardwheat, white flour*) or it can be specified as a range (*1 to 2 slices dark bread*). There are also relatively vague units of measurement:

(2.27)   a.   a bunch of watercress

        b.   a handful of raisins

        c.   a dash of sugar

        d.   a drop of tabasco

        e.   a little butter

        f.   a few drops of wine vinegar

The cardinality of a countable set can also be left imprecise, as in *a few chopped nuts* and *a few lettuce leaves*; finally, in some cases, there is no specification of quantity at all, as in *honey*, *sea salt* and *chopped fresh herbs*. The quantity of a compound ingredient can be specific while the amounts of the component ingredients are left unspecified:

(2.28)   350 g mixed raisins, sultanas, and currants

All of the above, with the exception of approximate measurements, will be expressible in our representation language.

2.2.4 Properties

The specification of an ingredient often includes properties of the ingredient other than the substance it consists of. As is to be expected, the properties mentioned are just those that are relevant from the point of view of cooking. Some of these properties are best thought of as properties of the way the ingredient is "packaged", whereas others are best thought of as properties of the substance itself; for example, we might be told that something is *large* or that something is *ripe*. Some properties of objects can be used to derive names of subtypes; for example, a *button mushroom* is a special type of mushroom whose name is derived from its shape. Thus, some properties would seem to license the construction of a type hierarchy for ingredients, whereas this seems to be less the case with other properties: *1 eating apple* sounds like an instance of the specialization of apple known as an eating apple; on the other hand, we might be less happy about saying that *a large onion* is a specialization of onion. This distinction can be expressed by means of the distinction between properties of packagings and properties of substances just described.

On occasion, we find that negative properties are specified:

(2.29)   a. 225 g cooking dates (not "sugar-rolled")
         b. 1.5 oz currants (not raisins)

A reason for the negative specification may be offered:

(2.30)   125 g light muscovado sugar (not the very dark one, as it's too treacly for this)

We will not, however, deal with properties specified by means of negatives in this book.

2.2.5 States and processes

Very often, some properties used in the specification of ingredients are properties arising from the application of some process to the ingredient; for example, we have *pitted ripe olives*, where the property of being pitted arises from a process of *pitting*. In such cases, the author of the recipe may intend that the reader carry out this processing, or that the ingredient be obtained already in this state. Sometimes one or the other is clear from what we know about ingredients: for example, it is relatively unusual to buy onions that have already been both peeled and chopped, so we would assume that an ingredient specified as *2 peeled and chopped onions* is intended to be taken by the reader as an instruction to peel and chop the onions. On other occasions, however, the description is ambiguous precisely because, as in the case of the *pitted ripe olives* above, the ingredient is widely obtainable both processed and unprocessed. The important thing, then, is that the ingredient should have the specified properties before the instructions in the recipe proper are carried out.

Sometimes the specification of preprocessing can be quite complex. For example, operations that are to be carried out on objects can be specified more precisely by means of adverbial modification, as in *freshly ground black pepper*, where it is important not only that the pepper has been ground but also that it was ground very recently; similarly, *450 g tender spinach, washed and finely shredded* must have been shredded *finely*. Things get more complex still. Consider (2.31).

(2.31) a. 1 cauliflower, washed and broken into florets
        b. 2 medium-sized aubergines sliced into 6 mm circles
        c. 225 g dried unsulfured apricots, washed and covered with boiling water, soaked overnight
        d. 2 oz wheat germ, toasted with honey
        e. 3 cloves garlic, put through a press

In these cases, processes as complex as some of those that appear within the body of the recipe appear to have migrated into the ingredients list. The specification of processing can also occur in conjunction with the kinds of structures noted above in our discussion of conjunctions and disjunctions:

(2.32) 450 g mixed vegetables: carrot, cut into rings; potato, swede, diced; celery, leeks, sliced; cauliflower, broken into largish sprigs

Here, what could have been an entire paragraph in a recipe finds itself realized as a noun phrase in the ingredients list.

One particularly troublesome aspect of the incorporation of processing information into a description has to do with the times at which particular forms of description are appropriate; for example, if we have *a carrot* which is subsequently grated, the result of this operation is best described as *some carrot*. However, it is not uncommon to find descriptions like *one carrot, grated* in a recipe, where the first part of the noun phrase (*one carrot*) describes the object in question *before* the processing described in the second part (*grated*) has been applied. Thus, describing an object may require knowing what is true of that object at different times.

Our representation language is capable of representing most of the above kinds of processing information.

2.2.6 Derived objects

Above, we saw that objects can be described in part by describing the processing that has been applied to them. A closely related phenomenon is that ingredients can be introduced as parts of other objects from which they are derived, as in *a slice of lemon*. These "derived objects" can be described in a number of different ways: for example, as being of a particular shape, as in the previous example; or as some proportion of the "ancestor" object, as in *half a carrot*. Alternatively, an object may be described as a structural part of another object:

(2.33)   a. an apple core
         b. an egg yolk
         c. the kernels from 1 fresh ear of corn
         d. seeds from 2 to 3 cardomom pods

Or an object may be described in terms of the process used to derive it:

(2.34)   a. a squeeze of lemon juice
         b. peels from 6 to 7 large, healthy potatoes

Notice that processing can be specified for either the ancestor object or the derived object:

(2.35)   a. grated orange rind
         b. grated rind of a well-scrubbed orange
         c. grated rind and juice of 1 small well-scrubbed orange

Disjunctions can also enter into specifications of this kind, as in *grated rind of 1 orange or lemon*. Properties of both the derived object and the ancestor object may be specified: in *half a fresh pimiento, thinly sliced*, it is the pimiento that is fresh but the half-pimiento that is thinly sliced.

An ingredient can also be specified as the *omission* of some part of something else:

(2.36)   a. 175 g whole wheat bread without crusts

        b. 225 g strawberries, stalks removed

The mechanisms described in this book are capable of representing a wide range of derived objects, although some of the more complex cases are not dealt with.

2.2.7   Some other observations

A number of other, less frequently occurring phenomena can be found in the specification of ingredients. These are mentioned here for completeness; none of the following are addressed by the representational mechanisms described in the rest of this chapter.

The specification of an ingredient sometimes states the function of that ingredient within the recipe, as in *lemon rings to garnish* and *lettuce leaves to serve*. Such statements of purpose are relatively rare, and for the most part they are restricted to ingredients that are in some way peripheral to the dish under construction; there are exceptions to this, however, such as *olive oil or ghee for frying*. A notion of functional role, as mentioned earlier, would be helpful here.

There are many other "adjuncts" to ingredient specifications. Sometimes an ingredient may be specified as optional:

(2.37)   a little honey to taste, optional

Some optional ingredients specify a condition that has to be satisfied in order for them to be included:

(2.38)   a. low-sodium yeast extract, if liked

        b. 1 teaspoon chopped fresh rosemary, thyme, or marjoram if available

Sometimes the source of an ingredient may be specified as a modifier, as in *450 g dried fruit salad mix, from health shops*. Finally, some ingredients cross-refer to other recipes, as in *1.5 pints aubergine pasta sauce (page 257)*. All of the above are sufficiently rare that we can ignore them in what follows without thereby imposing any serious limitations on the coverage of the representation language.

2.3 Generalized Physical Objects

The remainder of this chapter presents a representation language that encompasses a wide range, although not all, of the examples discussed in the previous section. The ontology encompasses two basic types: eventualities (corresponding to states, actions, and events) and generalized physical objects (corresponding to individuals, masses, and sets of individuals). The focus in this section is on physical objects; in section 2.4 we will consider eventualities.

2.3.1 The generalized physical object

As has already been emphasized, it is insufficient to assume that all we need in order to represent the kinds of objects that occur in recipes is the notion of a singular individual. Nonetheless, each item in an ingredients list (with some exceptions to be discussed below) does appear to function as a distinct object in a recipe, irrespective of how that ingredient is composed; thus, if we have an ingredient introduced as *3 lbs of carrots*, some *part* of that ingredient will be referred to relatively rarely; the carrots are typically used subsequently in the recipe as if (at least from the point of view of describing them) they constitute an indivisible object.

In the light of the earlier discussion concerning the individuation of objects in recipes, the ontology developed here echoes Hobbs' (1985: 61) suggestion that we should multiply the kinds of entities we allow in our ontology "by allowing as an entity everything that can be referred to by a noun phrase." Complications arise in taking this view to its extremes; for example, it would require that in (2.39) we posit the existence of a disjunctive entity corresponding to *either Michael or Mary*.

(2.39)   Either Michael or Mary will feed the cat.

For simplicity, we will ignore this possibility in the present work, and consider only specific individuals described by singular, plural, and mass terms; as was stated earlier, there are problems in dealing with disjunctions.

We view each ingredient in a recipe as a **generalized physical object**, or, for short, a **physobj**. A physobj is defined as follows:

(2.40)   A generalized physical object is any (not necessarily contiguous) collection of contiguous regions of space occupied by matter.

Thus, a physobj consists of one or more "conventional" physical objects. It is convenient to think of a physobj as a collection of physical objects brought together for the purpose of referring to them (although a physobj need not be referred to in order to exist). Entities that exist because they consist of molecules brought together in the nature of the world (e.g., the referent of *an onion*) and entities brought together for the purpose of referring to them by means of noun phrases (e.g., the referent of *two onions*) are physobjs of equal standing. This means that each of the following noun phrases has as its referent a physobj:

(2.41)   a. an onion
         b. two pounds of rice
         c. Michael and Mary

Nothing in the definition of a physobj requires that the constituent physical objects be made of the same substance, or that they be connected or in proximity: a physobj is just some collection of matter that is conveniently viewed as an individual.

Although the notion of a physobj is more general than that of an ordinary physical object, it is not as general as Hobbs' more promiscuous notion of an entity (mentioned above). Quite apart from the question of how we deal with disjunctions, Hobbs' notion of an entity does not require that the entity have any sort of physical existence; here, in contrast, we do not consider abstract objects.

By the above definition, the noun phrase *Jon and William* describes a single physobj irrespective of whether Jon and William are near each other; so, *Jon and William* describes an object in each of the following:

(2.42)   a. Jon and William went to the supermarket together.
         b. Jon and William have not yet met.

Ultimately, we may not require every NP to specify an object in this way; but the notion of a physobj provides a framework where it is possible. We can restrict this possibility later if this seems desirable.

2.3.2   The count/mass distinction

As we noted earlier, some objects are described by *count* noun phrases
and some by *mass* noun phrases,[2] as in *a large carrot* and *some grated
carrot*, respectively. It is tempting to suggest that an ontological distinction underlies this linguistic one, and indeed this intuition would seem
to be borne out in the general case: mass noun phrases tend to be used
to describe gases, liquids, powders, and collections of objects (such as
grains of rice) that are sufficiently small for it to be inconvenient to view
them as individuals in their own right; count noun phrases, on the other
hand, are used to describe objects that have identifiable boundaries.
However, positing an ontological basis for the count/mass distinction is
not without its problems. For example, Lyons (1968: 282) argues that
the count/mass distinction is primarily a linguistic one, evidence for this
being drawn from cross-linguistic data: some substances are denoted by
count nouns in one language but by mass nouns in another. Thus, the
English word *grape* is a count noun, whereas the German *Traube* and
the Russian *vinograd* are mass terms.

Another problem is that there are borderline cases in which there
appears to be a conflict between the naive ontology and the linguistic facts. Speaking ontologically, there appears to be little difference
between individual rice grains and individual lentils: although they consist of different substances, they are both small objects of roughly the
same size. However, when describing quantities of these we use a mass
noun in the first case but a count noun in the second case:

(2.43)   a. four ounces of rice

         b. four ounces of lentils

If the count/mass distinction were ontologically based, we would expect
these descriptions to be either both count or both mass.

It is more plausible to suggest that what we require is a *conceptual*
distinction: we want to encode whether or not something is *conceived of
as* count or mass. Leech and Svartvik (1975: 45) take a similar view:

> Some mass nouns, we might argue, should "really" be count,
> because the "substance" is divisible into separate things.

---

2. In the literature, the terms "count" and "mass" tend to be predicated of nouns
rather than noun phrases; however, by extension, we can say that a count noun
phrase is one that has a count noun as its head and a mass noun phrase is one that
has a mass noun as its head.

> ... But PSYCHOLOGICALLY we think of such things as indi-
> visible when we use a mass noun.

The idea, then, is that physobjs are not inherently count or mass, but
are *viewed* as being count or mass: we say that a physobj may be viewed
from either a mass or a count **perspective**. Thus, a specific physobj
can be viewed at one time as a mass and at another time as a countable
object: when cooking I will in all likelihood view a quantity of rice as
a mass, but if I am a scientist examining rice grains for evidence of
pesticide use I may view that same quantity of rice as a countable set
of individuals. In the domain of cooking, there is very rarely any need
to use or maintain more than one perspective on a given object, and so
for purposes of the work described here we can view the countability or
otherwise of an object as if it were an objective property of that object;
however, at the end of this chapter we will consider some circumstances
under which this approach is inadequate.

2.3.3 Representing quantities of stuff

Each object in the domain is represented by means of a **knowledge
base entity**, or KB entity for short. For the purposes of exposition, we
will begin by using first-order predicate calculus (FOPC) as a formalism
for representing the information contained in KB entities; however, the
system described later makes use of **feature structures** as its core
representational mechanism, and so we will quickly shift to a feature-
structure notation. In some cases below, both the FOPC form and the
corresponding feature structure will be shown in order to demonstrate
the relationships between the two.

Objects In the real world, we might take the view that any two entities that have exactly the same properties are, in fact, the same entity.
However, in our subjective appreciation of that world—where incomplete
information about an object is the rule rather than the exception—it is
entirely possible that two distinct entities may share all the same properties. For each entity in the domain, then, we introduce a unique symbol,
which serves as a locus of information that describes that entity. This
symbol is the entity's **index**. Properties of the entity are predicated
of this symbol. The most important property of an entity is its basic ontological type: every object is either a physobj or an eventuality.
For convenience, we use sorted indices here: the indices x, y, z and

subscripted versions thereof should be read as representing physobjs, and the indices e, f, g and subscripted versions thereof as representing eventualities. Every ingredient in a recipe is a physobj and is therefore represented by a symbol of the form x_i.

Irrespective of whether an ingredient is described by means of a count or a mass expression, it consists of some **quantity** of some **substance** (although in some circumstances the quantity may not be specified). These properties of the object, which are akin to Link's **invariant properties** (1983: 304–305), are unchanging throughout the life of the object, whereas any other properties of the object may change. This simplifies the process of generating subsequent referring expressions: in general, it is very easy to determine whether we are talking about the same entity as was mentioned on a specific previous occasion. However, this approach leads to complications when one is dealing with entities described by noun phrases, such as *the soup*, where the constituency of the object, and therefore the collection of substances of which it consists, changes during the process of the soup's being cooked.

Substances   The substance of an object is specified as one of a set of constants forming a hierarchy of substances; thus, an ingredient that is a quantity of low-fat milk has its substance specified as

(2.44)   substance(x, low-fat-milk)

where we specify separately that low-fat milk is a kind of milk and that milk is a kind of liquid:

(2.45)   ako(low-fat-milk, milk)
         ako(milk, liquid)

As noted above, entities are represented within the system as feature structures. The KB entity representing the information in (2.44) is then as shown in (2.46).

$$(2.46) \quad \begin{bmatrix} \text{index: } x \\ \text{spec: } \begin{bmatrix} \text{substance: low-fat-milk} \end{bmatrix} \end{bmatrix}$$

In the feature-structure representation, all properties predicated of an entity are attribute-value pairs within the value of the entity's **spec** (i.e., **specification**) attribute.

Quantities   The quantity of an ingredient may be specified in a number of ways, typically by weight or volume. A weight or a volume is specified as a tuple consisting of a unit of measurement and a number specifying how many units of that type there are. Thus, we represent the quantity of substance of the ingredient described by *4 oz cheese* as

(2.47) $\exists x$ substance$(x,$ cheese$) \land$ quantity$(x, \langle 4,$ ounce$\rangle)$

We permit a wide range of units of measurement that can be used to specify the quantity of an ingredient; we make no syntactic distinction between standard units of measurement, such as *ounces, grams, liters,* and *pints,* and more informal measures, such as *teaspoons, cups,* or even *handfuls* or *dashes* (although lexical information will determine whether, for example, we should say *one teaspoon* but *a dash*). So, for example, we represent the quantity of substance described by *a dash of tabasco* as

(2.48) $\exists x$ substance$(x,$ tabasco$) \land$ quantity$(x, \langle 1,$ dash$\rangle)$

We can also specify the quantity of an ingredient as a **range** (where a range consists of an upper limit and a lower limit, each expressed as a quantity tuple). The quantity of substance described by *1–2 tablespoons honey* is therefore represented as

(2.49) $\exists x$ substance$(x,$ honey$) \land$
         quantity$(x,$ range$(\langle 1,$ tablespoon$\rangle, \langle 2,$ tablespoon$\rangle))$

For ease of manipulation, the feature-structure representation of this information is slightly more structured; see figure 2.1. Note that the index of an entity is essentially *extensional*, whereas the specification is essentially *intensional*. There can be many entities with the same specification, but no two entities can have the same index. The specification of an entity can thus be viewed as a concept or a type.

2.3.4   States

Apart from the constant properties described in the previous section, an object may also have properties that are true of that object only at certain times. We say that a property is true of a given object in a specific **state**, where a state is a partial description of the world at some point in time. A state can be characterized by a formula as follows:

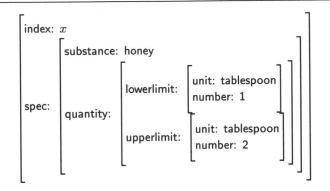

Figure 2.1
The KB entity corresponding to *1-2 tablespoons of honey*.

$$(2.50) \quad P_1 \wedge P_2 \wedge \ldots \wedge P_n$$

where each P_i is a proposition that is true in that state. Rather than represent states as long conjunctions of propositions, we represent them in a piecemeal way by stating that some proposition **holds** in a given state; thus, if we know that an object x is hot in the state s, we say

$$(2.51) \quad \text{holds}(s, \text{hot}(x, +))$$

Thus, the characterization of a state presented in (2.50) is equivalent to (2.52), where we suppose that s is the state described.

$$(2.52) \quad \text{holds}(s, P_1) \wedge \text{holds}(s, P_2) \wedge \ldots \wedge \text{holds}(s, P_n)$$

States are temporally ordered; thus, if we assume a function time that maps a state into the temporal location it describes, the relationship illustrated in (2.53) holds for any two states s_i and s_j.

$$(2.53) \quad [\text{time}(s_i) < \text{time}(s_j)] \vee [\text{time}(s_i) = \text{time}(s_j)] \vee [\text{time}(s_i) > \text{time}(s_j)]$$

The invariant properties mentioned earlier hold true of the objects of which they are predicated in all states[3]; thus, a more correct represen-

---

3. In reality, of course, objects are not eternal, even if the particles they consist of are. However, it is convenient to view ingredients as existing for the duration of a recipe, even if they lose their status as distinct objects, and so we can take s to range over the set of states that occur during the execution of a recipe.

tation of the quantity of substance described by *4 oz cheese* is as shown in (2.54).

(2.54) $\exists x \forall s$ holds(s, substance(x, cheese)) $\wedge$
                 holds(s, quantity(x, $\langle 4$, ounce$\rangle$)))

In order to be able to describe an object, we must also know what its **structure** is. An object's structure represents the particular perspective taken upon an object, and has one of three possible values: **bounded individual** (**individual** for short), **set**, and **mass**. It follows from the above discussion that the structure of a physobj is intended to correspond not to any objective attribute of the physobj, but to the way in which the object is most conveniently described at some point in time; as a result, an object's structure may be different at different times. Thus, the singular noun phrase *a carrot* describes a physobj whose structure is currently **individual**; the plural noun phrases *three carrots* and *three pounds of carrots* describe physobjs whose structures are both currently **set**; and the mass noun phrase *some grated carrot* describes a physobj whose structure is currently **mass**. We use the predicate **current** to indicate the state that represents the present moment in time:

(2.55) $\forall s$ current(s) $\leftrightarrow$ [time(s) = NOW]

The ingredient described as *4 oz cheese* is then fully represented as in (2.56).

(2.56) $\exists x \forall s_i$ holds(s_i, substance(x, cheese)) $\wedge$
                 holds(s_i, quantity(x, $\langle 4$, ounce$\rangle$)) $\wedge$
                     $\exists s_j$ current(s_j) $\wedge$ holds(s_j, structure(x, mass))

Again, for ease of manipulation, the feature-structure representation is slightly different. Each feature structure effectively provides a snapshot of a given object in a particular state, thus providing a way of accessing information objects by pairs of the form $\langle Index, State \rangle$. The feature structure corresponding to (2.56) is shown in figure 2.2.

2.3.5   Bounded individuals and packaging

The objects described by *a carrot* and *a slice of carrot* are both bounded individuals whose substance is carrot matter, but nothing in the foregoing discussion provides a way of representing the difference between the

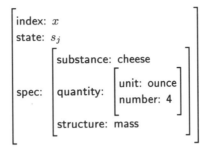

$$\begin{bmatrix} \text{index: } x \\ \text{state: } s_j \\ \text{spec:} \begin{bmatrix} \text{substance: cheese} \\ \text{quantity:} \begin{bmatrix} \text{unit: ounce} \\ \text{number: 4} \end{bmatrix} \\ \text{structure: mass} \end{bmatrix} \end{bmatrix}$$

Figure 2.2
The KB entity corresponding to *4 oz cheese*.

two objects. In the case of objects whose current structure is **individual**, we must also have some notion of the way the object is *packaged*.

The **packaging** of an object may also change through time, and so is predicated of an object in a particular state. In a similar fashion to the examples presented above, we represent the mass-structured ingredient described simply as *sugar* as in (2.57).

(2.57) $\exists x \forall s_i$ holds(s_i, substance(x, sugar)) $\wedge$
$\exists s_j$ current(s_j) $\wedge$ holds(s_j, structure(x, mass))

However, if we have the ingredient described as *a sugar cube*, then we have a bounded individual, packaged in a particular way. This packaging information is relative to the current situation (since it may change), and is represented by a tuple specifying the **shape** and the **size** of the package:

(2.58) $\exists x \forall s_i$ holds(s_i, substance(x, sugar)) $\wedge$
$\exists s_j$ current(s_j) $\wedge$ holds(s_j, structure(x, individual)) $\wedge$
holds(s_j, packaging(x, $\langle$cube, regular$\rangle$))

As a feature structure, this is represented as in figure 2.3.

The **size** of an entity's packaging can be one of a number of values. For example, the ingredient described as *one large sugar cube* is represented as in (2.59).

(2.59) $\exists x \forall s_i$ holds(s_i, substance(x, sugar)) $\wedge$
$\exists s_j$ current(s_j) $\wedge$ holds(s_j, structure(x, individual)) $\wedge$
holds(s_j, packaging(x, $\langle$cube, large$\rangle$))

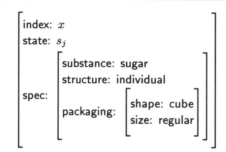

Figure 2.3
The KB entity corresponding to *a sugar cube*.

Many ingredients that are best viewed as bounded individuals in this framework tend to be described in such a way that their packaging is not explicitly stated, as in *a carrot*. In such cases we say that the packaging used is the default for that substance, and so it is typically omitted when the object is described. By convention, the default shape of an object consisting of a particular substance is represented by the same symbol used to represent that substance. The object described by *a carrot* is then represented as in (2.60).

(2.60) $\exists x \forall s_i$ holds(s_i, substance(x, carrot)) $\wedge$
$\qquad\qquad \exists s_j$ current(s_j) $\wedge$ holds(s_j, structure(x, individual)) $\wedge$
$\qquad\qquad$ holds(s_j, packaging(x, ⟨carrot, regular⟩)))

This can be read as saying that *a carrot* is a carrot-shaped package of carrot matter.

Note that (2.60) states basically the same information as the isa expressions we considered at the beginning of this chapter; in general, the following equivalence holds:

(2.61) holds(s, isa(x, y)) $\equiv$ holds(s, substance(x, y))
$\qquad\qquad\qquad\qquad\qquad\quad \wedge$ holds(s, structure(x, individual))
$\qquad\qquad\qquad\qquad\qquad\quad \wedge$ holds(s, packaging(x, ⟨y, regular⟩)))

where y is the substance of which ys are made.

Although many ingredients come in what we have called default packagings, this is not always the case. Celery, for example, comes in either heads or sticks. We would represent *one head of celery* as

(2.62) $\exists x \forall s_i$ holds(s_i, substance(x, celery)) $\wedge$
             $\exists s_j$ current(s_j) $\wedge$ holds(s_j, structure(x, individual)) $\wedge$
                holds(s_j, packaging(x, $\langle$head, regular$\rangle$)))

and *one stick of celery* as

(2.63) $\exists x \forall s_i$ holds(s_i, substance(x, celery)) $\wedge$
             $\exists s_j$ current(s_j) $\wedge$ holds(s_j, structure(x, individual)) $\wedge$
                holds(s_j, packaging(x, $\langle$stick, regular$\rangle$)))

As we saw in the case of the sugar cube, this form of representation is not restricted to "natural" packagings: we can also represent *an onion ring* as in (2.64).

(2.64) $\exists x \forall s_i$ holds(s_i, substance(x, onion)) $\wedge$
             $\exists s_j$ current(s_j) $\wedge$ holds(s_j, structure(x, individual)) $\wedge$
                holds(s_j, packaging(x, $\langle$ring, regular$\rangle$)))

We represent ingredients such as *a garlic clove* and *a fennel bulb* in the same way.

Another way in which ingredients can be described reflects the fact that certain individuals are composed of parts that are given specific names. For example, an avocado has as its parts a skin, a stone, and a quantity of avocado flesh. We represent entities that are parts of other entities as having a **part** attribute. The parts of a particular avocado are then represented by the three KB entities shown in figure 2.4. Note that only the third of these entities has its **substance** specified as avocado; this reflects the fact that the flesh itself may be referred to as *the avocado*, but that the stone and the skin may not. We do not encode the fact that an entity has parts directly as a property of that entity; rather, we have axioms that allow us to infer the existence of those parts whenever necessary. For example, the axiom in (2.65) allows us to infer the existence of a stone from an avocado.

(2.65) $\forall x$ substance(x, avocado) $\wedge$ structure(x, individual) $\wedge$
             packaging(x, $\langle$avocado, regular$\rangle$) $\supset$
                $\exists x_1$ structure(x_1, individual) $\wedge$ part(x_1, stone) $\wedge$
                    packaging(x_1, $\langle$stone, regular$\rangle$) $\wedge$ ancestor(x_1, x)

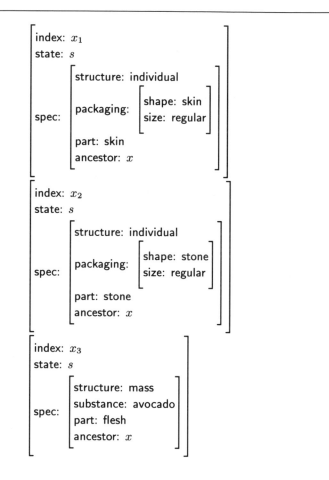

Figure 2.4
The KB entities corresponding to the parts of an avocado.

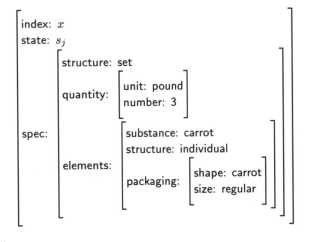

Figure 2.5
The KB entity corresponding to *3 lbs of carrots*.

2.3.6   Sets of objects

The third kind of object we have to be able to represent is the plural individual, or **set**. A set is any physobj that is made up of a number of other physobjs, although we do not need to be aware of the identity of these constituent physobjs.

There are a number of ways in which sets can be described. In those situations where we are not aware of the constituents' identities (as in *3 lbs of carrots*), or, more generally, where all the constituents are the same (as in *3 carrots*) and so could be listed separately but with much duplication of information, we may quantify over the elements of the set in order to specify their properties. The ingredient described as *3 lbs of carrots* is then represented as in figure 2.5.

Sets specified by cardinality   In the previous example, we specified the amount of the set using a statement of **quantity**, just as in the case of mass physobjs. Sets may also, however, be specified by means of their cardinality. In such cases, note that the cardinality is state-dependent, since a quantity of some substance can be repackaged into different sets at different times. Thus, the ingredient described as *3 carrots* can be represented as in figure 2.6.

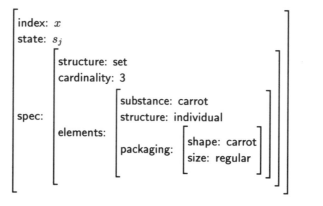

Figure 2.6
The KB entity corresponding to *three carrots*.

Just as in statements of quantity, we can state cardinality as a range. The cardinality of *3–4 carrots* is represented as

(2.66)   holds(s, cardinality(x, range(3, 4)))

where s is the current state.

Cardinality need not be numeric; it may also be specified as one of a limited number of *vague* values, so that the cardinality of the set described by *a few nuts* in state s can be represented as follows[4]:

(2.67)   holds(s, cardinality(x, few))

Sets specified by constituency   Finally, the constituents of a set need not all be of the same type. In such cases, we can explicitly list the constituents of the set. Given our very general definition of a physobj, we have an equally general definition of what it is to be a constituent of a physobj:

(2.68)   Given a physobj x, any portion of matter that is a proper part of the portion of matter that makes up x is also a physobj, and is said to be a **constituent** of x.

---

4. The formalism described here deals only with existentially quantified ingredients; thus, no representation is offered for expressions like *few nuts*.

The number of ways of partitioning a given physobj into different sets of constituents is thus limited only by our ability to break an object into smaller and smaller objects. In practice, however, only certain partitionings are of interest to us. As before, we use language as our guide to which partitionings are of use.

The simplest examples of this are objects that are themselves conjunctions of other objects, as in *350 g mixed raisins, sultanas, and currants.* This is represented as a set that itself consists of three sets:

(2.69) $\exists x \forall s_i$ holds(s_i, quantity(x, $\langle 350,$ grams$\rangle$)) $\wedge$
   holds(s_i, constituents(x, $[x_1, x_2, x_3]$)) $\wedge$
   $\exists s_j$ current(s_j) $\wedge$ holds(s_j, structure(x, set)) $\wedge$
    holds(s_j, structure(x_1, set)) $\wedge$
    [$\forall z$ holds(s_j, element(z, x_1)) $\supset$
     holds(s_j, substance(z, raisin)) $\wedge$
     holds(s_j, structure(z, individual)) $\wedge$
     holds(s_j, packaging(z, $\langle$raisin, regular$\rangle$))] $\wedge$
    holds(s_j, structure(x_2, set)) $\wedge$
    [$\forall z$ holds(s_j, element(z, x_2)) $\supset$
     holds(s_j, substance(z, sultana)) $\wedge$
     holds(s_j, structure(z, individual)) $\wedge$
     holds(s_j, packaging(z, $\langle$sultana, regular$\rangle$))] $\wedge$
    holds(s_j, structure(x_3, set)) $\wedge$
    [$\forall z$ holds(s_j, element(z, x_3)) $\supset$
     holds(s_j, substance(z, currant)) $\wedge$
     holds(s_j, structure(z, individual)) $\wedge$
     holds(s_j, packaging(z, $\langle$currant, regular$\rangle$))]

Notice that the constituents of the top-level object are constituents not only in the current state but in all states; this reflects the fact that the constituent objects in question are physical constituents irrespective of whatever other properties are true of the objects. As a result, the top-level object is represented by the feature structure shown in figure 2.7, with the constituent objects represented by distinct feature structures.

Hayes (1985: 481) distinguishes two types of objects in the world on the basis of their composition: **homogeneous objects** are composed of a single piece of homogeneous stuff, and can be broken or divided into pieces; **composite objects**, on the other hand, are made out of pieces each of which is an object, and can be disassembled and assem-

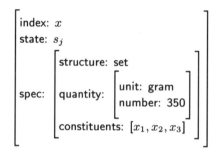

Figure 2.7
The KB entity corresponding to *350 g mixed raisins, sultanas, and currants.*

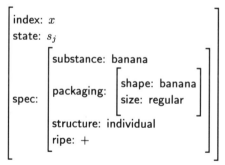

Figure 2.8
The KB entity corresponding to *a ripe banana.*

bled. This distinction cuts across the structural distinctions described here. In our framework, homogeneous objects will generally be viewed as having mass or individual structure, whereas composite objects will generally be viewed as having the structure set. Sometimes, however, the correspondence will break down, since Hayes' distinction is based on "naive ontology" rather than on the way in which things are described.

2.3.7   Representing simple properties

Simpler properties of objects are represented in a straightforward way. Thus, an ingredient specified as *a ripe banana* is represented as shown in figure 2.8. Attributes such as *ripe* are binary-valued, the possible values being "+" and "−". We carry this representation over to the FOPC description of the structures; hence the use of ripe$(x, +)$ instead of the simpler form ripe(x).

Many of the properties predicated of objects are true of those objects by virtue of some processing's having been carried out. In the simplest cases, we know that some processing has been applied to an object, but we do not know anything about the object's previous state, as in *some grated carrot*. This is represented, analogously to the previous example, as follows:

(2.70) $\exists x \forall s_i$ holds$(s_i,$ substance$(x,$ carrot$)) \land$
$\qquad \exists s_j$ current$(s_j) \land$ holds$(s_j,$ structure$(x,$ mass$))$
$\qquad$ holds$(s_j,$ grated$(x, +))$

However, we often also need to represent information about the object in different states. In the case of *one carrot, grated*, the representation for the object at the time it is described is exactly the same as in the case of *some grated carrot*; note, however, that this representation does not indicate how many carrots were involved. We also need to represent the object as it was *prior* to the grating process:

(2.71) $\exists x \forall s_i$ holds$(s_i,$ substance$(x,$ carrot$)) \land$
$\qquad \exists s_j$ time$(s_j) <$ NOW $\land$ holds$(s_j,$ structure$(x,$ individual$)) \land$
$\qquad$ holds$(s_j,$ packaging$(x, \langle$carrot, regular$\rangle))$

We will return to the representation of properties resulting from processing once we have addressed the representation of eventualities.

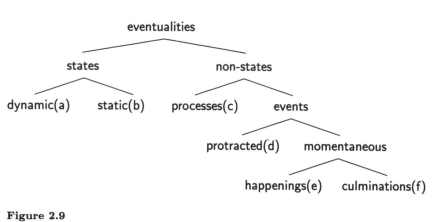

Figure 2.9
A taxonomy of eventualities (from Bach 1986: 6).

2.4 Eventualities

2.4.1 Eventualities and objects

Objects do not exist in a vacuum; they participate in relations which we
may informally call states and events. In the ontology developed here,
any collection of objects and the state or event in which they participate
is referred to as an **eventuality**, after Bach 1986. Bach presents a more
complete taxonomy of eventualities derived from Carlson 1981: this is
shown in figure 2.9. Typical examples of each kind of eventuality are
given in (2.72). (The examples are Bach's own.)

(2.72) a. dynamic states: sit, stand, lie +LOC
        b. static states: be drunk, be in New York, own x, love x, re-
            semble x
        c. processes: walk, push a cart, be mean (agentive)
        d. protracted events: build x, walk to Boston
        e. happenings: recognize, notice, flash once
        f. culminations: die, reach the top

In the recipe domain, we simplify things by dealing only with Bach's
general category of **events** (i.e., eventualities of types d, e, and f above);
however, in principle the representation can be extended to deal with the

other categories. In particular, the relationship between events and the kinds of states discussed earlier is not fully worked out here, although if we were to adopt Bach's analysis in its entirety we would need to take the view that (in our terms) the "process stuff" underlying any given event can be viewed from a state perspective, and vice versa. The ramifications of this approach remain to be worked out.

It has often been noted that strong parallels can be drawn between the logic of objects and the logic of events. Mayo (1961) argues that events are ontologically the exact reverse of material objects with respect to time and space. Thus, a given piece of matter must be at only one place at any one time, but the same piece of matter can be in different places at different times; a given piece of process (for example, the French Revolution), however, can be in different places at the same time, although it cannot be at the same place at different times. Zemach (1979: 69ff) suggests, in fact, that we do not need to talk of both objects (in his terminology, **continuants in time**) and processes (**continuants in space**), since each way of talking reflects a particular ontology that is sufficient in itself. However, for our day-to-day purposes it is more convenient to make use of both ontologies, and for ease of expression we will borrow from both in the ontology presented here. Nevertheless, as we will see, it turns out that there are many similarities between our consideration of objects and our consideration of events.

2.4.2   The representation of eventualities

Just as in the case of objects, we represent each eventuality by an index, and then predicate properties of that index as a means of representing information about the eventuality in question. We use the indices e, f, g, and subscripted versions thereof for eventualities.

In addition, just as a physobj has a specification of substance, so too does each eventuality. The substance of an eventuality is the "process stuff" in which it consists; thus, an instance of cycling can be represented by the feature structure shown in (2.73).

$$(2.73) \quad \begin{bmatrix} \text{index: } x \\ \text{spec: } \begin{bmatrix} \text{substance: cycling} \end{bmatrix} \end{bmatrix}$$

Just as for the substances that make up physical objects, the substances that make up eventualities are arranged in a taxonomic hierarchy[5]; thus, we know (for example) that cycling is a kind of moving:

(2.74)   ako(cycling, moving)

In order to describe an eventuality, we have to know how it is to be viewed; thus, just as for physobjs, we have a specification of **structure**. Here our treatment is somewhat simpler than in the case of physobjs, since we deliberately restrict ourselves to one particular eventuality structure, the **event**, and we assume that the structure of an eventuality is fixed and unchanging.

Each eventuality also has a beginning and an end; we say that it **occurs** between a begin-state and an end-state. If an eventuality begins in the state s_0 and ends in the state s_1, we write

(2.75)   occurs(s_0, s_1, e)

with the proviso that

(2.76)   time$(s_0) \leq$ time(s_1)

Finally, each eventuality has one or more arguments corresponding to the participants in the eventuality: there are a finite set of possible participants in an eventuality, each identified by the **role** it plays in the eventuality (see, for example, Fillmore 1968 and Bruce 1975b). The particular roles played by the participants in an eventuality will depend on the nature of the eventuality; thus, a sleeping event will have an agent but no object, whereas a shutting event will have both an agent and an object (both will, of course, have other participants as well). We do not need to explicitly state the identity of all the participants: as a result, an eventuality will typically be only partially specified.

As an example, we represent the eventuality describe by sentence (2.77a) as (2.77b), where j and d are the indices for Judy and the door, respectively. (The representation of the participating individuals is omitted here.)

(2.77)   a. Judy shut the door.

---

5. See Lehrer's (1969, 1972) analysis of the semantic structure of cooking vocabulary.

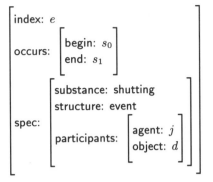

$$\left[\begin{array}{l} \text{index: } e \\[6pt] \text{occurs: } \left[\begin{array}{l}\text{begin: } s_0 \\ \text{end: } s_1\end{array}\right] \\[12pt] \text{spec: } \left[\begin{array}{l}\text{substance: shutting} \\ \text{structure: event} \\ \text{participants: } \left[\begin{array}{l}\text{agent: } j \\ \text{object: } d\end{array}\right]\end{array}\right] \end{array}\right]$$

Figure 2.10
The KB entity corresponding to *Judy shut the door.*

b. $\exists e, s_0, s_1 \forall s_i$ occurs(s_0, s_1, e) $\wedge$
   holds$(s_i,$ substance$(e,$ shutting$))$ $\wedge$
   holds$(s_i,$ structure$(e,$ event$))$ $\wedge$
   holds$(s_i,$ agent$(e, j))$ $\wedge$ holds$(s_i,$ object$(e, d))$

The corresponding feature structure is then as shown in figure 2.10.

The similarity between the representation of objects and that of eventualities allows the possibility of generating nominalizations.[6] The eventuality described by sentence (2.78a) is represented as (2.78b), where w is the index corresponding to William, and the agent of the upsetting event is the embedded shutting event (in other words, the shutting event causes the upsetting event).

(2.78) a. Judy's shutting the door upset William.

   b. $\exists e_0, e_1, s_0, s_1, s_2, s_3 \forall s_i$ holds$(s_i,$ eventuality$(e_0))$ $\wedge$
      occurs(s_0, s_1, e_0) $\wedge$ holds$(s_i,$ substance$(e_0,$ shutting$))$ $\wedge$
      holds$(s_i,$ structure$(e_0,$ event$))$ $\wedge$
      holds$(s_i,$ agent$(e_0, j))$ $\wedge$ holds$(s_i,$ object$(e_0, d))$ $\wedge$
      occurs(s_2, s_3, e_1) $\wedge$ holds$(s_i,$ substance$(e_1,$ upsetting$))$ $\wedge$
      holds$(s_i,$ structure$(e_1,$ event$))$ $\wedge$
      holds$(s_i,$ agent$(e_1, e_0))$ $\wedge$ holds$(s_i,$ object$(e_1, w))$ $\wedge$
      time$(s_0) \leq$ time(s_2)

---

6. This idea is taken a little further in Oberlander and Dale 1991.

Notice that the only temporal constraint specified is that the shutting
event did not begin after the upsetting event. Thus, the sentence is
compatible with a situation where it was Judy's turning the door handle
at the very beginning of the shutting event that upset William (perhaps
he was hanging onto the other side), and also with a situation where it
was the bang made by the door closing that upset William.

2.4.3   Plans

We can view a recipe as a prescribed sequence of eventualities (specif-
ically, events) that must take place for some desired goal state to be
reached: in other words, it is a specification of a plan of action. The
system described in the rest of this book generates descriptions of recipes
viewed as plans of action; thus, before going on to show how this relates
to our representation of objects and eventualities, it will be useful to review some of the essential elements of planning as it is conceived within
AI.[7]

Planning has been an active area of research within AI for over two
decades, and planning systems technology has achieved a fair degree of
sophistication as a result. The basic elements of any planning system are
some specification of an initial world state, an explicitly specified goal
state, and a set of operators that can be used to achieve the transitions
between world states. The task of the planning system is to specify some
sequence of actions providing a path from the initial state to the goal
state.

Operators, in their simplest form, consist of a specification of some
preconditions (those facts about the world that must hold *before* the
action represented by the operator can be carried out) and some **postconditions** (those facts about the world that will be true *after* the
action has been carried out). By chaining operators either backward or
forward between world states, a planning system can determine which
sequence of actions is required in order to achieve the goal state. As an
example, consider the simple blocks-world scenario shown in figure 2.11.
The initial state here might be represented as in (2.79a) and the goal
state as in (2.79b).

---

7. For a step-by-step introduction to the basic issues in planning, see chapter 9 of
Charniak and McDermott 1985; for an overview of the planning literature, see Tate
1985.

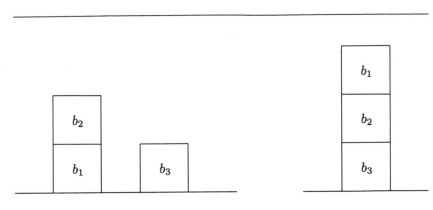

Initial state s_0 Goal state s_1

Figure 2.11
A simple block stacking problem.

(2.79)   a. on(b_1, table) $\land$ on(b_2, b_1) $\land$ clear($b_2, +$) $\land$ on(b_3, table)
         $\land$ clear($b_3, +$)
         b. on(b_1, b_2) $\land$ on(b_2, b_3) $\land$ on(b_3, table) $\land$ clear($b_1, +$)

Suppose our planner has two operators at its disposal, called **pickup**
and **puton**. The **pickup** operator takes an object as argument and is
defined as in (2.80).

(2.80)   Action: Do(A,**pickup**(x))
         Preconditions: on(x, *SomethingElse*)
                            clear($x, +$)
         Postconditions: holding(A, x)
                            clear($x, -$)
                            $\neg$on(x, *SomethingElse*)

The **puton** operator takes an object x and a location y as arguments,
and is defined as in (2.81).

(2.81)   Action: $\text{Do}(A,\textbf{puton}(x,y))$
          Preconditions: $\text{holding}(A,x)$
                             $\text{clear}(y,+)$
          Postconditions: $\text{clear}(x,+)$
                             $\text{on}(x,y)$
                             $\neg\text{holding}(A,x)$
                             $\text{clear}(y,-)$

Then, the goal state can be achieved by applying the following sequence of actions in the initial state[8]:

(2.82) $\text{Do}(A,\textbf{pickup}(b_2)) \wedge \text{Do}(A,\textbf{puton}(b_2,b_3)) \wedge$
          $\quad\quad \text{Do}(A,\textbf{pickup}(b_1)) \wedge \text{Do}(A,\textbf{puton}(b_1,b_2))$

Following Cohen and Levesque 1980, we define an action term to be an eventuality from which the agent has been abstracted, thus allowing the planner to ignore the identity of the agent when this is not of importance. We notate the action term corresponding to a particular type of event by writing the name of that event in bold face; thus, "putting-on" events are described by the operator whose name is **puton**. Most planning systems assume that there is a single agent in the world, with the result that the agent of actions can be left implicit. As will be seen in the next chapter, EPICURE allows for the possibility of multiple agents.

All of the above can be represented within the formalism we have already introduced for eventualities. Thus, each planning operator defines a change of state, where the preconditions provide a partial description that must be true of the state in which the operator is applied and the postconditions provide a partial description of the state that results from applying the operator. In the above example, the sequence of actions resulting in the goal state is then described as follows:

(2.83) $\exists s_0, s_1, s_2, s_3, s_4, e_0, e_1, e_2, e_3, b_1, b_2, b_3, A \forall s_i$
          $\quad\quad \text{occurs}(s_0, s_1, e_0) \wedge \text{holds}(s_i, \text{substance}(e_0, \text{picking-up})) \wedge$
          $\quad\quad\quad \text{holds}(s_i, \text{agent}(e_0, A)) \wedge \text{holds}(s_i, \text{object}(e_0, b_2)) \wedge$
          $\quad\quad \text{occurs}(s_1, s_2, e_1) \wedge \text{holds}(s_i, \text{substance}(e_1, \text{putting-on})) \wedge$
          $\quad\quad\quad \text{holds}(s_i, \text{agent}(e_1, A)) \wedge \text{holds}(s_i, \text{object}(e_1, b_2)) \wedge$
          $\quad\quad\quad \text{holds}(s_i, \text{destination}(e_1, b_3)) \wedge$

---

8. Strictly speaking, the sequence of actions should be explicitly ordered, a fact not represented in (2.82).

$$\text{occurs}(s_2, s_3, e_2) \land \text{holds}(s_i, \text{substance}(e_2, \text{picking-up})) \land$$
$$\text{holds}(s_i, \text{agent}(e_2, A)) \land \text{holds}(s_i, \text{object}(e_2, b_1)) \land$$
$$\text{occurs}(s_3, s_4, e_3) \land \text{holds}(s_i, \text{substance}(e_3, \text{putting-on})) \land$$
$$\text{holds}(s_i, \text{agent}(e_3, A)) \land \text{holds}(s_i, \text{object}(e_3, b_1)) \land$$
$$\text{holds}(s_i, \text{destination}(e_3, b_2))$$

A more concise form of (2.83) is given as (2.84).

(2.84) $\exists s_0, s_1, s_2, s_3, s_4, b_1, b_2, b_3, A$
$$\text{occurs}(s_0, s_1, \text{Do}(A, \mathbf{pickup}(b_2))) \land$$
$$\text{occurs}(s_1, s_2, \text{Do}(A, \mathbf{puton}(b_2, b_3))) \land$$
$$\text{occurs}(s_2, s_3, \text{Do}(A, \mathbf{pickup}(b_1))) \land$$
$$\text{occurs}(s_3, s_4, \text{Do}(A, \mathbf{puton}(b_1, b_2)))$$

We can axiomatize the preconditions of the **pickup** operator as in (2.85a), and the postconditions as in (2.85b).[9]

(2.85)   a. $\forall A, s_1, s_2, x \ \text{occurs}(s_1, s_2, \text{Do}(A, \mathbf{pickup}(x))) \supset$
$$\text{holds}(s_1, \text{clear}(x, +)) \land \exists y \ \text{holds}(s_1, \text{on}(x, y))$$
   b. $\forall A, s_1, s_2, x \ \text{occurs}(s_1, s_2, \text{Do}(A, \mathbf{pickup}(x))) \supset$
$$\text{holds}(s_2, \text{holding}(A, x)) \land \text{holds}(s_2, \text{clear}(x, -)) \land$$
$$\neg \exists y \ \text{holds}(s_2, \text{on}(x, y))$$

2.4.4   Actions and eventualities

Changing an object's state   The basic ideas described above can be applied fairly straightforwardly to the domain of cooking. Some cooking operators are very simple and do no more than change the state of an object in much the same way as the blocks-world operators described above. Take, for example, the **peel** operator, which takes an ingredient and peels it. Recall from the previous section that when an ingredient is peeled it changes state; thus, the **peel** operator is specified as in (2.86).

(2.86)   Action: $\text{Do}(A, \mathbf{peel}(x))$
         Preconditions: $\text{peeled}(x, -)$
         Postconditions: $\text{peeled}(x, +)$

In reality, things are a little more complex than this. In particular, some objects apply directly to individuals only: thus, if the **peel** operator

---

9. This is essentially the same as the approach taken by Appelt (1985: 42).

is applied to an ingredient whose structure is **set**, it is the *element* specification that changes rather than that of the set itself.

Changing an object's structure   Some operators change the structure of an object. Since the structure is a property of an object like any other, such operators also have very simple definitions. Thus, the **grate** operator is defined as follows:

(2.87)   Action: Do(A,**grate**(x))
         Preconditions: grated($x, -$)
         Postconditions: grated($x, +$)
                                   structure(x, mass)

In other words, grating something changes it from an object that is perceived as a bounded individual to one that is perceived as a mass.

Deriving new objects   Some operators are more complex, in that they may create new objects. There are two general ways in which this can be done: by combining two or more objects and by breaking an existing object into parts. Both kinds of operators change the object population of the world. Modeling the use of these operators requires the notion of a **working set**; that is, a list of the identifiably distinct objects in the domain at any point in time. The working set is itself represented as a distinguished physobj whose constituents are just the ingredients in the recipe. Thus, for any state s, we have a proposition of the form

(2.88)   holds(s, constituents($WorkingSet$, $[x_0, x_1, \cdots, x_n]$)))

where x_0 through x_n are the identifiably distinct objects in the domain in state s. Operators that create new objects manipulate the working set, adding and/or removing objects.

The simplest operator that combines two or more objects is called **add**. It takes a base object and one or more objects that are to be added to this base, and the result is a new object. The operator is defined in (2.89).

(2.89)   Action: $\text{Do}(A, \text{add}(x, y))$
         Preconditions: $x \in WorkingSet$
                            $y \in WorkingSet$
         Postconditions: $\text{constituents}(z, [x, y])$
                            $x \notin WorkingSet$
                            $y \notin WorkingSet$
                            $z \in WorkingSet$

A simple example of an operator that creates a number of objects from a single object is the **half** operator, defined in (2.90).

(2.90)   Action: $\text{Do}(A, \text{half}(x))$
         Preconditions: $x \in WorkingSet$
         Postconditions: $\text{part}(x_1, half)$
                            $\text{part}(x_2, half)$
                            $\text{ancestor}(x_1, x)$
                            $\text{ancestor}(x_2, x)$
                            $x \notin WorkingSet$
                            $x_1 \in WorkingSet$
                            $x_2 \in WorkingSet$

Thus, when a new object is added to the working set, we also have some indication of which object it was derived from. As a more complex example of this kind of operation, consider the process of obtaining the kernels from an ear of corn. We will call this operation **get-kernels**, although it has no particular name in English, and define it as in (2.91).

(2.91)   Action: $\text{Do}(A, \text{get-kernels}(x))$
         Preconditions: $x \in WorkingSet$
         Postconditions: $\text{structure}(y, \text{set})$
                            $\text{ancestor}(y, x)$
                            $[\forall z : z \in y \supset \text{structure}(z, \text{individual}) \land$
                            $\qquad\qquad\qquad \text{packaging}(z, \langle \text{kernel}, \text{regular} \rangle)]$
                            $x \notin WorkingSet$
                            $y \in WorkingSet$

Thus, the process of getting the kernels from an ear of corn removes the ear in question from the working set, and adds an object which is a set of kernels. The use of operators like **get-kernels** allows us to represent derived objects. The object described as (2.92a) is then represented as (2.92b).

(2.92) a. the kernels from a fresh ear of corn

b. $\exists x, s_0, s_1, e, \forall s_i$ holds(s_i, substance(x, corn)) $\land$
holds(s_0, structure(x, individual)) $\land$
holds(s_0, packaging(x, $\langle$ear, regular$\rangle$)) $\land$
holds(s_0, fresh(x, $+$)) $\land$ occurs(s_0, s_1, e) $\land$
holds(s_i, substance(e, getting-kernels)) $\land$
holds(s_i, object(e, x)) $\land$ holds(s_i, ancestor(y, x)) $\land$
holds(s_i, substance(y, corn)) $\land$
holds(s_1, structure(y, set)) $\land$
[$\forall z$ holds(s_1, element(z, y)) $\supset$
holds(s_1, structure(z, individual)) $\land$
holds(s_1, packaging(z, $\langle$kernel, regular$\rangle$)))]

In English, this is glossed as follows: We have a physobj y whose structure is **set**, and whose elements are all individuals which are packaged as kernels; this physobj was derived from another physobj, x, by a GettingKernels event e, where x was a quantity of fresh corn packaged as an ear.

2.4.5   Action Decomposition

Modern planning systems embellish the basic apparatus described above in a number of ways. Two particular embellishments are of interest here. First, in hierarchical planners[10] we find the introduction of macro actions (also known as skeletal plans, plan schemas, and scripts) which aggregate a number of more primitive actions. These higher-level actions can then be used to plan at a higher level of abstraction; the lower level detail is filled in later. Second, we can distinguish "linear" planners from more recent "nonlinear" planners. Linear planners adopt what is known as the "linearity assumption": that solving the subgoals in a task can be performed in a strictly sequential fashion. Nonlinear planners, on the other hand, represent a plan as a partially ordered network, introducing temporal links between nodes in the plan only when absolutely necessary. (See Tate 1976 for a description of nonlinear planning.)

For simplicity, the system described in this book assumes that all the plans to be described are linear. Some issues relating to linearity are relevant to the part of the text generation mechanism that is responsible

---

10. The best exposition of the basic ideas used in hierarchical planning is found in the original work of Sacerdoti (1974, 1977).

for reordering of information before the generation of the final output; these are discussed in the next chapter but are not important here. The notion of hierarchical planning is of particular importance, however.

In the examples above, all the planning operators considered were *atomic* in the sense that they were assumed primitive and not open to decomposition. Whether an action is viewed as primitive depends entirely upon the context in which it is used; thus, a more detailed explanation of what it means to grate something might be required for a robot that understood only commands expressed in a language oriented toward describing simple movements of its limbs.

Within the planning literature, it is now generally accepted that constructing plans in realistic domains requires planning at different levels of abstraction. Thus, in a hierarchical planning system, we also have nonprimitive operators. In addition to preconditions and postconditions, each nonprimitive operator has a **body**. This provides a way of expanding the action described to produce a number of lower-level actions. Thus, we might have the body of the **prepare-beans** action defined as in (2.93).

(2.93)   **soak**$(x) \land$ **drain**$(x) \land$ **rinse**(x)

The body of a plan operator thus provides a way of looking at the process that makes up the original action at a smaller grain size. More precisely, if a plan P has a body, then it can be decomposed into a number of subtasks, each of which can be represented by schemas P_1 through P_n, where

- the start state for P_1 is the same as the start state for P,
- the end state for P_n is the same as the end state for P, and
- for each i where $n - 1 > i > 0$, the end state for P_i is the same as the start state for P_{i+1}.

In other words, execution of P_1 through P_n exhausts execution of P. Recursively, each P_i may also be decomposable.

Strictly speaking, there are infinitely many ways in which an action can be decomposed into smaller events: the process stuff that makes up an action can be partitioned in infinitely many ways. Here we have another similarity between objects and events (recall our earlier discussion of the constituency of an object). Just as in the case of ingredients we saw that there were difficulties in the individuation of objects, similarly there are difficulties in the individuation of actions and events. Consider, for example, the action described in (2.94).

(2.94)   Peel and chop the onion and carrots.

In the appropriate circumstances, we can reexpress this as any of the following:

(2.95)   a. Prepare the vegetables.
         b. Peel and chop the onions.
             Peel and chop the carrots.
         c. Peel the onions and carrots.
             Chop the onions and carrots.
         d. Peel the onions.
             Peel the carrots.
             Chop the onions.
             Chop the carrots.

Do we have one event, two events, or four events? Similarly, does (2.96) describe three adding actions, or one?

(2.96)   Add the milk, the stock and the beans.

Ultimately, as in the case of physobjs, it depends on how the action is viewed. In the present framework, this is determined by the level of detail used in the plan that constitutes the recipe in question; thus, we say that

(2.97)   Peel and chop the onions and carrots.

describes one event decomposed into four lower-level events, which have been collected together for the purposes of description.

In the real world, not all event decompositions are equal. Some are preferred over others, for a number of reasons:

- Some events are temporally related to others.

- Similarly, some events are more naturally related because they talk about the same entities.

- Some events are clustered because the language provides ways of talking about them.

Given that certain event decompositions are of more value than others, we can view the expansions for actions provided by the bodies of plan operators as corresponding to particular ways of decomposing one action into a number of other actions.

We can represent the eventuality corresponding to an instance of the execution of the **bean-preparing** action as

(2.98) $\exists e, s_0, s_3 \forall s$ holds(s, substance(e, bean-preparing)) $\wedge$
  occurs(s_0, s_3, e) $\supset$
    $\exists e_0, e_1, e_2, s_1, s_2$ holds(s, constituents(e, [e_0, e_1, e_2])) $\wedge$
      occurs(s_0, s_1, e_0) $\wedge$ holds(s, substance(e_0, soaking)) $\wedge$
        occurs(s_1, s_2, e_1) $\wedge$ holds(s, substance(e_1, draining)) $\wedge$
          occurs(s_2, s_3, e_2) $\wedge$ holds(s, substance(e, rinsing)) $\wedge$
            time(s_0) $<$ time(s_1) $<$ time(s_2) $<$ time(s_2)

We noted earlier that current planning systems allow the representation of partially ordered plans. Here, we always assume that a linearization has been adopted.

2.5   The Representation Language Summarized

2.5.1   Entities in general

1. The domain consists of a finite set of entities. Each entity is represented by a distinct symbolic constant called its index.

2. An entity is either a physobj or an eventuality. For convenience, physobjs are represented by the indices x, y, z and subscripted versions thereof; eventualities are represented by the indices e, f, g and subscripted versions thereof.

3. Every entity has, in addition to its index, a spec. This specification of the entity provides all the information known about that entity.

4. Every entity also has, as part of its specification, a substance. In the case of physobjs, the substance is the kind of matter from which the object is made; in the case of eventualities, the substance is the kind of process stuff that makes up the eventuality. There is a finite but extensible set of substances and process stuffs represented by means of symbolic constants; these are organized into a taxonomic graph structure.

5. As part of its specification, every entity has a **structure**. This corresponds to the way in which the entity is perceived.

   - If the entity is a physobj the structure is either **individual, set,** or **mass**.
   - If the entity is an eventuality, the structure is always **event**.[11]

6. An entity may have any number of additional properties specified as part of its specification, where those additional properties are drawn from a finite but extensible set of properties. These properties are binary-valued features, "+" and "−" being the possible values.

2.5.2 Physobjs

1. A physobj is any (not necessarily contiguous) collection of contiguous regions of space occupied by matter.

2. If it has been derived from some other physobj in the domain, a physobj has a specification of the latter physobj as its **ancestor**.

3. If a physobj has structure **individual**, then it also has a **packaging** as part of its specification. A packaging is a tuple consisting of a **shape** and a **size**. The possible values of **shape** and **size** are drawn from two finite but extensible sets.

4. If a physobj is a mass, it may or may not have a **quantity**.

5. If the physobj is a **set**, it may have either a **cardinality**, a **quantity**, an explicit list of **constituents**, or none of these (in which case it can be described only by a bare plural).

6. Cardinality is specified as a numerical value, or as a range of numerical values where the range consists of a **lowerlimit** and an **upperlimit**.

7. The quantity of a physobj is specified as a tuple consisting of some unit of weight or other form of measure and a number, or as a range consisting of two such tuples (one for the lower limit and one for the upper limit). The possible values for the **unit** feature are drawn from a finite but extensible set.

---

11. In a more complete system, each of the categories identified by Bach (1986) would be permitted as a value of the **structure** attribute; however, a single structure is adequate in the present circumstances.

8. If a physobj whose structure is set has the feature **constituents**, the value of this feature is a list of symbolic constants which are the indices of just those entities that are constituents of the set.

9. If a physobj whose structure is set does not have an explicit list of constituents, then it will have an **elements** feature. This provides a specification that is true of all the elements of the physobj.

10. Properties hold true of physobjs in **states**. The invariant properties (**substance** and **quantity**) hold true of an object in all states; all other properties of objects may change.

11. In general, any two states are linked by the occurrence of an eventuality.

12. There is a privileged physobj, called the **working set**, that has as its constituents the set of identifiably distinct objects in the recipe at some state (i.e., at a given time).

2.5.3 Eventualities

1. By analogy with physobjs, an eventuality is defined to be any (not necessarily contiguous) collection of contiguous regions of time occupied by process stuff.

2. Every eventuality **occurs** from a **begin** state to an **end** state.[12]

3. An eventuality may have, as part of its specification, a finite but extensible set of **participants**. These are collected into two substructures, corresponding to the **in** participants and the **out** participants: the **in** participants are those participants that exist in the **begin** state of the eventuality, and the **out** participants are those participants that exist in the **end** state of the eventuality. Each participant role has as its value a symbolic constant which is the index of an entity in the domain.

4. Corresponding to each eventuality there is an operator that defines the preconditions and postconditions of the type of action described by the eventuality, and which may also include a possible decomposition of the eventuality into its constituent eventualities.

---

12. This and the following properties are necessarily true only of eventualities whose structure is **event**.

2.6   Limitations

2.6.1   Perspectives

It was suggested above that whether we view a given quantity of matter as a mass or as a bounded individual seems to depend on the context, rather than on any intrinsic property of the quantity of matter itself. In principle, any countable object can be put through a "Universal Grinder" (Pelletier 1979) and made into a mass object: given something describable by *a dog*, we can convert it into a quantity of something described as *dog*. Similarly, given a "Universal Packager", we can convert any mass object into a countable object; thus, we can convert some quantity of something described as *coffee* into some individual described as *a coffee*.

In the representation language presented here, a given physobj may have only one structure at any one time; more precisely, we permit only one **perspective** on a given physobj at any one time. However, there are situations where this restriction may be too strong. Discussing this phenomenon, Link (1983: 303–304) argues that our guide in ontological matters has to be language itself:

> ... if we have, for instance, two expressions *a* and *b* that refer to entities occupying the same place at the same time but have different sets of predicates applying to them, then the entities referred to are simply not the same. From this it follows that my ring and the gold making up my ring are different entities.

Similarly, Link regards the following two noun phrases as denoting the same portion of matter, but wants to say that the individuals described are distinct:

(2.99)   a. the cards

       b. the deck of cards

On Link's view, an individual lies between a noun phrase and the denotation of that noun phrase. The notion of a physobj developed here corresponds to Link's notion of a portion of matter; we might identify the notion of a **discourse entity** as corresponding to Link's notion of an individual. A discourse entity could be said to provide a **perspective** on a physobj, and to be realized by means of a noun phrase. On this view, a discourse entity consists of a pair $\langle X, P \rangle$, where X is a physobj and P is a perspective. A discourse entity then provides one way (among potentially many) of describing a physobj. Then, if we view a physobj from two different perspectives, we have two discourse entities. Under this approach, Link's *the cards* is a noun phrase describing a physobj from a set perspective and his *the deck of cards* is a noun phrase describing the same physobj from a bounded-individual perspective. Notice that we can also view the same physobj as a mass individual: if I am collecting waste paper and cardboard for recycling, and I find an unwanted deck of cards, I can say

(2.100) I found some card.

Similarly, the same physobj can be described either in terms of a collection or in terms of the individuals that make up that collection: compare *a bouquet garni* and *some herbs*.

Note the difference here between *a pound of carrots* and *a deck of cards*: although the surface forms appear the same, the first describes a physobj from a set perspective (where we have a measure of the set but do not know its cardinality), whereas the latter is a statement of constitution, much closer to a noun phrase like *a stick of celery*, and therefore describes a bounded individual. This distinction is borne out by the following:

(2.101) a. a stick of celery

           b. a celery stick

(2.102) a. a deck of cards

           b. a card deck

(2.103) a. a pound of carrots

           b. *a carrot pound

In practice, the ability to switch between multiple perspectives on a physobj is rarely of any real benefit in the recipe domain; for simplicity, then, only one perspective is used at a time in EPICURE. However, in more complex domains it might be of value to introduce the additional distinct level of abstraction corresponding to the notion of a discourse entity just described.

Another use of the term *perspective* can be found in the literature; let us call this **functional** perspective to distinguish it from the notion discussed above, which could more properly be called **structural** perspective. Thus, one and the same individual may be seen as *a father*, *an architect*, and *an owner of a yacht*, and different properties may be applicable depending on the functional perspective taken. This point has been discussed by Grosz (1981: 100), and has been recognized by developers of knowledge representation languages. For example, KRL (Bobrow and Winograd 1977) provides a way of describing different roles that an entity can perform, and KL-ONE provides the notion of a **nexus** (Brachman 1979) as a way of connecting together different views of a particular individual. Thus, I can be viewed as a programmer, a cyclist, a guitar player, and so on; we may then encode the fact that I am a lazy cyclist while preventing the inference that I am therefore a lazy programmer or a lazy guitar player. McCoy (1985) notes some of the problems associated with attempts to make use of the notion of perspectives, and suggests a modified approach. The machinery required in order to make use of structural perspectives might also be applicable to functional perspectives; the major problems lie in deciding how structural and functional perspectives are related.

2.6.2   Disjunctions

As was pointed out above, disjunctions are surprisingly common in recipes; however, our representation language does not attempt to deal with them. This section explains why the current formalism does not support disjunctions, and make some observations on the usefulness of a notion of function in the representation of recipes.

We noted earlier that ingredients in recipes can be viewed as *specifications* for participating objects. On this view, we might suggest that each of the physobjs we have described is really a specification for a more abstract entity—which, for convenience, we will call a **marker**— and that the recipe instructions operate on these markers rather than operate on the physical instantiations of the ingredients directly. Thus, for each marker there is a corresponding specification, but the nature of the specification is not of fundamental importance: what the operators in the plan operate upon are markers. Any effects of operators, such as changes of state, will then have to be propagated onto the specifications themselves. Thus, we would need to state explicitly which markers were realized by which physobjs.

Adding this extra level of representation suggests a way of dealing with disjunctive specifications of ingredients. We can suggest that an ingredient described as

(2.104) 1 teaspoon of salt or 1 tablespoon of soy sauce

provides a number of **alternate specifications** for a marker. These might be represented in the following way:

(2.105) specifications(marker, $[x, y]$) $\wedge$
  substance(x, salt) $\wedge$ quantity(x, $\langle 1$, teaspoon$\rangle$) $\wedge$
  substance(y, soy-sauce) $\wedge$ quantity(y, $\langle 1$, tablespoon$\rangle$)

Here, the second argument to the specifications clause should be interpreted as a list of mutually exclusive specifications.

However, such a representation ultimately throws up yet more problems. Suppose, for example, that our disjunctive specification includes a process, as in (2.106).

(2.106) 75 g chopped almonds or toasted cashews

We have a problem here if we want to maintain that our operators apply only to markers and not to particular specifications, since the implied **toast** operator here applies to the cashews and not to the almonds. On the other hand, if we suggest that our operators apply, instead, to specifications, then wherever a disjunctive specification appears the arguments to our operators start to become unwieldy. In the case of the ingredient just described, an instruction to *Add the nuts* would be represented as something like **add**($[x \vee y]$); at the very least, this obscures the fact that we are talking about one functional participant in the recipe.

We have only just brushed the surface here. It is possible that we might be able to circumvent these problems if we describe the entire recipe at the functional level, rather than the physical level, along with correspondingly abstract operations upon the participants. Such an approach would help in other areas of recipe generation too. For example, many noun phrases that appear in recipes appear to be functional descriptions: thus we see references to *the seasoning*, *the sauce*, and so on. There is also a problem in the modeling of recipes concerning the creation of new objects: in the work described here, an object is assumed to be the same object through any *state* change, but if the substance is changed—for example, if two substances are added together, or an object is broken into pieces—then we bring new objects into existence. Yet, we typically find in recipes that, if we add (for example) some salt to some cooking carrots, we still refer to the result of this addition operation as *the carrots*. In EPICURE this is dealt with by assuming that in such cases one constituent of the object created by an addition operation is the major constituent, and using this constituent as the basis of any references generated. However, this is really only slipping a functional approach in by the back door.

3 The Generation of Connected Discourse

3.1 An Overview of EPICURE

In order to generate connected discourse, EPICURE makes use of four distinct processing modules (a **discourse planner**, a **discourse generator**, a **clause generator**, and a **domain modeler**) and six distinct knowledge sources (a **plan library**, a **hearer model**, a **discourse model**, a **world model**, a **lexicon**, and a **grammar**). The overall structure of the system is as shown in figure 3.1.[1] The role of each of the components is introduced below, and described in more detail in the rest of this chapter.

3.1.1 The plan library

EPICURE starts out with a particular goal to be achieved. In the present context, this is the goal of producing the result of a particular recipe. In order to be able to do this, EPICURE has to know what actions are necessary to achieve this goal. The actions known to EPICURE are defined, in terms of their preconditions and effects, in the **plan library**. In addition, if the action is a macro-operator rather than a primitive action, the definition contains a body (more precisely, a list of **constituents**) specifying the subactions that make up that action. From the point of view of the macro-operator, these subactions are primitives; however, each subaction may also have an entry in the plan library specifying its subactions, and so on. Thus, in principle, any action may be decomposed into lower-level actions.

The information held in operator definitions is used by EPICURE in two specific ways:

- In conjunction with knowledge of the hearer's capabilities, the **constituents** information is used by the discourse planner in order to determine just how much detail is required in the description of a plan of action.

- The **effects** information is used by the domain modeler to update

---

1. To reiterate the conventions used in this diagram: Data structures are represented by long flat boxes, whereas process modules are represented by the more squat boxes. An arrow pointing from box A to box B is intended to show that data flows from A to B.

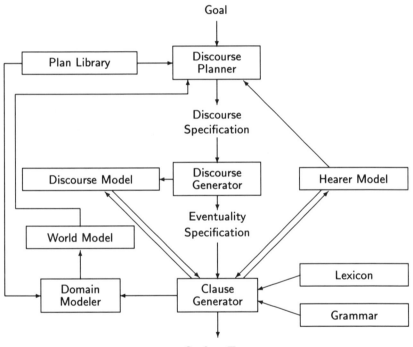

Figure 3.1
The overall structure of EPICURE.

the world model so that its state is consistent with the effects of the operations described.

3.1.2 The world model

At any time, the domain in which the system operates is in some particular state As we saw in chapter 2, a state can be characterized by a formula

(3.1) $\quad P_1 \wedge P_2 \wedge \ldots \wedge P_n$

where each P_i is a proposition that is true in that state. These propositions describe properties of the entities in the domain. As the description of a plan proceeds, the properties of entities may change; some entities may even disappear, and new entities may be created. In order to describe an entity, EPICURE must know what properties are true of that entity at a given time. Within the system, the current state of each entity is modeled by a knowledge base object representing all the properties that are true of that entity in that state; the world model is just that collection of such objects that describes all the entities in the domain. Whenever an action takes place, this collection of objects is updated by the domain modeler, as described in section 3.3.

3.1.3 The hearer model

The hearer model is a data structure specifying those propositions that EPICURE assumes the hearer believes to be true. Strictly speaking, the discourse model (described below) is essentially part of the hearer model by this definition; however, for convenience, we model the two as distinct data structures. We will refer to the part of the system's knowledge base that models the hearer's knowledge other than that derived directly from the discourse as the hearer model. The hearer model contains various kinds of information:

- For each action in the domain, if the hearer is assumed to know how to carry out that action, this fact is specified in the hearer model. The discourse planner makes use of this knowledge in determining the level of detail at which a plan should be described.

- For each entity in the domain, if the hearer has any knowledge of that entity apart from that gained from the discourse, then this information is specified in the discourse model. In the current domain, this information is minimal: the hearer is assumed to know that both he or she and the speaker are present in the domain—in Prince's (1981) terminology, that they are **situationally evoked**).

- The hearer is assumed to know the information maintained in the taxonomy of substances, so that, for example, a superordinate term such as *seasoning* can be used to describe an ingredient whose substance is *salt*.

- The hearer is also assumed to know a number of axioms of inference, so that he or she can infer the existence of entities that have not been explicitly introduced into the discourse. The use of this information is described in chapters 4 and 5.

The hearer model therefore plays two distinct roles:

- It provides EPICURE with the means to determine the level of detail necessary to describe the plan.

- It provides EPICURE with justification for using definite noun phrases to refer to a class of entities that are assumed to be mutually known outside the discourse, either directly or by virtue of inference, and allows it to use superordinate terms when describing ingredients.

Given a goal state S, modifying the contents of the hearer model will cause EPICURE to describe the plan required to achieve that goal differently, both in terms of the level of detail at which the plan is described and in the way in which objects participating in that plan are described.

3.1.4   The discourse planner

The discourse planner is the component of EPICURE that determines "what to say" at the topmost level; that is, it determines which particular actions should be described. This is done using the information stored in the plan library and the hearer model, as described above; the process is described in more detail in section 3.2.

The result of this process is a tree-structured discourse specification corresponding to the hierarchical decomposition of the plan it describes. Some discourse-level optimization is then carried out on this structure, primarily for the purposes of making the resulting text more fluent. This involves massaging the structure to allow the use of ellipsis and conjunction in the linguistic description of the plan.

3.1.5 The discourse generator

Once the optimized discourse specification has been constructed, it is passed to the discourse generator. This component has two responsibilities, which it fulfills as it walks around the discourse structure in a breadth-first fashion:

- The discourse model is constructed as a hierarchy of focus spaces matching the structure of the discourse specification.

- The eventuality specifications constituting the leaf nodes of the discourse specification are passed to the clause generator for realization.

This process is described further in section 3.3.

3.1.6 The discourse model

The discourse model is a repository for all the information made available in the discourse, and is used by the clause generator to determine how to refer to entities in the domain. In structure, the discourse model consists of a hierarchy of focus spaces: the approach to discourse modeling adopted here is based on the view of discourse structure proposed by Grosz and Sidner (1985, 1986). The construction of the discourse model is addressed in sections 3.3 and 3.4, and its use in generating referring expressions is described in chapter 5.

3.1.7 The clause generator

The process of generating clauses from eventuality specifications is described in section 3.4. The clause generator takes each basic eventuality specification provided by the discourse generator and builds two intermediate levels of structure, which result in the production of a surface linguistic string. First, a structure that represents the **recoverable semantic content** is constructed; from this, an **abstract syntactic structure** is derived, and this is then unified with the linguistic knowledge represented in the grammar and the lexicon to produce a surface string. The basic elements of this process for the overall construction of a sentence are described in the present chapter, although the details of the processes used in constructing noun phrase referring expressions are left until chapter 4.

3.1.8   The domain modeler

Before deciding on the semantic content of the description of an event, the clause generator passes the eventuality specification to the **domain model**. The domain modeler retrieves the operator definition corresponding to the eventuality from the plan library, and uses the information about the effects of the operator to update the world model appropriately. This process is described in section 3.3.

3.2   Deciding What to Say

3.2.1   Language as planned behavior

An increasingly widespread view found in computational linguistics is that language can be viewed as planned behavior, the ultimate goal of which is to effect some change in the state of mind of the hearer. Of course, this view of language is not new within work in linguistics and the philosophy of language, for at its heart lies the work of Austin (1962) and Searle (1969) on speech-act theory. The basic ideas of speech-act theory have been formalized and examined in ever more detail by a number of researchers in computational linguistics, beginning with the early work of Bruce (1975a); the best-known work is that of Allen, Perrault, Cohen, and Levesque (Allen and Perrault 1978; Cohen and Perrault 1979; Perrault and Allen 1980; Cohen and Levesque 1980; Cohen 1981; Allen 1983). This work has shown that speech acts can usefully be modeled as operators in a planning system, with the consequence that physical and speech acts can be integrated within the same framework.

Three major types of speech acts discussed in the literature are those of

- informing someone of some fact,
- asking someone a question, and
- requesting someone to carry out some action.

These are typically realized by means of the declarative, interrogative, and imperative sentence forms, respectively. However, by means of an **indirect speech act**, a speaker can perform an action other than that normally associated with a particular surface form; thus, in an appropriate context, the interrogative

(3.2)   Is there any salt?

may in fact convey a request to someone to pass the salt, although the surface form is more normally associated with the asking of a question.

In a planning framework, the direct speech act of informing is typically represented as in (3.3).[2]

(3.3)   Action: $Do(S, \textbf{inform}(H, Proposition))$
         Preconditions: $\textsf{Believes}(S, Proposition)$
         Body: $Do(S, \textbf{s-inform}(H, Proposition))$
         Postconditions: $\textsf{Believes}(H, \textsf{Believes}(S, Proposition))$

Similarly, the direct speech act of requesting might be represented as in (3.4).

(3.4)   Action: $Do(S, \textbf{request}(H, Action))$
         Preconditions: $\textsf{Believes}(S, \textsf{CanDo}(H, Action))$
         Body: $Do(S, \textbf{s-request}(H, Action))$
         Postconditions: $\textsf{Believes}(H, \textsf{Believes}(S, \textsf{Wants}(Action)))$

Here, **s-inform** and **s-request** are intended to represent surface informs and requests (i.e., declaratives and interrogatives). Having these specified as the bodies of the higher-level speech acts permits the representation of indirect speech acts; thus a request can be performed indirectly by means of a surface question, as we saw above. Within work in this area, the asking of a question is typically represented as a request to perform some kind of **inform** action. Thus, a *yes-no* question is a request to the hearer to inform the speaker whether or not some proposition is true:

(3.5) $Do(S, \textbf{request}(H, \textbf{informif}(S, Proposition)))$

Speech-act definitions like those given above are typically supported by subsidiary definitions, and rely on a number of simplifying assumptions. For example, in cooperative dialogue we might make the assumption that speakers do not tell lies, and that hearers cooperate by carrying out any actions requested of them. Various researchers complicate these definitions in various ways; Cohen and Perrault (1979), for example, distinguish **cando** preconditions and **want** preconditions, and Appelt

---

2. In this example and the following, S is the speaker and H is the hearer.

(1982, 1985) distinguishes effects on knowledge (**k-effects**) and physical effects (**p-effects**). Complications of this sort are necessary in order to model the effects of these actions on the states of mind of hearers.

Within EPICURE, we are not directly concerned with the intricacies of modeling the hearer's state of mind with respect to intentions (as opposed to the hearer's state of knowledge). This permits us to make some simplifying assumptions:

The Successful Communication Assumption Whenever the system requests an action, the hearer always understands that the speaker wants the action carried out.

The Cooperation Assumption The hearer always cooperates: whenever the hearer is requested to carry out some action, he or she will not refuse to execute it.

The Successful Action Assumption Actions which are requested are always carried out successfully: this simplifies the process of modeling what happens in the domain.

The System's Omniscience of the Hearer's Capabilities The system's knowledge of the hearer's capabilities is correct: if EPICURE thinks that an agent is capable of an action, then the agent is capable of that action.

It is fair to ask whether *all* language can be viewed as planned behavior. Indeed, some work has focused on the distinctions between planned and unplanned discourse (Ochs 1979; Sibun 1990), although the concern there is more with the mechanisms underlying extended discourse: the basic elements of a plan-based approach can still be relevant where smaller units of discourse are at issue. Hobbs and Evans (1979) apply the planning approach to conversational discourse and conclude that conversation can be viewed in this way, although some modifications to the planning mechanisms used in AI are necessary. Although the initial work on speech acts in a computational linguistics framework attempted to cover a very wide range of speech acts in a variety of social contexts (see Bruce 1975a), some more recent work has focused on **task-oriented dialogues** (see, for example, Cohen 1984a), typically in situations where an expert describes to an assistant how to execute some task. Many of the concepts developed in the planning literature seem to fit well here, particularly where the task itself has a structure that is amenable to hierarchical planning as described in chapter 2.

3.2.2   Hierarchical planning and reasoning about what to say

Sacerdoti (1977: 69ff) describes how, within a dialogue, a plan may be described in increasing detail in response to the user's requests. Suppose we have a hierarchical structure representing a planned task and its subtasks. Sacerdoti's NOAH then executes the plan by means of the following algorithm.

(3.6)   To execute a plan of action:

- Ask the user to accomplish the action represented by the node at the top of the plan.
- If the user responds positively, assume the action has been accomplished, and so the current plan has been successfully executed.
- If the user responds negatively, assume he or she needs a more detailed breakdown of the execution of the action, and so execute in turn all the subtasks of the current plan.

Thus, the description of the plan unfolds recursively, to a depth determined by the user's knowledge. Of course, Sacerdoti's work was not particularly concerned with language generation, and so in his system asking the user to accomplish an action amounted to no more than outputting some canned information associated with the corresponding plan node. A more formal description of a variation of Sacerdoti's basic method used by EPICURE as a means of constructing a hierarchically structured **discourse specification** that mirrors the structure of the plan being described is presented below.

Like any planning system, EPICURE takes as input a specified initial state and a specified goal state. In the domain of cooking tasks, the specified goal state is the preparation of food in some manner, this being the result of the execution of a recipe. In order to motivate the generation of discourses, we do not give EPICURE the capability of carrying out any actions other than making requests of someone else; as a result, the only way in which the system can achieve its goal is to describe to the hearer how to execute the cooking task in question. In order to do this,

EPICURE has to build a plan that specifies the requesting actions to be carried out.

Reasoning about action decomposition In order to determine what to say, EPICURE's discourse planner uses information in the hearer model and the plan library in conjunction with a number of axioms that allow the system to reason about what must be requested of the hearer.

Recall that the plan library specifies information about achieving particular goal states given particular initial states. In a proper planning system, we would use the preconditions and effects specified within the definitions of these operators in order to construct an appropriate sequence of actions to achieve the desired goal state.[3] In EPICURE, however, this aspect of the problem is not a central concern, and so the plan library also contains very-high-level operators corresponding to the particular recipes to be generated. Thus, given specific descriptions of an initial state s_0 and a goal state s_1, we stipulate that the system knows that a particular action will achieve the desired result:

(3.7)   Knows(EPICURE, occurs(s_0, s_1, e))

where e might be glossed as something like *making avocado salad*. This can be read as saying that the system knows that eventuality e occurring in state s_0 will result in state s_1, where states s_0 and s_1 are specified independently.

EPICURE's goal is then to ensure, or **guarantee**, that the event e takes place. In the context of planning, it is more convenient to talk of actions than of events. The execution of an action is an event, and so in what follows we will use the symbol T_i for the action corresponding to the event e_i. Intuitively, an agent A can guarantee that an action T will be executed if A is known to be able to find some way of seeing that T is executed; we state this as

(3.8)   CanGuarantee(A, T)

This may involve the agent carrying out the action, or getting someone else to execute the action; the means are irrelevant. Thus, the execution of an action can be delegated to anyone who can guarantee it, who may in turn be able to delegate it to someone else, and so on.

---

3. In theory, at least. Cooking is very complicated, however, and even working out the preconditions and effects of the necessary primitives would be a considerable task.

In order to determine what must be requested of the hearer in order
to ensure that the eventuality e takes place, EPICURE makes use of a
number of **planning axioms**: axioms that control the planning of the
discourse by providing a number of strategies for achieving the execution
of a specified action. In order to build a plan, EPICURE must find a
guarantor for each action in that plan. Thus, given a high-level action
T that leads to a specified goal state, the goal state can be achieved if
EPICURE can guarantee performance of T:

(3.9)   CanGuarantee(EPICURE, T)

The first strategy EPICURE makes use of is the **simple action strategy**.
If the required action is one that an agent is physically capable of, then
that agent can guarantee that action:

(3.10) $\forall A,\ T$ PhysicallyCapable$(A, T) \supset$ CanGuarantee(A, T)

We say that an agent is **physically capable** of an action if that agent
knows how to perform that action and is capable of doing so.

Information about the hearer's capabilities is one kind of knowledge
recorded in the hearer model. Thus, we would represent the fact that
the hearer knows how to perform **soaking** actions, and is physically
capable of doing so, by the following proposition:

(3.11)   PhysicallyCapable(hearer, **soaking**)

Note that this representation requires that an agent who is capable of
performing an action at all be capable of performing it irrespective of
the object or objects to which the action is applied; this is, of course, an
oversimplification.

The second strategy available to EPICURE is the **delegation strategy**: if an agent B can guarantee an action, and agent A is capable of
requesting B to carry out that action, then this means that agent A can
guarantee the action. This is expressed by the following axiom:

(3.12)   PhysicallyCapable$(A, \textbf{request}(B, T)) \wedge$ CanGuarantee$(B, T) \supset$
         CanGuarantee(A, T)

The third axiom deals with actions that can be decomposed into smaller
units, and is referred to as the **action decomposition strategy**: if
an agent knows a possible decomposition for a complex action, and can
guarantee each of the subactions in that decomposition, then it follows
that the agent can guarantee the higher-level action.

(3.13)   Knows(A, constituents($T, [T_1, T_2, \ldots, T_n]$)) $\wedge$
$\qquad$ [$\forall T_i : T_i \in [T_1, T_2, \ldots, T_n]$ ⊃ CanGuarantee(A, T_i)] ⊃
$\qquad$ CanGuarantee(A, T)

Some simplifications Together, the simple action strategy, the delegation strategy, and the action decomposition strategy provide the potential for complex dialogues between multiple agents attempting to achieve a mutually held goal. To simplify things in our domain, we impose a number of restrictions. First, the *only* action that EPICURE is capable of is requesting someone else to carry out some action; so, the only statement of EPICURE's capabilities present in the knowledge base is the following[4]:

(3.14) $\forall A, T$ PhysicallyCapable(EPICURE, **request**(A, T))

The hearer, however, is not capable of requesting anything of the system:

(3.15) $\neg \exists T$ PhysicallyCapable(hearer, **request**(EPICURE,T))

This restriction prevents the construction of plans that involve infinite regresses of mutual requests (i.e., where A requests B to request A to request B to ...). If we wanted to build a system that performed multi-agent planning and permitted the possibility of dialogue, we could augment the mechanism with some means of preventing circularity, but this is beyond the scope of the present work.

3.2.3 Building a plan

EPICURE creates an entire plan before attempting to realize any of that plan linguistically. In principle, it would be possible to interleave the two stages of plan construction and description; however, it is easier to treat them as distinct. This choice is purely an implementational issue from the standpoint of the present work.

Using the axioms described in the previous section, along with the information in the plan library and the hearer model, EPICURE can determine precisely which actions have to be described to the hearer in order to achieve a specific goal. Together, the axioms provide a way of implementing the following algorithm:

---

4. We adopt a "negation as failure" approach to the knowledge held in the knowledge base: i.e., if a particular proposition is neither in the knowledge base nor inferrable from the contents of the knowledge base, then it is assumed to be false.

$$
\begin{bmatrix}
\text{substance : bean-preparing} \\[4pt]
\text{participants :} \begin{bmatrix} \text{in : [object : } X] \\ \text{out : [result : } X] \end{bmatrix} \\[12pt]
\text{constituents :} \begin{bmatrix}
\begin{bmatrix}
\text{index : } E_1 \\[4pt]
\text{occurs :} \begin{bmatrix} \text{begin : } S_0 \\ \text{end : } S_1 \end{bmatrix} \\[8pt]
\text{spec :} \begin{bmatrix} \text{substance : soaking} \\ \text{participants :} \begin{bmatrix} \text{in : [object : } X] \\ \text{out : [result : } X] \end{bmatrix} \end{bmatrix}
\end{bmatrix} \\[20pt]
\begin{bmatrix}
\text{index : } E_2 \\[4pt]
\text{occurs :} \begin{bmatrix} \text{begin : } S_1 \\ \text{end : } S_2 \end{bmatrix} \\[8pt]
\text{spec :} \begin{bmatrix} \text{substance : draining} \\ \text{participants :} \begin{bmatrix} \text{in : [object : } X] \\ \text{out : [result : } X] \end{bmatrix} \end{bmatrix}
\end{bmatrix} \\[20pt]
\begin{bmatrix}
\text{index : } E_3 \\[4pt]
\text{occurs :} \begin{bmatrix} \text{begin : } S_2 \\ \text{end : } S_3 \end{bmatrix} \\[8pt]
\text{spec :} \begin{bmatrix} \text{substance : rinsing} \\ \text{participants :} \begin{bmatrix} \text{in : [object : } X] \\ \text{out : [result : } X] \end{bmatrix} \end{bmatrix}
\end{bmatrix}
\end{bmatrix}
\end{bmatrix}
$$

Figure 3.2
The KB entity corresponding to the process of bean preparation.

(3.16)   To achieve execution of a task T:

- if A is physically capable of T, then **request**(A, T);
- otherwise, for each $T_i \in T$, achieve execution of T_i.

As we saw in chapter 2, operators are modeled by means of knowledge base structures corresponding to partially specified eventualities (more precisely, eventualities in which the **participants** and **begin** and **end** states have not been instantiated). If the operator is not a primitive, then the definition will also specify a decomposition by means of a **constituents** feature. So, for example, the expansion of **bean-preparing** as a combination of the operations of **soak**ing, **drain**ing, and **rins**ing is controlled by the structure shown in figure 3.2, where the index of the top-level structure is E, the **begin** state is S_0, and the **end** state is S_3.[5] If the hearer is believed to understand what it means to prepare beans, the hearer model will contain the proposition in (3.17).

(3.17)   PhysicallyCapable(hearer,**bean-preparing**)

In such a situation, the constituency information specified in the operator definition can be disregarded by the planning mechanism. However, if the hearer does not know how to prepare beans, then each constituent action becomes a goal to be achieved by EPICURE. Each of these actions will have a more complete definition, specifying preconditions and effects as well as any further possible decomposition, as a separate entry in the plan library. When this information is required by EPICURE, it is obtained by **unifying** the plan structure being constructed with additional information held in the plan library. The unification of these more complete specifications with those provided in the mother goal's **constituents** slot allows EPICURE to gradually build a plan structure of increasing detail.

Note that these expansion specifications permit the distribution of participants across constituent operations, so that when an operator definition is unified with a particular working set the appropriate entities are threaded through the constituent actions.[6] Suppose, for example, that we have a recipe for making instant coffee. The input working set

---

5. The **index** and **occurs** attributes are omitted here for the sake of brevity.
6. Recall from chapter 2 that each operator is applied to a particular working set: the set of objects which appear within the **in** slot of the **participants** slot.

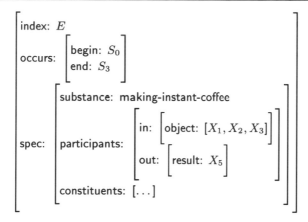

Figure 3.3
The KB entity corresponding to the process of making instant coffee.

here might consist of three ingredients: a quantity of water, some coffee granules, and some milk; the resulting working set is a single entity, the cup of coffee. The constituent actions of this simple recipe could be described by the following discourse:

(3.18)   Boil the water.
         Stir in the coffee granules.
         Add the milk.

The corresponding operator definition for **making-instant-coffee** might then look like that shown in figure 3.3 (some detail has been elided here). This structure specifies that a **making-instant-coffee** event E can be carried out beginning in a state S_0 and ending in a state S_3, applied to objects X_1, X_2 and X_3, and resulting in object X_5. The constituents feature, shown in figure 3.4, specifies the subactions involved. Each of these operators may be further specified by means of distinct entries in the plan library. Although the entity resulting from the **boiling** action is the same entity that the action is applied to, the **stirring-in** action results in a new entity, X_4, which then serves as one of the inputs to the **adding** action. The use of shared variables in the planning operator definitions thus ensures that, when actions are decomposed, the constituent actions will be applied to the appropriate entities.

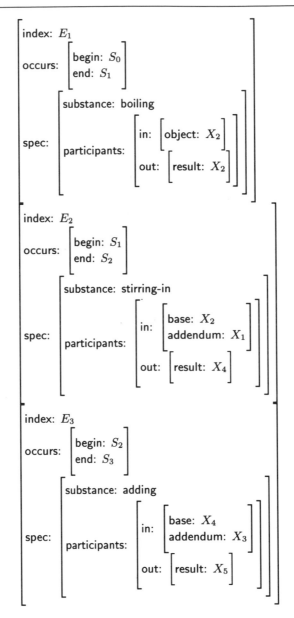

Figure 3.4
The constituents of making instant coffee.

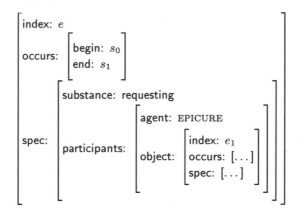

Figure 3.5
The form of a **requesting** eventuality.

The discourse specification   The discourse planning algorithm terminates when the entire plan is composed of actions of which the hearer is believed to be physically capable. The result is a tree-structured plan where the terminal nodes in the tree are those actions that must be requested of the hearer. Each such action can therefore be embedded with a **request** operation whose agent is EPICURE itself; the resulting **discourse specification** is thus a structured set of speech acts of the form

$$(3.19) \quad [T_1, T_2, \ldots, T_n]$$

where each T_i is either a primitive speech act or an embedded discourse specification. So, we might have a structure like

$$(3.20) \quad [T_1, T_2, [T_{31}, T_{32}, \ldots, T_{3n}], T_n]$$

where the structure of the discourse specification matches that of the task itself. Each primitive T_i is a **requesting** eventuality of the form shown in figure 3.5, where the embedded OBJECT is the requested eventuality. The representation of **requests** is somewhat simpler than that of physical actions, since the simplifying assumptions we made earlier remove the need to reason about the effects of speech acts on the hearer's state of mind.

To simplify the process of modeling the effects of actions in the domain, we also make the **begin** and **end** states of the **requesting** eventuality the same as the **begin** and **end** states of the requested eventuality. Of course, this is hardly an accurate representation of what happens in the real world; in general, execution of a requested action begins *after* the request itself has ended. However, this is of no consequence in the current framework.

3.2.4   Massaging the discourse specification

It has often been noted that knowledge representations used by programs which are not concerned primarily with language generation are often far from ideal with respect to the needs of a language generator. Mellish (1988: 137–138), for example, describes a **message optimization** phase in the language generation process; the purpose of this phase is to modify and simplify the output data produced by a planner so that it is more convenient for the purposes of the generator. Mellish's optimization rules are, in the main, not linguistically oriented; rather, they perform a role analogous to that of **critics** (Sacerdoti 1977) in nonlinear planning systems, watching out for and removing redundancies in the plan structure. EPICURE, on the other hand, is primarily oriented toward discourse generation, and so any massaging of the message that it carries out always has linguistic goals in mind. Currently, this aspect of the system is very primitive, and does no more than modify the structure produced by the discourse planner to allow the clause generation process to make use of conjoined verbs.[7] Further optimizations could be added, however. In particular, if integrated with a nonlinear planning system, one of the functions of the massaging process would be to determine the best order in which to present information. In the context of recipe description, the order of presentation of actions does not always match the order of execution. Often, the most useful temporal ordering of the actions is sabotaged by the author of the recipe, perhaps in the interests of compactness, so that actions relating to the same objects are often described together even if they are temporally quite distant from each other. Consider the following recipe, for example.

---

7. There are similarities here with the collapsing together of moves as carried out by Davey's (1978) program PROTEUS.

(3.21)   Cook the rice; cool.
         Sprinkle apple and banana with lemon juice and add to rice.
         Steep raisins in a little boiling water for half an hour to plump;
         drain, and add to rice with sunflower seeds, mixing well.
         Fry onion in oil with curry powder for 10 minutes.

Here, the instruction to *steep the raisins* comes after the instruction to
add the apple and banana to the rice, although it would obviously be
more sensible to start steeping the raisins earlier.

   In EPICURE, message optimization rules operate only on sequences of
primitive **requests**. This is necessary in the current framework, since
otherwise the structure of the resulting discourse specification may de-
viate substantially from the structure of the underlying task. Thus, we
have an optimization rule that checks to see if a sequence of eventualities
has the same participants; if so, the description of these eventualities
can be collected together, resulting in the generation of a number of
conjoined verbs. In the case of bean preparation discussed earlier, for
example, the following are all primitive actions:

(3.22)   a.   Do(EPICURE, **request**(hearer, **soak**(x)))

         b.   Do(EPICURE, **request**(hearer, **drain**(x)))

         c.   Do(EPICURE, **request**(hearer, **rinse**(x)))

However, since all three **requests** are sisters in the discourse specification, they can be collected together. The result is a single **request**
eventuality which has the **object** shown in figure 3.6. As a result, instead
of generating the sequence of sentences in (3.23), we can generate the
single sentence in (3.24).

(3.23)   Soak the butterbeans.
         Drain them.
         Rinse them.

(3.24)   Soak, drain and rinse the butterbeans.

Optimization rules closer in spirit to those used by Mellish would be appropriate for collecting clauses into complex sentences. Brée and Smit
(1986) specify rules for incorporating subordinate clauses into sentences,
and Scott and Souza (1990) suggest various heuristics for clause combining in the framework of Rhetorical Structure Theory; these would

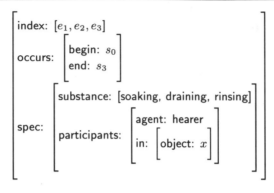

Figure 3.6
The result of message optimization.

be particularly useful if we were to generate recipes that included more detailed descriptions of actions that incorporate information such as specifications of duration and manner. Incorporating the necessary information is far from trivial, however, and it is beyond the scope of the work presented here.[8] In what follows, we will generate only single-clause sentences.

A final modification made to the discourse specification involves the addition of a **describe** speech act to the front of the structure for each entity in the working set of the top-level action in the plan. Thus, a series of structures of the form shown in figure 3.7 are added. The complete discourse specification then has the form

(3.25) $[D_1, D_2, \ldots, D_n, R]$

where each D_i is a **describe** action, and R is either a primitive **request** (in the limiting case where a single action is to be requested) or a discourse specification. In principle, the working set required by each individual action could be described immediately before that action; however, it is more convenient to describe all the ingredients of a recipe at the beginning of a recipe; and so, in general, no **describe** acts will appear other than at the top level of the discourse specification.[9]

---

8. In this connection, see Karlin (1988) on the variety of semantic case roles that are common in recipes.

9. This is analogous to a situation in programming, where we might decide to declare all variables as global, rather than local to the procedures that use them.

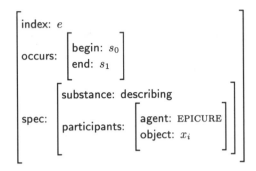

$$\begin{bmatrix} \text{index: } e \\ \text{occurs: } \begin{bmatrix} \text{begin: } s_0 \\ \text{end: } s_1 \end{bmatrix} \\ \text{spec: } \begin{bmatrix} \text{substance: describing} \\ \text{participants: } \begin{bmatrix} \text{agent: EPICURE} \\ \text{object: } x_i \end{bmatrix} \end{bmatrix} \end{bmatrix}$$

Figure 3.7
The form of a **describe** action.

3.3 Discourse Generation and Domain Modeling

3.3.1 The discourse model

It is generally recognized that the salience or information status of an entity is a crucial factor in determining the kind of linguistic expression that can be used to refer to that entity. Our primary concern is with modeling the information status of those entities that have been explicitly introduced into the discourse; i.e, those entities which have been, in Prince's (1981) terminology, **textually evoked**. Most computational models of discourse understanding or generation model this aspect of information status by means of a discourse model of some kind. Typically, this structure is used to determine

- when a pronoun can be used to refer to an entity

and

- when a definite referring expression, as opposed to an indefinite referring expression, can be used to refer to an entity.

In most cases, the discourse model is no more than a list of the entities that have been mentioned in the discourse. Assuming a very simple pronominalization heuristic, then, if we have a discourse model D and an intended referent x, we might have a simple algorithm along the following lines:

(3.26)   **if** x was mentioned in the previous sentence
          then use a pronoun
          else if $x \in D$ **then** use a definite noun phrase
          else use an indefinite noun phrase

However, another aspect of the meaning of the definite determiner is the uniqueness of the description contained in the noun phrase; the above algorithm has nothing to say about this.[10] Ideally, our discourse model should have something to say about how the relevant intended context of interpretation is determined.

Below, we first note some of the requirements we would like to see met by a discourse model, and then go on to describe the structure of the discourse model used by EPICURE.

The requirements to be met by the discourse model Some anaphoric phenomena, such as *one*-anaphora, verb phrase ellipsis, and most instances of pronominalization, appear to obey a kind of locality constraint, in that the antecedent material required for their resolution tends to occur within the previous few sentences of the discourse. Full definite noun phrase reference, on the other hand, does not appear to be restricted in this way.

Apart from simply recording which entities have been mentioned in the discourse, we would like our discourse model to have something to say about the fact that anaphoric phenomena appear to fall into these two broad categories. One suitable distinction we might embody within the discourse model, then, is that—suggested by Grosz (1977)—between local and global focus. Work in psycholinguistics lends support to the view that the hearer's memory for text consists of two parts, referred to as syntactic and semantic memory. Guindon (1985) has explicitly used Grosz's distinction as a model in a number of experiments. Some work on anaphora in linguistics has also supported this general view: Hankamer and Sag (1976) draw a distinction between **deep anaphora** and **surface anaphora**, corresponding to the distinction between semantic and syntactic memory. The most common anaphora are surface anaphora, which are always generated (and thus interpreted) with respect to the contents of syntactic memory. Other anaphora are deep

---

10. We could also take issue with the simple approach to pronominalization incorporated here. We will return to this in chapter 5.

anaphora, and are concerned with the "semantic memory" part of the discourse model.

Adopting this distinction then raises a number of questions:

- What part of the preceding discourse corresponds to local focus?

- What kinds of information are stored in the element of the discourse model corresponding to the local focus?

- What internal structure, if any, does the component of the discourse model corresponding to global focus have?

- What kinds of information are stored in the element of the discourse model corresponding to the global focus?

The answers we give to these questions should take account of as many anaphoric phenomena as possible; the extent to which our chosen model achieves this goal, and how it does so, will be examined in chapter 5. Below, we describe the basic structure of the model we adopt.

The structure of the discourse model   Our discourse model distinguishes two principal components, corresponding to Grosz's (1977) distinction between local focus and global focus.

We will call that part of the discourse model corresponding to the local focus **cache memory**. We assume that cache memory contains the lexical, syntactic, and semantic detail of the current (major) clause being generated, and the same detail for the previous (major) clause. The significance of the clause as the primary unit of discourse modeling can be questioned. It has often been suggested that the basic unit of communication is the sentence (see, for example, Winograd 1983: 469), but there are various other measures we might have chosen: apart from the contents of a single sentence, clause, or utterance, we might have specified a fixed number of words, morphemes, or even phonemes. Ultimately, all these suggestions have something to offer, but how the differing demands they make might be reconciled will not be pursued here.

As was stated at the outset of this work, psychological plausibility is not one of our aims. This does not mean, however, that work in psychology and psycholinguistics is of no relevance. We might note, then, that a considerable amount of research in this area has argued that the sentence, or the clause, or some closely related unit, constitutes the basic

planning unit in language production. In this connection, see Bernardo
(1977) on the cognitive relevance of the sentence, and Taylor (1969),
Butterworth (1975), MacNeilage (1973), Danks (1977), and Lindsley
(1975, 1976) on the size of planning units.

Corresponding to global focus, our discourse model will consist of
a number of **focus spaces**. These focus spaces record the semantic
content, but not the syntactic or lexical detail, of the remainder of the
preceding discourse. As suggested by Grosz and Sidner's work (Grosz
1977; Grosz and Sidner 1986), some of these focus spaces will be arranged
in a focus stack that models the focus of attention in the discourse;
however, our discourse model must provide a history of the relevant
detail from all the discourse, not just those parts currently in focus, and
so we also require a structure that consists of those focus spaces that
have been removed from the focus stack.

A major motivation for the adoption of a discourse model of this kind
is that it fits well with the approach we have taken to the generation of
discourses from underlying plans, i.e., by means of recursive expansion of
plan operators into their components. As we will see, there are a number
of ways in which this basic model can be used; and, as will be discussed
in chapter 5, it may help to provide an explanation for long-distance
pronominalization.

More precisely, our discourse model has the following structure. First,
cache memory consists of three parts[11]:

Current Clause Work Space This contains the recoverable semantic structure corresponding to the current clause, and both the
abstract and surface syntactic structures generated from it (the
format of these structures will be described later).

Previous Clause Contents This contains the recoverable semantic
structure of the previous clause generated.

The Current Center This contains the index of the current discourse
center, intuitively similar to the notion of centering suggested by

---

11. Our use of the term "cache memory" is slightly different from that proposed by
Guindon (1985: 218), who uses the term to refer to a memory structure that contains
"a subset of the meaning units expressed in the previous sentences." For her, cache
memory is one part of short-term memory: the other part, called the **buffer**, holds a
representation of the incoming sentence. Thus, Guindon's short-term memory is our
cache memory; her cache is our previous clause contents structure; and her buffer is
our current clause workspace.

Grosz, Joshi, and Weinstein (1983)—i.e., something like the focus of attention. In recipes, we take the center to be the result of the previous operation performed; because of this, the centre may not always be realized linguistically. The effects of this will be seen later.

The global focusing component of the discourse model also consists of two distinct parts:

The Focus Stack This contains a focus space for each discourse segment that has not been closed. Each focus space consists of a set of structures, one for each entity (object or event) mentioned in that focus space. These structures are partially specified knowledge base structures, as defined in chapter 2; they are intended to represent the hearer's knowledge of the entities introduced in the discourse.

The Closed Focus Space List This structure contains the focus spaces that have been popped from the focus stack as a result of the closing of the corresponding discourse segments.

Within EPICURE, the discourse model is assumed to be identical for both the speaker and the hearer. This permits us to make use of one data structure for modeling the discourse, instead of having to maintain one discourse model for the speaker and one for the hearer. It also means that we adopt what has been called the **standard name assumption** (Appelt and Kronfeld 1987: 641): that is, that the internal names used to represent real-world entities are the same for both speaker and hearer. So, if the system constructs the referring expression *the black olives* in order to refer to the entity x, then the act of reference succeeds if the hearer associates the entity x with this description. Appelt and Kronfeld point out that, in general, this assumption is too strong, and attempt to eliminate it; however, we adopt it for the present purposes. Thus, by consulting the discourse model to ascertain the relative salience of an entity to be referred to, the speaker can assume that the entity will have a similar degree of salience in the hearer's discourse model.

Note that the assumption means that there is no scope in the present system for modeling **communication failure**, whereby the discourse participants believe themselves to be talking about the same entity when in fact they are talking about different entities (in this connection, see

the work by Goodman [1985, 1986] on reference repair). These concerns
are beyond the scope of the present work.

3.3.2   The discourse generation algorithm

Once the discourse planner has constructed the discourse specification,
each element of this structure has to be passed to the clause generator.
In conjunction with this, the basic elements of the discourse model must
also be manipulated. Coordinating the construction of the discourse
model with the dispatch of eventuality specifications to the clause generator is the task of the discourse generator component.

Recall from section 3.2 that a discourse specification has the following
structure:

$$(3.27) \quad DS = [D_1, D_2, \ldots, D_n, R]$$

where each D_i is a **describe** action, and R is either a primitive **request** (in the limiting case where a single action is to be requested) or
a discourse specification. Given a discourse specification DS produced
by the discourse planner, the process of generating a discourse proceeds
as follows.

- Push a focus space for this discourse onto the focus space stack,
  and make it the current focus space (CFS).

- For each **describe** action in DS:

    - Build a recoverable semantic structure which describes x_i, the
      object of the **describe** action.[12] The recoverable semantic
      structure represents all the information that the hearer should
      be able to recover from the resulting noun phrase.

    - Add a knowledge base structure for x_i to CFS, where that
      knowledge base structure contains the information chosen for
      inclusion in the recoverable semantic structure.

    - Pass the recoverable semantic structure to the surface gen-
      erator. This will construct an abstract syntactic structure
      suitable for input to the grammar.

---

12. The processes involved in building the recoverable semantic structure and the
abstract syntactic structure are described in chapter 4.

Once all the initial descriptions have been dealt with, we turn to the remainder of the discourse specification. The algorithm is shown in (3.28).

(3.28)   To describe R:

- If R is a primitive **request**, pass it to the clause generator.
- If R is a list of specifications, then do the following.
  Push a new focus space onto the stack and make it the CFS.
  Describe each $R_i \in R$.
  Pop the focus stack and add the popped focus space to the closed focus space list.

The net effect is that the top-level mechanism recursively builds a focus space structure that follows the embedding of the discourse structure.

3.3.3   Modeling the domain

In order to be able to compute appropriate referring expressions, the system's world model must be accurate at the time those descriptions are computed. Ensuring that this is the case is the task of the **domain modeler**. Before the clause generator attempts to construct a clause describing an eventuality specification, it first passes the eventuality specification to the domain modeler. This models the effect of the action about to be described. This means that, when clause generation proceeds, EPICURE has at its disposal information describing the states of the world *before* the action to be described took place and *after* the action to be described took place. This is necessary in the construction of clauses like (3.29), where the entity referred to by *the stalks* is not present explicitly in the domain until after the **destalking** action has taken place.

(3.29)   Remove the stalks from the strawberries.

Recall that the state of all the entities in the domain can be characterized as a conjunction of propositions of the form

(3.30) $\mathsf{holds}(s, P)$

where P is a predication of some property of an entity and s is the state in which this predication holds true. A serious problem for any system that models a dynamically changing domain is the **frame problem**: for any change that takes place as the result of some event, how do we model the fact that most other things do not change?

In the current framework this problem is not severe, since we are dealing with a small number of entities at any one time. We thus have a **frame axiom** which states that, other things being equal, nothing changes: given an event e such that

(3.31) $\mathsf{occurs}(s_0, s_1, e)$

then in the general case

(3.32) $\forall P\ \mathsf{holds}(s_0, P) \supset \mathsf{holds}(s_1, P)$

In other words, everything that was true before the event took place is also true after the event took place. Of course, some things *do* change as the result of events' having occurred. Within a procedural model, this poses no significant problems. EPICURE models the effects of an action by means of **add** and **delete** lists (this method dates back to the STRIPS system (Fikes and Nilsson 1971)): the **add** list specifies those propositions that have to be added to the new state description, and the **delete** list specifies those propositions that have to be removed from the state description. Thus, for the operator **soak**, we have the following information:

(3.33)   Add: $\mathsf{soaked}(x, +)$
           Delete: $\mathsf{soaked}(x, -)$

Let A be the add list for a given operation, and let D be the delete list for that operation. The domain model is then updated as follows whenever an eventuality e causes a transition from state s_0 to state s_1:

- For each P such that $\mathsf{holds}(s_0, P)$, add $\mathsf{holds}(s_1, P)$.
- For each $P \in D$, remove $\mathsf{holds}(s_1, P)$.
- For each $P \in A$, add $\mathsf{holds}(s_1, P)$.

Within EPICURE, the effects of an action are modeled as **delete** and **add** lists included as part of the **spec** of the operator in question. So, for example, the **delete** and **add** lists of the **soaking** operator are as shown in figure 3.8. Using the frame axioms described above, updating the world model then involves creating new knowledge base structures for

$$\begin{bmatrix} \text{delete}: & \begin{bmatrix} \begin{bmatrix} \text{index}: X \\ \text{state}: S_2 \\ \text{spec}: \begin{bmatrix} \text{soaked}: - \end{bmatrix} \end{bmatrix} \end{bmatrix} \\ \\ \text{add}: & \begin{bmatrix} \begin{bmatrix} \text{index}: X \\ \text{state}: S_2 \\ \text{spec}: \begin{bmatrix} \text{soaked}: + \end{bmatrix} \end{bmatrix} \end{bmatrix} \end{bmatrix}$$

Figure 3.8
The **delete** and **add** lists for the **soaking** operator.

each object in the domain (i.e., each object in the global working set), identical to the old knowledge base structures except that the value of the **state** feature is changed from the **begin** state of the event in question (say S_1) to the **end** state of that event (say S_2). Then we apply the following algorithm.

- For each element d in the event's **delete** list:

    - Obtain the knowledge base structure indexed by $\langle d$ index$\rangle$ and $\langle d$ state$\rangle$.
    - For each element in the **spec** feature in d, remove that element from the knowledge base structure (if it is there: it may not be present).

- For each element a in the **add** list:

    - Obtain the knowledge base structure indexed by $\langle a$ index$\rangle$ and $\langle a$ state$\rangle$.
    - For each element in the **spec** feature in a, add that element to the knowledge base structure.

Execution of an action also causes the current working set to be updated. The constituency of the working set is determined by the operator defini-

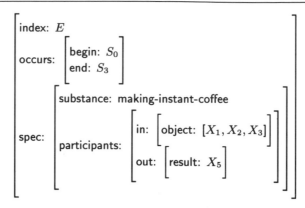

Figure 3.9
The KB entity corresponding to the process of making instant coffee.

tion itself. Recall the **making-instant-coffee** operator we saw earlier,
repeated in figure 3.9; all the distinct objects that appear in the in structure are constituents of the working set at the **begin** state, whereas all
the distinct objects that appear in the **out** structure are constituents of
the working set at the **end** state. Suppose we have a **making-instant-
coffee** event occurring from state s_0 to state s_1; then we have

(3.34) $\text{holds}(s_0, \text{constituents}(x, [x_1, x_2, x_3]))$

before the event, and

(3.35) $\text{holds}(s_1, \text{constituents}(x, [x_5]))$

afterwards where x is the global working set.

3.4   Generating Clauses

We now turn to the question of how an eventuality specification, as
produced by the discourse generator, is realized as a sentence by the
clause generator. The main issue here is the determination of the semantic content of the sentence to be output, along with the specification
of additional information that determines ordering or particular grammatical choices. Within EPICURE, there are two intermediate levels of
representation corresponding to a given surface string; we call these

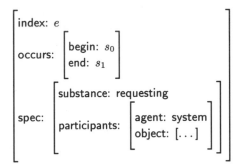

Figure 3.10
The KB entity corresponding to a **request**.

the **recoverable semantic structure** and the **abstract syntactic structure**. The distinctions between these levels of representation are described below.[13]

3.4.1   Levels of representation

The input provided to the clause generator by the discourse generator is a particular kind of knowledge base (KB) structure, namely an eventuality specification that specifies a speech act. In the current context, this is always a **request**. The input structure is therefore something like that shown in figure 3.10, where the embedded **object** is the particular eventuality to be requested. Realizing this request as a surface linguistic form involves the construction of two intermediate levels of representation, as follows.

Recoverable semantic structure   As has often been noted, a representational formalism that is useful for one task may be inappropriate for other tasks (see, for example, Swartout 1983). So, in a situation where a generation system is acting as a front end to some other application, it may be necessary to provide some mapping from the particular structures used by the application to structures that are more appropriate to

---

13. At an earlier stage in the development of this work, the recoverable semantic structure was referred to as **deep** semantic structure, and the abstract syntactic structure was referred to as **surface semantic** structure; thus, the two intermediate levels of structure were both viewed primarily as semantic structures. However, although the abstract syntactic structure does indeed encode what we might call semantic information, it is motivated primarily by syntactic concerns; hence its name.

the needs of the generation system itself.

In the case of EPICURE, the particular structures that are useful for modeling the domain for the purposes of planning are not the most appropriate for the generation of text. More particularly, an eventuality specification as provided by the discourse generator, since it is consists of an instantiated plan operator, may include information that is not required in the description of that eventuality; in this sense, the structure is overspecified. In another respect, the structure may be underspecified; in particular, the participants in the eventuality are specified by means of their indices alone, with no associated information attached.

Thus, given an eventuality specification, the clause generator uses a set of **mapping rules** (described below) to build a **recoverable semantic structure**. This specifies, in a relatively flat form, the semantic content of the utterance to be generated. In this structure, the indices of objects are replaced by structures which describe the semantic content of the noun phrases that will describe these objects; and any participants and other information in the eventuality which are not to be described will have been omitted. Thus, the mechanism used to build the recoverable semantic structure represents the bridge between knowledge representation and semantic representation, where the latter is a linguistically motivated construct. The semantic representation is intended to be domain-independent: the particular mechanism used by EPICURE to construct the recoverable semantic structure in the current domain could be replaced by a different mechanism to permit it to generate text for other applications.[14]

As the name suggests, the recoverable semantic structure corresponding to an event to be described represents the semantic content which should be recoverable from the utterance by the hearer: this does not mean that all of this semantic content need be explicitly *realized* by the clause generator. So, for example, the use of of *one*-anaphora and verb phrase ellipsis is not represented at the level of recoverable semantic structure; for related reasons, it is the recoverable semantic structure that is integrated into the discourse model.

---

14. As things are set up at the moment, any such application would have to provide knowledge base structures that are expressible as single clause sentences. In practice, it is probably more desirable to interface application and generation system at a higher, or more abstract, level: see, for example, the work of Moore and Mann (1979, 1982).

Abstract syntactic structure   A second set of mapping rules is then applied to the recoverable semantic structure, resulting in the construction of an **abstract syntactic structure**. This structure is much closer to the syntax of the linguistic form that will eventually be produced: it incorporates ordering information, and takes account of the scope for *one*-anaphora and other forms of ellipsis. The mapping from recoverable semantic structure to abstract syntactic structure is one-to-many: so, for example, the recoverable semantic structure will specify which illocutionary act is to be performed by the utterance being generated, but will not specify which particular surface form is to be used to realize this act.

Making use of two intermediate levels of representation in this way is not without precedent. Webber (1979) does this, for example, and for reasons not unrelated to those that motivate the distinction here: in particular, she found it useful to distinguish a level of representation that does not include anaphoric elements from one that does.

The abstract syntactic structure is then unified with the grammar, as described later in this section, resulting in the production of a surface string.

The clause generation process therefore consists of a series of transducers, as shown in figure 3.11. These levels could be compiled together, but it is conceptually simpler to deal with them as distinct processes, described below.

3.4.2   Building the recoverable semantic structure

Recoverable semantic structure   The domain of the KB→RS mapping rules is the universe of knowledge base structures, and the range is the universe of recoverable semantic (RS) structures. The set of possible RS structures is defined by the grammar in (3.36).

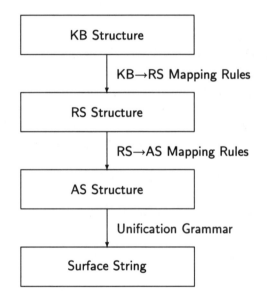

Figure 3.11
The levels of representation in clause generation.

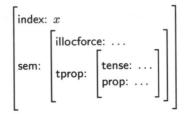

Figure 3.12
The basic form of a recoverable semantic structure corresponding to a speech act.

(3.36)	RS	::-	index sem
	index	::-	x_i | e_i | $\langle$ *a list of indices* $\rangle$
	sem	::-	illocforce tprop
	illocforce	::-	*requesting, informing,* ...
	tprop	::-	tense prop
	tense	::	*present, past, inf* ...
	prop	::-	substance participants
	substance	::-	$\langle$ *a basic substance* $\rangle$
	participants	::-	[agent] [in] [out]
	in	::-	[object] ...
	out	::-	[object] ...

The recoverable semantic structures corresponding to the individual participants are not included in this grammar, but will be described in chapter 4.

So, the basic form of a recoverable semantic structure corresponding to a speech act eventuality is that shown in figure 3.12.

Mapping rules The mapping from knowledge base structure to recoverable semantic structure is one-to-many: the end result of this stage depends on the particular mapping rules used.

Mapping rules within EPICURE always take the same basic form: they specify an input pattern, and a resulting output pattern. The left-hand side of each rule is some partially specified structure in the domain of the rule; the right-hand side of each rule is some partially specified structure in the range of the rule. Instantiating a rule against a particular input structure and a particular output structure results in the output structure's becoming more fully specified as a result of the rule's having applied.

Mapping rules are collected together into ordered sets, such that for any given input structure only the first rule in each set that matches the input structure will be used. By forcing the system to backtrack, subsequent rules which match the input structure can be used, thus producing multiple output structures for a given input structure. The algorithm for building a recoverable semantic structure from a knowledge base structure then applies a number of sets of rules to the input structure in turn.

Within the current context, there are effectively four sets of rules that are used, with the following functions:

1. Build the basic recoverable semantic structure for the utterance to be generated, specifying the illocutionary force to be used.

2. Determine the tense to be used in the utterance.

3. Determine which participants in the eventuality are to be mentioned or described in the utterance.

4. Build recoverable semantic structures corresponding to the participants to be described.

This last step is essentially recursive, and will be described in detail in chapter 4. The first three steps are outlined below.

Determining the illocutionary force   The illocutionary force to be used depends straightforwardly upon the substance of the eventuality specification itself (recall that the eventuality specification passed to the clause generator is essentially a specification of a speech act, with the propositional content of the utterance being the object of that act). The only mapping rule in this set is the following:

$$(3.37) \quad \text{KB:} \begin{bmatrix} \text{index: } X \\ \text{spec: } \begin{bmatrix} \text{substance: } F \end{bmatrix} \end{bmatrix} \Rightarrow \text{RS:} \begin{bmatrix} \text{index: } X \\ \text{sem: } \begin{bmatrix} \text{illocforce: } F \end{bmatrix} \end{bmatrix}$$

This rule establishes that the recoverable semantic structure corresponding to an eventuality that is a speech act is a structure whose illocutionary force is the speech act in question.

Mapping rules as path equations Mapping rules can also be represented as sets of **path equations**. A **path** in a feature structure is a sequence of features that picks out some part of that structure. We notate a path by means of a sequence of symbols enclosed between angle brackets, where the first symbol is an identifier for the feature structure itself and the second and subsequent symbols are feature names. Thus, given a structure F, the path

(3.38) $\langle F \; a \; b \; c \rangle$

picks out the value of the feature c in that structure which is the value of the feature b in that structure which is the value of the feature a in the structure F.

Corresponding to the mapping rule presented above, then, we have the following set of path equations:

(3.39) $\langle$RS index$\rangle$ = $\langle$KB index$\rangle$
         $\langle$RS sem illocforce$\rangle$ = $\langle$KB spec substance$\rangle$

In general, those path equations whose left-hand side specifies a path in the input structure and whose right-hand side specifies an atomic value are effectively conditions on the application of the rule represented by the set of path equations. That this is not made explicit in the formalism is deliberate, since it means that the equations can be read declaratively and thus could, in theory, be used in reverse (i.e., to construct knowledge base structures from recoverable semantic structures).

In what follows, mapping rules will be specified as sets of path equations.

Determining tense The propositional content (tprop, for tensed proposition) of the recoverable semantic structure consists of two parts: the tense and the prop (for proposition). Ideally, the tense of the proposition should be determined by the relative temporal indices of the speech time, the event time and the reference time (Reichenbach 1947). However, we make use of a much simplified rule here, since only imperative sentences are realized in the current context:

(3.40) $\langle$KB spec illocforce$\rangle$ =   requesting
         $\langle$RS sem tprop tense$\rangle$ =   inf

Choosing the participants In order to choose the participants to be described, for each **substance** we have a verb **case frame** (Fillmore 1968; Bruce 1975b) specifying the correspondences between KB participants and RS participants. The frame for **peel** is as follows[15]:

(3.41) **Peel** **Verb Case Role** **Eventuality Participant**
object [oblig +]   in:object

This states that the object in the recoverable semantic structure is the value of ⟨in object⟩ in the knowledge base structure. Verb case roles are marked as to whether they are **obligatory**: nonobligatory elements may, under circumstances to be described later, result in null NP constituents. This information can also be specified by means of path equations, as in (3.42).

(3.42) ⟨RS sem tprop prop participants object index⟩
        = ⟨KB spec participants in object index⟩
        ⟨RS sem tprop prop participants object spec status oblig⟩ = +

Since the participants to be included in the recoverable semantic structure may be drawn from either the ⟨participants in⟩ or the ⟨participants out⟩ features of the event to be described, the verb case frames also determine whether an entity is to be described as it was before or after the event in question. This permits us to generate sentences like (3.43) even though the stalks do not exist explicitly in the model at the outset of the action.

(3.43) Remove the stalks from the strawberries.

The corresponding verb case frame in this case is

(3.44) **remove** **Verb Case Role** **Eventuality Participant**
object [oblig +]   out:result
indobject [oblig −]   in:object

The output of this phase of the processing is a recoverable semantic structure that might look something like figure 3.13.[16] This might be the recoverable semantics underlying the utterance

---

15. Again, the case frames described here are simplified in that we assume that the agent will not be explicitly mentioned in the surface linguistic form. This is acceptable in the current context since we only ever generate imperative sentences.
16. The value of the object feature here has been elided. Its detail is worked out as explained in chapter 4.

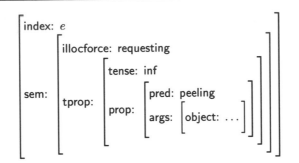

Figure 3.13
The recoverable semantic structure once participants have been chosen.

(3.45)   Peel the potatoes.

However, before this sentence form can be generated, we have to construct an abstract syntactic structure.

3.4.3   Building the abstract syntactic structure

Just as there is a one-to-many mapping from KB structures to RS structures, there is a one-to-many mapping from RS structures to AS structures: the recoverable semantics of an utterance underspecify the particular realization of that utterance. The domain of the RS→AS rules is the universe of recoverable semantic structures, and the range is the universe of abstract syntactic structures. The set of possible AS structures is defined by the following grammar:

(3.46)

AS	::-	index sem
index	::-	$x_i \| e_i \| \langle a\ list\ of\ indices \rangle$
sem	::-	mood tprop
mood	::-	*imp, decl, interr*
tprop	::-	tense prop
tense	::-	*present, past, inf* ...
prop	::-	agent action args
action	::-	$\langle a\ basic\ eventuality\ substance \rangle$
args	::-	[object] [indobject] ...

Again, we leave the definition of the abstract syntactic structures that correspond to participants until the next chapter.

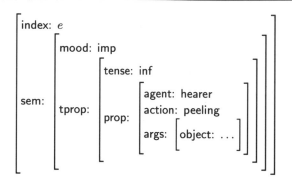

Figure 3.14
The AS structure corresponding to *Peel the potatoes*.

The AS structure is very close to the surface syntactic structure of
the eventual utterance. For direct speech acts, there are straightforward
mapping rules which determine the sentence type on the basis of the
illocutionary force of the required utterance:

(3.47)   ⟨RS sem illocforce⟩   =   requesting
          ⟨AS sem mood⟩   =   imp

(3.48)   ⟨RS sem illocforce⟩   =   informing
          ⟨AS sem mood⟩   =   decl

Obviously this simple correspondence could be made more complicated
by allowing indirect speech acts to be performed.

The RS→AS mapping rules also determine whether the resulting sentence will be active or passive. The fully specified AS structure for the
utterance (3.49) might then look like that shown in figure 3.14, where
we have again omitted the structure corresponding to *the potatoes* for
the sake of brevity.

(3.49)   Peel the potatoes.

Note that the propositional content consists of an **agent** and an **action**,
rather than a predicate and a number of arguments: this intermediate
representation mirrors the standard subject-predicate form of sentences
more closely than ordinary first-order predicate calculus. This structure
would be more useful for the generation of VP ellipsis, since it makes it

very easy to compare the underlying structures corresponding to verb phrases.

Once complete, the abstract syntactic structure is then unified with the grammar to produce a surface linguistic form.

3.4.4   The unification grammar

Linguistically founded grammars in natural language generation   By and large, most work in natural language generation does not make use of linguistically founded grammatical formalisms. A major reason for the *ad hoc* nature of grammatical knowledge encoded in these systems is that most mainstream grammatical formalisms do not represent the kinds of information required in the generation process (specification of focus, rhetorical force, etc.); in the absence of an existing tool with the desired specification, the researcher's response is often to grow his or her own linguistic-structure-building mechanisms.

There are some exceptions to this: some approaches to grammar do embody the right kinds of information. Thus, the systemic tradition (Halliday 1973, 1985) is well represented within the field of natural language generation, and most developed in the NIGEL system (Mann 1983; Matthiessen 1981, 1984). Functional unification grammar (FUG) (Kay 1975) has also proved popular among researchers in NLG, since it too addresses functional aspects of language rather than simply being concerned with the derivation of semantic content in a narrow sense. More recently, there has been work that has tried to integrate the well-established and broad coverage of systemic grammar with the more formally robust work in FUG (Matthiessen and Kasper 1987; Mellish 1987). A different direction can be found in some recent work by McDonald and Pustejovsky (1985), which uses Joshi's (1983, 1985) **tree adjoining grammar**.

Unification now plays a central role in a number of grammar formalisms with a bewildering variety of similar-sounding names: unification categorial grammar (UCG) (Zeevat, Klein, and Calder 1987; Calder, Klein and Zeevat 1988), categorial unification grammar (CUG) (Uszkoreit 1986), dependency unification grammar (Hellwig 1986), and tree unification grammar (Popowich 1988); doubtless there are others. Shieber (1986) provides a good introduction to the area. The extent to which these newer unification grammars have been used in NLG work is still somewhat limited, but this is unlikely to remain the case for long, since the declarative nature of the formalisms lends itself well to the development of grammars that can be used bidirectionally (Shieber 1988).

EPICURE's unification grammar   The grammatical formalism used in the present work adheres to the unification approach, and has been influenced by generalized phrase structure grammar (GPSG) (Gazdar et al. 1985). The mapping from the abstract syntactic structure to a surface syntactic form is achieved by unifying the abstract syntactic structure with the grammar. In an approach like FUG, this is achieved by representing the grammar by means of a feature structure, and unifying this with the representation of the semantic structure to be realized. This is the mechanism used in Appelt's TELEGRAM grammar.[17]

In EPICURE, the grammar consists of phrase structure rules annotated with path equations which determine the relationships between abstract syntactic units and surface syntactic units: the path equations specify arbitrary constituents (either complex or atomic) of feature structures. The phrase structure rules are expressed here in a PATR-like formalism (Karttunen 1986; Shieber 1986), although within EPICURE they are encoded as PROLOG definite clause grammar (DCG) rules (Clocksin and Mellish 1981).

Suppose, for example, we wish to realize the abstract syntactic structure shown in figure 3.15 by means of a declarative sentence. Here, j and c are standing in for more detailed representations of the participants in the event described. The corresponding surface string is then

(3.50)   Judy grated some cheese.

This is an instance of the simple sentence form expressed by the phrase-structure rule

(3.51)   S   →   NP VP

In order to generate the surface form, we annotate the phrase-structure rule with path equations that determine how the elements of the abstract syntactic structure are to be distributed through the surface syntactic constituents:

---

17. For a detailed exposition of how this mechanism is used, see Appelt 1985: 103–112.

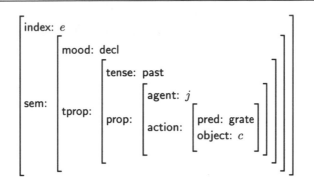

Figure 3.15
The AS structure corresponding to *Judy grated some cheese.*

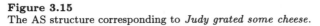

(3.52)　S　→　NP VP

$\langle$NP sem$\rangle$　　　=　$\langle$S sem tprop agent$\rangle$

$\langle$VP sem$\rangle$　　　=　$\langle$S sem tprop prop action$\rangle$

$\langle$VP tense$\rangle$　　=　$\langle$S sem tprop tense$\rangle$

$\langle$NP syn agr$\rangle$　=　$\langle$VP syn agr$\rangle$

The abstract syntactic structure is first constrained to unify with any grammar rule whose left-hand side is S (i.e., the structure must be realized as a sentence). The path equations then cause the appropriate component structures to be passed to the rules that generate NPs and VPs, and ensure that these constituents agree syntactically.[18]

EPICURE is interested primarily in generating imperative sentences, for which we have the following rule:

(3.53)　S　→　VP

$\langle$S sem tprop tense$\rangle$　=　inf

$\langle$VP tense$\rangle$　　　　=　$\langle$S sem tprop tense$\rangle$

$\langle$VP sem$\rangle$　　　　　=　$\langle$S sem tprop prop action$\rangle$

Here, the first constraint ensures that the rule will unify only with abstract syntactic structures intended to be realized as imperatives.

---

18. The grammar rules sometimes contain other constraints, not shown here, to reduce inefficiency in the use of the grammar.

3.4.5   The clause generation algorithm

We are now in a position to summarize the clause generation algorithm and its interaction with the discourse model. Given a knowledge base structure that specifies a primitive request I, the algorithm is as follows.

First, we manipulate the basic elements of the discourse model, and ensure that the world model is updated appropriately:

- Flush the previous clause contents memory.

- Move the contents of the current clause workspace into the previous clause contents memory.

- Put I into the current clause workspace.

- Pass the **object** of I (an eventuality specification) to the domain modeler so that it can update the world model.

EPICURE now has access to information about the state of the world both before and after the event to be described has taken place. A recoverable semantic structure corresponding to the event to be described can then be constructed as follows:

- Apply the KB→RS mapping rules to build the basic recoverable structure structure R from I, as detailed above.

- Retrieve the verb case frame corresponding to the **substance** of the **object** of I.

- For each role specified in the verb case frame do the following:

    - Get the corresponding participant x_i from I.
    - If x_i is the current center then add the attribute **center** with value + to this participant in R.

- Set the **center** to be the **result** of the **object** of I.

- For each of the participants in R:

    - If the participant has a **center** value of '+' then set the **spec** to be ϕ (i.e., no semantic content is necessary for NPs which are the focus of attention: they may be realized by means of pronouns or null NPs, as determined later).
    - Otherwise, build an appropriate recoverable semantics for the noun phrase.

The resulting RS structure is then passed to the mechanism that constructs abstract syntactic structures. This applies the RS→AS mapping rules to build a basic AS structure A, and then applies the rules described in the next chapter to construct the appropriate abstract syntactic structures for the noun phrases to be generated. The abstract syntax constructor can choose to omit entire participants, just as it can choose to omit chunks of semantic content to make use of *one*-anaphora. In particular, as we will see in chapter 5, any participant having the features [oblig,−] and [center,+] can be omitted from the abstract syntactic structure entirely.

4 Generating Referring Expressions

4.1 Introduction

In this chapter, we turn to the generation of noun phrase referring expressions. Just as in the case of clause generation, there are two steps involved in this process: first we have to construct a recoverable semantic structure representing the semantics of the noun phrase that will eventually be realized, and then from this we have to construct an abstract syntactic structure that can be passed to the grammar for linguistic realization. Owing to the emphasis of the present work on referring expressions, the mapping rules used in the generation of noun phrases are considerably more complex than those used in the generation of clauses; consequently, this chapter provides a considerable amount of detail. The principal aim of the chapter is to describe the process of generating initial referring expressions of various kinds, corresponding to the variety of knowledge base structures presented in chapter 2; the mechanisms used by EPICURE for generating pronouns and *one*-anaphora and for determining the content of definite referring expressions are described in chapter 5.

4.2 Referring

4.2.1 Initial and subsequent reference

For the purposes of generating referring expressions, McDonald (1980: 216) draws a distinction between initial reference and subsequent reference. These notions are intuitive enough: we use initial reference when we refer to an entity for the first time, and subsequent reference whenever we refer again to an entity already mentioned. In the present work, **initial reference** is the name given to an act of reference that introduces an entity into the discourse model; thus, the point of an initial reference is to establish a symbol that can be used as a "conceptual coathook."[1] **Subsequent reference** is the name we give to an act of reference that picks out an entity already present in the discourse model: a speaker uses an act of subsequent reference when he or she wants to

---

1. Webber (1988) attributes this term to William Woods.

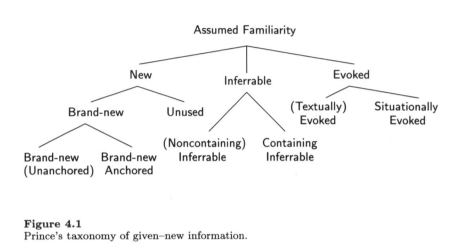

Figure 4.1
Prince's taxonomy of given–new information.

identify a discourse entity in order to say something more about it.

Before it has been introduced into the discourse model, it is possible that the entity being referred to is already known to the hearer. An entity is known to a discourse participant if that discourse participant already has an internal symbol corresponding to that entity. If an entity is known to both discourse participants, then we say that the entity is **mutually known**.[2] In the present system, all entities in the domain are known to EPICURE, but not all entities are known to the hearer.

The distinction between initial and subsequent reference seems to correspond fairly straightforwardly to the normal uses of the terms **new** and **given**. However, a number of intermediate levels of givenness can be hypothesized, as described by Prince's (1981: 237) taxonomy of assumed familiarity, shown in figure 4.1.

Prince's categories represent different statuses that a given entity can have with respect to a discourse. As defined above, the term subsequent reference applies only to those entities that have been textually evoked, since entities falling under the other categories are not present in the dis-

---

2. Mutual knowledge is a thorny problem: see, for example, Clark and Marshall 1981. We assume a very simple model of mutual knowledge, whereby an entity is said to be mutually known if the system knows of the existence of an entity and the system believes that the user knows of the existence of that entity.

course model when they are referred to; thus, in these terms, the other categories describe forms of initial reference. However, in terms of the kinds of referring expressions used, the relevant distinction appears to be between brand-new references and all the other categories: indefinite noun phrases are used for the former and definite noun phrases for the latter. To put this another way: what is new to the discourse is not necessarily new to the hearer; he or she may already have prior knowledge of the entity in question. As we will see, the mechanisms used for initially referring to evoked and inferrable entities have a great deal in common with subsequent reference to textually evoked entities.

4.2.2   The principles of reference

We can view the process of constructing a referring expression as being governed by a number of principles, very like the conversational maxims of Grice (1975), which we will call the principles of **sensitivity**, **efficiency**, and **adequacy**.

The principle of sensitivity   A speaker should always be *sensitive* to his or her hearers. The principle of sensitivity requires that, in constructing a referring expression, the speaker must pay heed to what the hearer can be presumed to know. At the broadest level, this gives rise to requirements such as the following:

- Use a language that the hearer understands.
- Use words and expressions that the hearer understands.

The principle also requires that the speaker acknowledge when an entity being referred to is already known to the hearer, since to do otherwise may be misleading. Thus, the principle requires that definite and indefinite referring expressions be used appropriately.

The principle of adequacy   A referring expression should identify the intended referent unambiguously, and provide sufficient information to serve the purpose of the reference. Thus, if there are two balls on a table, and I wish you to pick up a particular one, then referring to it as *the ball* is unlikely to be adequate: I must distinguish the particular ball I have in mind from the other ball, perhaps by making reference to its color, size, or location.

The adequacy of an act of reference is dependent upon the purpose of the reference: a referring expression that is sufficient to permit the hearer to construct or retrieve a mental entity corresponding to the intended referent may not be adequate for actually locating the referent in the real world. In view of the latter purpose, if there is only one tin of cat food in the kitchen and I say to you

(4.1)   Bring me <u>the tin of cat food</u>.

then the referring expression I have used will be adequate only if I have provided sufficient information to enable you to find the tin of cat food in question within the referring expression itself. If the tin of cat food is hidden in an unusual location, then a referring expression like that in the request

(4.2)   Bring me <u>the tin of cat food that is in the bucket on the shelf.</u>

may be necessary in order to satisfy the principle of adequacy.

The principle of efficiency   The principle of efficiency requires that the referring expression used not contain more information than is necessary for the task at hand; thus, it pulls in the opposite direction from the principle of adequacy. This is not just a question of the speaker's saving his or her breath; saying more than is necessary is likely to mislead the hearer into thinking that something else is encoded in the message.[3] Satisfying this principle requires some way of measuring the amount of information in a referring expression. We will return to this question in section 5.2, where we introduce the notion of **discriminatory power**.

4.2.3   The hearer model

We noted in the previous chapter one particular kind of knowledge about the hearer that the speaker needed to have in order to be able to plan a discourse: knowledge about the hearer's capabilities with respect to the actions in plans. From the above discussion, we can identify other kinds of knowledge of the hearer that the speaker must have:

1. The speaker must know what language the hearer understands.

2. The speaker must know what words and expressions in that language the hearer understands.

3. The speaker must know which entities are known to the hearer by virtue of having been explicitly mentioned in the discourse.

---

3. Some of the issues here are discussed in depth by Reiter (1990).

4. The speaker must know which entities are known to the hearer, be-sides those which have been explicitly mentioned in the discourse.

5. The speaker must know what entities the hearer can infer the existence of.

6. The speaker must know what entities are assumed by the hearer to be, in Prince's terms, situationally evoked.

In the present system, we ignore the problems presented by cases 1 and 2 above: we assume that the hearer understands English, and that she understands all the vocabulary available to EPICURE.

In case 3, the system's knowledge of which entities are known to the hearer by virtue of having been explicitly mentioned is modeled by the shared discourse model introduced in chapter 3.

In case 4, entities which are known to the hearer but which have not been mentioned in the discourse are present in the hearer model by virtue of assertions in EPICURE's knowledge base of the following form:

(4.3)   Knows(hearer, holds($s, A(x, V)$))

where x is some entity, A is an some attribute of that entity, and V is the value of A for x. Thus, if the hearer knows anything at all about an entity x, then x is known to the hearer.

In order to deal with entities whose existence can be inferred (case 5), we have assertions in EPICURE's knowledge base regarding the axioms known to the hearer.[4] So, if the hearer knows that corresponding to every avocado there is a stone, and EPICURE knows that the hearer knows this, then we have

(4.4)   Knows(hearer, [$\forall x$ avocado(x) $\supset$
$\exists y$ stone(y) $\wedge$ associated-with(y, x)])

Finally, to deal with case 6, we have assertions regarding those entities which are situationally evoked. In the present work, only the speaker and the hearer are considered to be situationally evoked:

(4.5)   Knows(hearer, holds(s, situationally-evoked(speaker)))
Knows(hearer, holds(s, situationally-evoked(hearer)))

The effect of this information is that the system can use pronouns to refer to itself and to the user.

---

4. The mechanisms required to use axioms like these are discussed in chapter 5, but are not present in the implemented version of the system described in chapter 6.

4.3   Building Noun Phrases

Various stages of processing are required in order to construct noun
phrases; the most important of these is that of deciding on the semantic
content to be realized in the noun phrase. We focus here on the question
of how information is transferred between the different levels of representation; as before, this is achieved by the use of mapping rules. We
describe a number of the mapping rules, but leave the question of how
EPICURE decides *which* rules to use until later in the present chapter. As
an example of how the mechanism operates, we will consider references
to singular individuals.

4.3.1   An overview of the process

Just as in the case of generating clauses as a whole, we distinguish several
levels of representation in the generation of a noun phrase:

- the knowledge base object corresponding to the entity to be described,

- the recoverable semantic structure chosen for the noun phrase that
  will describe that entity,

- the abstract syntactic structure of the noun phrase that will describe that entity, and

- the surface syntactic structure of the resulting noun phrase.

Again, just as in the case of clause generation, we have two sets of mapping rules that create the two intermediate levels of structure. However,
in the case of the generation of noun phrase referring expressions these
are considerably more complex than the rules used in clause generation. In building the recoverable semantic structure, the system has
to decide what the hearer should understand the noun phrase to mean
once any anaphoric elements have been resolved. This involves choosing
the particular KB→RS mapping rules that will have the desired effect.
Constructing the abstract syntactic structure is then relatively straightforward, since the applicability of RS→AS rules is tightly constrained by
the recoverable semantic structure. This stage of the process is nonde-
terministic, however, since different rules may apply to one recoverable
semantic structure, producing different results. Thus, for example, the

two noun phrases in (4.6) have the same recoverable semantic structure
but different abstract syntactic structures.

(4.6)   a. a Glasgow-bound plane
         b. a plane to Glasgow

In order to demonstrate the various stages of constructing a noun phrase
referring expression, we consider below the construction of simple indefinite and definite referring expressions like those in (4.7).

(4.7)   a. a mouldy carrot
         b. the carrot

These two referring expressions represent an initial and a subsequent reference to a singular individual; we will also deal with references of both
kinds to more complex entities. In each case, the stages of processing
involved are as follows:

- Given a knowledge base structure, EPICURE has to construct a
  recoverable semantic structure that contains the information to be
  conveyed to the hearer.

- Once a recoverable semantic structure has been constructed, EPI-
  CURE then constructs an abstract syntactic structure that specifies
  what is to be realized in the noun phrase.

- Unification of this structure with the grammar and lexicon then
  results in a surface string that realizes the required semantics.

We describe each of these stages in turn.

4.3.2 Determining the recoverable semantics

Given a knowledge base structure, we construct recoverable semantic
structure by applying a set of KB→RS mapping rules. The recoverable
semantic structure has to represent two kinds of information about the
intended referent:

- information indicating the **discourse status** of the entity, and

- a description of the entity.

A grammar that defines the possible set of recoverable semantic structures will be presented later; for the moment, the fragment of the recoverable semantics grammar that is relevant to the current example is

RS	::-	index sem
index	::-	x_i
sem	::-	status spec
status	::-	given [unique]
given	::-	$+|-$
unique	::-	$+|-$
spec	::-	agr type
agr	::-	[number] countable
countable	::-	$+|-$
number	::-	sg|pl|$1 \ldots n$
type	::-	category [props]
category	::-	⟨*a basic semantic category*⟩
props	::-	⟨a_1, v_1⟩, …, ⟨a_n, v_n⟩

Figure 4.2
A fragment of the grammar for recoverable semantic structures.

shown in figure 4.2. The particular rules required in order to derive the information to be encoded in a referring expression depend on the type of knowledge base structure to be described, and on some contextual factors. Initial RS structures are created from KB structures by the following mapping rule:

(4.8)   ⟨RS index⟩ = ⟨KB index⟩

Below, we show how different information is added to the basic RS structure created by this rule depending upon whether an initial or a subsequent reference is being made.

Discourse status   Determiners in English specify two things:

- whether the entity described is considered to be mutually known; and

- whether the description supplied is uniquely true of the intended referent in the relevant context.

This information is specified in the recoverable semantics by the **status** features. We will return to how the values of the **status** features are actually determined later; for the moment, it is sufficient to note that when a brand new entity is introduced into the discourse the value of the status feature in the corresponding recoverable semantic structure is as shown in (4.9).

$$(4.9) \quad \left[\text{given: } - \right]$$

Whenever an entity is subsequently referred to, however, the value of the given feature in the corresponding recoverable semantic structure will be "+". If the semantic content of the description constructed to refer to that entity picks it out uniquely (by means of a process that will be described below), then this is also noted in the status feature; the result is the structure shown in (4.10).

$$(4.10) \quad \begin{bmatrix} \text{given: } + \\ \text{unique: } + \end{bmatrix}$$

As we will see below, these two structures result in indefinite and definite determiners, respectively. If a unique description cannot be constructed, then the following structure is set to be the value of the status structure·

$$(4.11) \quad \begin{bmatrix} \text{given: } + \\ \text{unique: } - \end{bmatrix}$$

This then also results in the use of an indefinite determiner.

Recoverable semantic content   Different rules are applied to build the recoverable semantic structure, depending upon the value of the KB structure's **structure** feature. For the moment, we will focus on objects whose structure is individual. The first rule to be applied adds the appropriate agreement features to the recoverable semantic structure:

(4.12)   ⟨KB spec structure⟩   =   individual
⟨RS sem spec agr countable⟩ =   +
⟨RS sem spec agr number⟩   =   sg

This ensures that the entity will be described as a singular individual.

Next, the semantic content of the description is determined. For objects whose structure is individual, the important information here consists of the object's **substance** and the **shape** of its **packaging**. If these

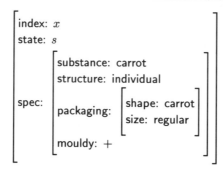

$$\left[\begin{array}{l} \text{index: } x \\ \text{state: } s \\ \\ \text{spec:} \left[\begin{array}{l} \text{substance: carrot} \\ \text{structure: individual} \\ \\ \text{packaging:} \left[\begin{array}{l} \text{shape: carrot} \\ \text{size: regular} \end{array}\right] \\ \\ \text{mouldy: } + \end{array}\right] \end{array}\right]$$

Figure 4.3
The KB entity corresponding to a single mouldy carrot.

are the same (i.e., the entity is packaged in the "standard way" for its substance), then the following rule applies:

(4.13)   ⟨KB spec substance⟩   =   ⟨KB spec packaging shape⟩
          ⟨RS sem spec type category⟩   =   ⟨KB spec substance⟩
          ⟨RS sem spec type props size⟩ =   ⟨KB spec packaging size⟩

Finally, other properties of the object may be added to the RS structure. Whether this is done, and which properties are added, depends on the context, and will be discussed further below. The addition of other properties to the recoverable semantic structure is performed by a set of rules of the form[5]

(4.14)   ⟨RS sem spec type props A⟩   =   ⟨KB spec A⟩

where the possible range of values for A is restricted (in particular, the substance or structure of an entity will not be added as a property). The particular values of A used are chosen on the basis of a notion of discriminatory power, as described in section 5.2.

Suppose we have the knowledge base structure shown in figure 4.3; this represents a single mouldy carrot. The recoverable semantic structure corresponding to an initial reference to our carrot might then be as shown in figure 4.4. The entity's property of being mouldy has been added here

---

5. Note that (4.14) is effectively a rule schema. In the system itself, we have a distinct rule for each property.

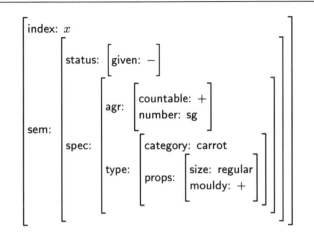

Figure 4.4
The RS structure corresponding to an initial reference to the mouldy carrot.

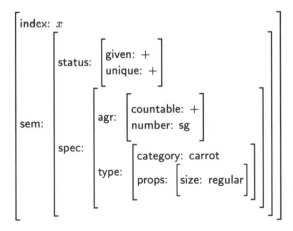

Figure 4.5
The RS structure corresponding to a subsequent reference to the mouldy carrot.

sign	::-	index phon sem syn
index	::-	x_i
phon	::-	$\langle$ *a string* $\rangle$
syn	::-	$\langle$ *a representation of the expression's syntax* $\rangle$
sem	::-	status spec
status	::-	given [unique]
given	::-	$+|-$
unique	::-	$+|-$
spec	::-	agr desc
agr	::-	countable [number]
countable	::-	$+|-$
number	::-	sg|pl|$1 \ldots n$
desc	::-	head [mod]
head	::-	$\langle$ *an atomic semantic category* $\rangle$ | mod head
mod	::-	head [mod]

Figure 4.6
A fragment of the grammar for abstract syntactic structures.

by an instance of the general property-addition rule we specified above, namely (4.15).

(4.15) $\langle$RS sem spec type props mouldy$\rangle$ = $\langle$KB spec mouldy$\rangle$

However, when the speaker is making a subsequent reference to the entity, the carrot's being mouldy might be irrelevant; the RS structure would then be as shown in figure 4.5.

4.3.3 Determining the abstract syntactic structure

The recoverable semantic structures introduced above cannot be realized directly by noun phrases. First, we must build the corresponding abstract syntactic structures. The abstract syntactic structures relevant to the present example are defined by the grammar fragment shown in figure 4.6 (again, a complete specification of abstract syntactic structures will be presented at the end of this section). Recall that the principal differences between the two levels of representation are these:

- The abstract syntactic structure is closer in structure to the surface syntax.

- Some information present in the recoverable semantic structure may be omitted from the abstract syntactic structure.

In the present example, the RS→AS mapping rules dealing with **status** and **agr** information are very straightforward:

(4.16) $\langle$AS index$\rangle$ $\quad = \quad \langle$RS index$\rangle$

$\langle$AS sem status$\rangle$ $\quad = \quad \langle$RS sem status$\rangle$

$\langle$AS sem spec agr$\rangle$ $\quad = \quad \langle$RS sem spec agr$\rangle$

In all the examples dealt with in the present work, we assume that the semantic number of an entity is the same as its syntactic number. However, the indirection provided by the use of two levels of representation would permit us to introduce a distinction between the two kinds of number, thus allowing us represent entities whose syntactic number seems at odds with their "conceptual" number. Thus, in the case of noun phrases like those in (4.17), the semantic number of the entities so described would be singular, whereas the syntactic number is plural.

(4.17) a. the trousers

b. the pliers

Adjective ordering   As just noted, a major difference in the two levels of representation is the way in which the various properties to be realized are structured. In the case of the recoverable semantic structure, we isolate the semantic category that will eventually be realized as the head noun and maintain all the other properties essentially as a flat list; in the abstract syntactic structure, however, the various properties are collected together in a way that mirrors exactly the embedding of modifiers in the noun phrase. The structure of the information in the recoverable semantics is, as we will see in section 5.3, particularly suitable for decisions concerning the use of *one*-anaphoric expressions. [6]

In order to build this part of the abstract syntactic structure, then, the generator has to know something about adjective ordering. The

---

6. The same consideration led to Webber's (1979) use of restricted quantification in her semantic representation, so that the property corresponding to the head noun in a noun phrase would be separated out from the other properties of the entity described by the noun phrase.

psychological data suggest that certain adjective orderings are preferred (Herrmann and Laucht 1976), although these orderings can easily be overridden (see, for example, Ney 1983). The most comprehensive discussion of adjective ordering is that presented by Vendler (1968), who groups adjectives into nine major categories, one of these categories being further subcategorized into 14 groups. Following Vendler, we annotate the major categories here as A_1 through A_9, with the subcategories of A_1 bearing alphabetic indices. Some examples of these categories follow.

A_9: *probably, likely, certain*

A_8: *useful, profitable, necessary*

A_7: *possible, impossible*

A_6: *clever, stupid, reasonable, nice, kind, thoughtful, considerate*

A_5: *ready, willing, anxious*

A_4: *easy*

A_3: *slow, fast, good, bad, weak, careful, beautiful*

A_2: contrastive/polar adjectives: *long-short, thick-thin, big-little, wide-narrow*

A_j: verb-derivatives: *washed*

A_i: verb-derivatives: *washing*

A_h: *luminous*

A_g: *rectangular*

A_f: color adjectives

A_a: *iron, steel, metal*

When realized in noun phrases, according to Vendler, adjectives are ordered as in (4.18).

(4.18) $A_9\, A_8\, \ldots A_2\, A_x\, A_m\, A_l\, A_k\, A_j\, A_i\, A_h\, A_g\, A_f\, A_e\, A_d\, A_c\, A_b\, A_a$

Within EPICURE, each adjective is given a numerical classification as suggested by Vendler's categorization.

Recall that the properties predicated of an entity appear as the value of the **props** feature in the recoverable semantic structure. This is essentially a list of attribute-value pairs of the form

(4.19) $[\langle a_1, v_1 \rangle, \langle a_2, v_2 \rangle, \ldots, \langle a_n, v_n \rangle]$

In order to integrate this information into the abstract syntactic structure, we have to omit any properties which the hearer should be able to infer, and embed the remaining properties in such a way that their ordering matches that specified by the adjective categorization. The hearer is assumed to be able to infer properties that are defaults for entities of the specified **substance** and **packaging**; for example, **regular** is assumed to be the default size of most entities.

The algorithm for integrating properties into the AS structure is as follows.

First, we construct a list L of the properties to appear in the abstract syntactic structure, determining the ordering category for the adjective that realizes the semantic content of each property to be realized, while also omitting those properties whose values can be assumed by the hearer.[7]

For each $\langle a_i, \ v_i \rangle$:

- If v_i is the default value of a_i for entities of the specified **substance** and **packaging**, then ignore this $\langle a_i, \ v_i \rangle$ pair.

- Otherwise, determine the ordering category A_i of a_i, and add the pair $\langle A_i, \ \langle a_i, \ v_i \rangle \rangle$ to the list L.

So, for example, if an entity which is an onion has the size **regular**, this information will not be included in the list of properties to be included in the abstract syntactic structure.

Next, we have to build the abstract syntactic structure. Suppose this is a feature structure with the name S. We use the list of annotated properties L to build S recursively as follows.

- If L is empty, then set $\langle$S head$\rangle$ to be the value of $\langle$RS sem spec type category$\rangle$.

- Otherwise:

    - Find the highest-valued A_i in L (this corresponds to the adjective that will be realized furthest away from the head noun).

---

7. Note that this means we assume that, if a given property is realizable by means of a number of different adjectives, then all those adjectives will belong to the same category. This is probably an oversimplification.

- Set $\langle$S mod head$\rangle$ to be the value of $\langle$RS sem spec type props $a_i\rangle$.
- Remove $\langle A_i, \langle a_i, v_i\rangle\rangle$ from L, and build $\langle$S head$\rangle$ using the new L.

Thus, we pick off the properties to be realized from L, building up the abstract syntactic structure as we go. The result of this process is a feature structure which then becomes the value of $\langle$AS sem spec desc$\rangle$. For our initial reference to our mouldy carrot, this results in the abstract syntactic structure shown in figure 4.7. The abstract syntactic structure for the subsequent reference, however, includes no additional properties, and so is as shown in figure 4.8. Note the content of the **status** feature here: we assume that, for the purposes of this example, the content of the **desc** feature is sufficient to identify the intended referent, and so the **unique** feature has the value "+".

4.3.4 Surface realization

Finally, we have to realize these abstract syntactic structures as surface linguistic forms. We analyze the surface syntactic structure of *the carrot* by the phrase-structure rules

(4.20)   NP   →   Det N1
          N1   →   N

and get the structure shown in figure 4.9; for noun phrases like *an old carrot*, we have the additional phrase-structure rules

(4.21)   N1   →   AP N1
          AP   →   Adv AP
          AP   →   A

which yield the structural analysis shown in figure 4.10. Since the phrase-structure rule that introduces adjectival phrases is recursive, the noun phrase *an old orange carrot* is given the structural analysis shown in figure 4.11.

As we saw in chapter 3 in the discussion of clause generation, the mapping from the abstract syntactic structure to the surface syntactic form is achieved by annotations on the phrase-structure rules: these distribute the elements of the abstract syntactic structures appropriately to the surface syntactic constituents. The surface string is then constructed

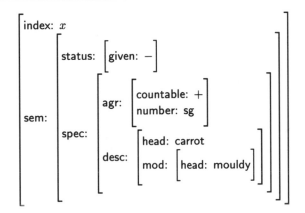

Figure 4.7
The AS structure corresponding to an initial reference to a mouldy carrot.

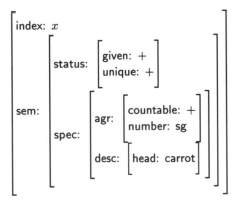

Figure 4.8
The AS structure corresponding to a subsequent reference to the mouldy carrot.

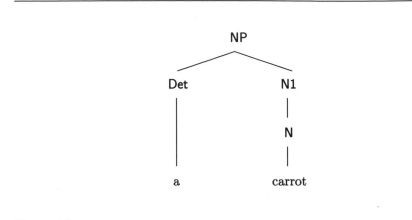

Figure 4.9
A simple noun phrase.

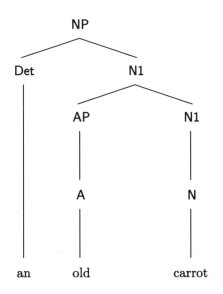

Figure 4.10
Simple adjectival modification.

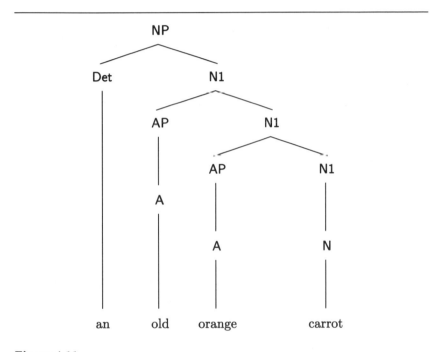

Figure 4.11
Embedded adjectival modification.

NP	→	Det N1	$\langle$Det sem$\rangle$	=	$\langle$NP sem status$\rangle$
			$\langle$NP syn agr$\rangle$	=	$\langle$NP sem spec agr$\rangle$
			$\langle$N1 syn agr$\rangle$	=	$\langle$NP syn agr$\rangle$
			$\langle$Det syn agr$\rangle$	=	$\langle$N1 syn agr$\rangle$
			$\langle$N1 sem$\rangle$	=	$\langle$NP sem spec desc$\rangle$
N1	→	N	$\langle$N sem$\rangle$	=	$\langle$N1 sem head$\rangle$
$N1_1$	→	AP $N1_2$	$\langle$AP sem$\rangle$	=	$\langle N1_1$ sem mod$\rangle$
			$\langle N1_2$ sem head$\rangle$	=	$\langle N1_1$ sem head$\rangle$
AP_1	→	Adv AP_2	$\langle$Adv sem$\rangle$	=	$\langle AP_1$ sem mod$\rangle$
			$\langle AP_2$ sem head$\rangle$	=	$\langle AP_1$ sem head$\rangle$
AP	→	Adj	$\langle$Adj sem$\rangle$	=	$\langle$AP sem head$\rangle$

Figure 4.12
A fragment of the NP grammar.

---

by concatenating the appropriate lexical items in the order specified by the phrase-structure rules. For our current examples, the relevant rules are shown in figure 4.12. Recall that the algorithm that constructs the **desc** structure in the abstract syntax (described in the previous section) constructs an embedding of modifiers corresponding to the embedding of adjectival modification; the **desc** for the noun phrase *the old orange carrot* is then as shown in figure 4.13. Mirroring the fact that adjectives themselves can be modified by adverbs, modifiers can also be modified in the abstract syntactic structure, as shown in figure 4.14. Accordingly, the noun phrase *the very old orange carrot* is given the surface syntactic analysis shown in figure 4.15.

4.3.5   Lexical realization

Terminal categories in grammar rules correspond to the values of the $\langle$syn cat$\rangle$ features of structures held in the lexicon. Thus, lexical insertion involves obtaining the lexical item with the appropriate semantics and syntactic category from the lexicon. Some examples of lexical items are

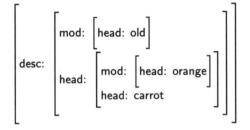

Figure 4.13
The desc for the noun phrase *the old orange carrot*.

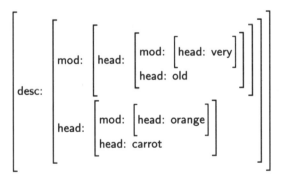

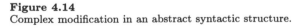

Figure 4.14
Complex modification in an abstract syntactic structure.

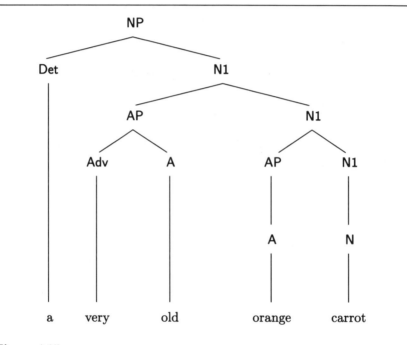

Figure 4.15
Complex embedded adjectival modification.

given below.

Nouns   Common nouns are represented in a fairly simple manner; for example, (4.22) represents the noun corresponding to the semantic category **carrot**.

$$(4.22) \quad \begin{bmatrix} \text{phon: carrot} \\ \text{syn:} \begin{bmatrix} \text{cat: noun} \\ \text{agr:} \begin{bmatrix} \text{number: sg} \end{bmatrix} \end{bmatrix} \\ \text{sem:} \begin{bmatrix} \text{head: carrot} \end{bmatrix} \end{bmatrix}$$

Determiners   The lexical item *the* is represented in (4.23).

$$(4.23) \quad \begin{bmatrix} \text{phon: the} \\ \text{syn:} \begin{bmatrix} \text{cat: det} \end{bmatrix} \\ \text{sem:} \begin{bmatrix} \text{given: +} \\ \text{unique: +} \end{bmatrix} \end{bmatrix}$$

Notice that no number-agreement features are specified here, so that the determiner can be used for both singular and plural noun phrases.

The indefinite determiner *a* has the following lexical entry:

$$(4.24) \quad \begin{bmatrix} \text{phon: a} \\ \text{syn:} \begin{bmatrix} \text{cat: det} \\ \text{agr:} \begin{bmatrix} \text{number: sg} \end{bmatrix} \end{bmatrix} \\ \text{sem:} \begin{bmatrix} \text{given: } - \end{bmatrix} \end{bmatrix}$$

In this entry, there is no specification for the **unique** feature, since whether or not the description used in conjunction with the determiner is unique is irrelevant.[8]

---

8. Note that the determiner *a* can also be used in nonspecific references. In the present framework, this would require a distinct lexical entry.

RS	::-	index sem
index	::-	x_i | $\langle a\ list\ of\ indices \rangle$
sem	::-	status spec
status	::-	given [unique]
given	::-	$+$|$-$
unique	::-	$+$|$-$
spec	::-	agr type |
		agr quant subst |
		agr part set
agr	::-	[number] countable
type	::-	category [props]
category	::-	$\langle a\ basic\ semantic\ category \rangle$
props	::-	$\langle a_1,\ v_1 \rangle,\ \ldots,\ \langle a_n,\ v_n \rangle$
quant	::-	agr type
subst	::-	agr type | $\langle a\ list\ of\ subst\ structures \rangle$
part	::-	agr type
set	::-	index sem

Figure 4.16
The complete grammar for recoverable semantic structures.

4.3.6   The levels of representation summarized

Above, we focused on some relatively simple semantic structures. Here, the complete specifications of the two levels of representation will be presented. The structure of RS objects corresponding to participants in described eventualities is described by the grammar shown in figure 4.16; the abstract syntax is similar in a number of respects to the recoverable semantics, and is described by the grammar in figure 4.17.

The remainder of this chapter will describe the mapping rules used in building the wider range of structures defined by these grammars.

4.4   Initial Reference

Within the literature on natural language generation, there is very little work that addresses the issues involved in initial reference in any great depth. The main problem is that of deciding what the semantic content

sign	::-	index phon sem syn
index	::-	x_i | e_i | $\langle$ *a list of indices* $\rangle$
phon	::-	$\langle$ *a string* $\rangle$
syn	::-	$\langle$ *a graph representation of the expression's syntax* $\rangle$
sem	::-	status spec
status	::-	given [unique]
given	::-	$+\|-$
unique	::-	$+\|-$
spec	::-	agr desc | $\langle$ *a list of spec structures* $\rangle$
agr	::-	countable [number]
countable	::-	$+\|-$
number	::-	$\text{sg}\|\text{pl}\|1 \ldots n$
desc	::-	head [mod] | spec_1 spec_2 | spec set
head	::-	$\langle$ *an atomic semantic category* $\rangle$ | mod head
mod	::-	head [mod]
set	::-	index phon sem syn

Figure 4.17
The complete grammar for abstract syntactic structures.

of an initial reference should be. In the present work, we adopt a fairly simple solution which is adequate in the domain addressed here, but which at the same time permits us to generate a wide range of surface forms for initial reference, corresponding to the wide variety of objects we saw in chapter 2.

4.4.1   The problem of initial reference

Deciding on the content of an initial reference to an entity is not a simple process. We might expect things to be simplest when the intended referent has a proper name that is known to both the speaker and the hearer; but even in this case there are subtle decisions that have to be made on the basis of contextual factors, as McDonald (1977: 119) points out:

> When I telephone one of my house-mates at their laboratory, context comes into play in deciding which name I use to refer to them. If I recognize who answers, I say "Is Jeanne there?". I use their first name because it is the friendly thing to do and because I'm sure they will know who I want. If I don't recognise them, then I use the full name, "Is Jeanne Margolskee there?". That is more formal and less likely to be confusing. Before I knew that there was no one else in that lab with the same first name, I always used the full name. If I should want to sound official, I would probably say "Is Dr. Margolskee there?".

If the intended referent does not have a mutually known name (and this is generally the case), then it will be described in terms of its properties; and which properties we use again depends very much on the context of use and the purpose of making the reference in the first place.

As was suggested at the end of chapter 2, descriptions of a given object are always mediated through a **perspective**. A crucial issue, then, when one is referring to an entity for the first time, is the choice of the perspective from which the entity is to be viewed. When referring to a friend's mother, for example, I have to decide whether to view her (for the purposes of the conversation) as an architect, a mother, or a mountain climber. The mechanisms underlying this choice are ill-understood, and essentially unexplored within computational linguistics; this is hardly surprising, given that all the systems extant at the time of writing operate within narrowly defined domains where perspective choice is unnecessary, with one perspective built into the system. EPICURE is no less deficient, since we assume that the entities within recipes are to be described as ingredients. This simplification does no harm in the present work.

Once the initial perspective to be taken has been determined, the search space of properties that can be used in describing an entity for the first time is reduced considerably. The purpose of the discourse remains a major factor in the particular choices made, however. For example, if we are talking about the variety of hobbies pursued by our friend's mothers, then the property of being a mountain climber might be the only relevant property I have to mention; but if we are talking about quality of mountain-climbing skill exhibited by people we know, I might introduce my friend's mother as *a very good mountain climber*. In general, the requirement seems to be to inform the hearer of those properties which are necessary to distinguish the intended referent from other entities that have been mentioned, and often (given sufficient prescience on the part of the speaker) those properties which are necessary to distinguish it from entities the speaker expects to be introduced later in the discourse.

4.4.2 Initial reference in EPICURE

Within EPICURE, two requirements guide the choice of the properties that are used in describing an ingredient for the first time:

- Sufficient information should be provided to distinguish the intended referent from all other entities that have already been mentioned, and also those that have yet to be mentioned.

- Those specific properties that are relevant in the context of cooking (namely substance, quantity, and any prior processing that is required) should be mentioned.

Recall that, at the outset of a description of a recipe, all the ingredients are elements of the **working set**. Each element of the working set is described by constructing a noun phrase that encodes the relevant information held in the knowledge base structure that represents this ingredient. As before, we do this by first constructing a recoverable semantic structure, and then developing from this an abstract syntactic structure which can be realized by the grammar.

As was mentioned in section 4.3, information about the discourse status of the entity being described, and the uniqueness-in-context of the description used, determine the contents of the status feature which is introduced in the recoverable semantic structure and then copied across to the abstract syntactic structure. For entities which are being referred to for the first time, the relevant status information is specified by the following mapping rule:

(4.25)   ⟨RS spec status given⟩   =   −

This rule applies whenever the entity to be referred to is brand new (that is, whenever it is not present in the discourse model, it is unknown to the hearer, and its existence cannot be inferred by the hearer). In the RS structures described below, we will assume that this feature has already been added.

4.4.3   Initial reference to individuals

The various steps involved in constructing an initial reference to an entity whose structure is individual were described in section 4.3; the only thing not specified there was the algorithm that determines the particular properties to be used. This is very straightforward.

If the structure of an entity x is individual:

- If x has an ancestor y, then include a description of y; otherwise, describe the substance of x.[9]

- Describe the packaging of x.

- Describe any other locally encoded properties of x.

A **locally encoded property** is any property of the entity, other than its structure, substance, packaging, and ancestor, that is represented as part of the entity's spec feature. The restriction to locally encoded properties prevents EPICURE from including information that might be inherited from other entities (such as the information that the entity in question is a member of the working set).

The procedure described in section 4.3 is therefore all that is involved for simple individuals as might be described by the following noun phrases:

---

9. Recall from chapter 2 that an entity may be represented as being derived from another entity, where that other entity is said to be the ancestor of the first.

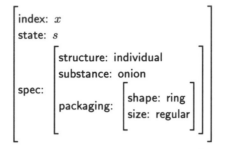

Figure 4.18
The KB entity corresponding to a ring of onion.

(4.26)   a. a carrot

          b. a ripe green pepper

However, there are two other kinds of individuals which are slightly more complex: entities whose **packaging** is not the "standard" packaging for entities made of that substance, as in (4.27), and entities which are described in terms of other entities from which they have been derived (their **ancestors**), as in (4.28).

(4.27)   a. a ring of onion

          b. a stick of celery

(4.28)   a. the juice of a lemon

          b. the kernels of a fresh ear of corn

We will return to the second category in the next chapter, since the mechanisms used are closer to those used for certain kinds of subsequent reference. Here, we show how the system constructs initial references to entities that belong to the first category.

Building the recoverable semantics   Recall from chapter 2 that the knowledge base structure corresponding to an entity describable as *a ring of onion* will look like that shown in figure 4.18. For entities of this kind, where the **substance** and the **shape** of packaging are not the same, we have the following mapping rule:

(4.29)   ⟨RS sem spec type category⟩ = ⟨KB spec packaging shape⟩

          ⟨RS sem spec type props substance⟩ = ⟨KB spec substance⟩

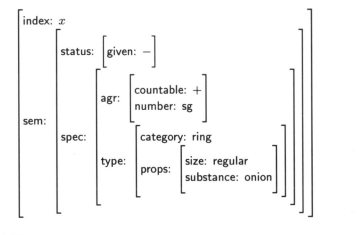

Figure 4.19
The RS structure corresponding to *a ring of onion*.

$$\langle \text{RS sem spec type props size} \rangle = \langle \text{KB spec packaging size} \rangle$$

The recoverable semantic structure that results from the application of these rules is shown in figure 4.19.

Building the abstract syntactic structure   The values for ⟨AS sem status⟩ and ⟨AS sem spec agr⟩ are the same as the status and agr features in the RS structure, and are specified by the mapping rules already presented. However, note that entities of this kind can be described in two ways: either as *a ring of onion* or as *an onion ring*. In order to account for this, we have two distinct abstract syntactic structures that correspond to the recoverable semantics, and therefore two sets of mapping rules. These can apply whenever the substance of an entity is specified as one of the props in the recoverable semantics.

To generate noun phrases like *a ring of onion* requires an abstract syntactic structure whose spec feature is of the general form shown in (4.30), where the embedded spec$_1$ feature corresponds to the packaging of the object and the embedded spec$_2$ feature corresponds to the substance of the object.

$$
(4.30) \quad
\begin{bmatrix}
\text{spec:} & \begin{bmatrix} \text{agr: } \ldots \end{bmatrix} \\
\text{desc:} & \begin{bmatrix}
\text{spec}_1: & \begin{bmatrix} \text{agr: } \ldots \\ \text{desc: } \ldots \end{bmatrix} \\
\text{spec}_2: & \begin{bmatrix} \text{agr: } \ldots \\ \text{desc: } \ldots \end{bmatrix}
\end{bmatrix}
\end{bmatrix}
$$

The RS→AS mapping rules that build this structure are as follows, where R is the value of $\langle$RS sem spec$\rangle$ and A is the value of $\langle$AS sem spec desc$\rangle$:

(4.31)

$$
\begin{aligned}
\langle\text{A spec}_1 \text{ desc head}\rangle &= \langle\text{R type category}\rangle \\
\langle\text{A spec}_1 \text{ agr}\rangle &= \langle\text{A agr}\rangle \\
\langle\text{A spec}_2 \text{ desc head}\rangle &= \langle\text{R type props substance}\rangle \\
\langle\text{A spcc}_2 \text{ agr countable}\rangle &= - \\
\langle\text{A spec}_2 \text{ agr number}\rangle &= \text{sg}
\end{aligned}
$$

The resulting abstract syntactic structure is then as shown in figure 4.20. In order to construct the abstract syntactic structure corresponding to *an onion ring*, we have a different set of mapping rules:

(4.32)

$$
\begin{aligned}
\langle\text{A head}\rangle &= \langle\text{R type head}\rangle \\
\langle\text{A mod head}\rangle &= \langle\text{R type props substance}\rangle
\end{aligned}
$$

Thus, in this case, the abstract syntactic structure is as shown in figure 4.21.

Building the surface syntactic structure The syntactic analyses provided for the simple noun phrases presented in section 4.3 were relatively uncontroversial. There is much less agreement within the linguistics literature, however, as to the correct analysis of noun phrases like *a ring of onion* (see, for example, Akmajian and Lehrer 1976 and Selkirk 1977).

Constructions like these are usually referred to as **pseudo-partitives** (Selkirk 1977: 302ff). The examples in (4.33) are all pseudo-partitives, whereas those in (4.34) are partitive NPs.

(4.33)   a. a number of giraffes

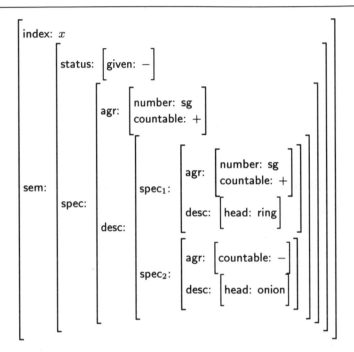

Figure 4.20
The AS structure corresponding to *a ring of onion*.

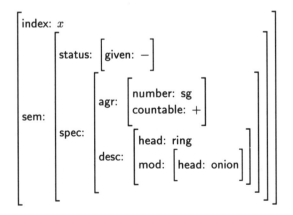

Figure 4.21
The AS structure corresponding to *an onion ring*.

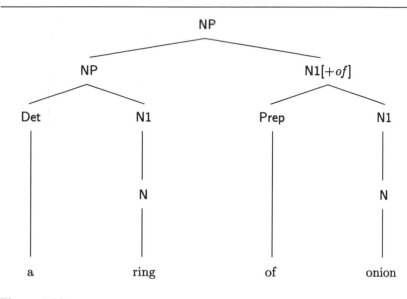

Figure 4.22
The structure of pseudo-partitive constructions.

     b. a cup of cucumber

     c. a piece of gnu

(4.34)   a. many of the giraffes

     b. some of the cucumbers

     c. one of the gnus

Intuitively, we want to say that a partitive noun phrase describes an entity which is derived from (usually, is part of) some other entity; whereas a pseudo-partitive noun phrase describes a quantity of some substance. We will discuss partitives in section 5.2, since they involve the use of strategies for subsequent reference (they correspond to Prince's category of **brand-new anchored**, where the anchor is a known entity).

In the present work, we analyze noun phrases like *a ring of onion* by means of the rule given in (4.35).

(4.35)   NP → NP N1[+*of*]

This results in the structural analysis shown in figure 4.22.

The annotations required to distribute the semantic content through the structure are then as shown in (4.36).

(4.36) $NP_1 \rightarrow NP_2 \ N1[+\textit{of}]$

$\langle NP_2 \ \text{sem} \rangle$ $=$ $\langle NP_1 \ \text{sem spec desc spec}_1 \rangle$

$\langle N1 \ \text{sem} \rangle$ $=$ $\langle NP_1 \ \text{sem spec desc spec}_2 \rangle$

$\langle N1 \ \text{syn agr} \rangle$ $=$ $\langle NP_1 \ \text{sem spec agr} \rangle$

$\langle NP_2 \ \text{sem status} \rangle$ $=$ $\langle NP_1 \ \text{sem status} \rangle$

The alternate form *an onion ring* is realized by means of a rule for noun-compounding:

(4.37) $N1_1 \rightarrow N1_2 \ N1_3$

$\langle N1_2 \ \text{sem} \rangle$ $=$ $\langle N1_1 \ \text{sem spec desc mod} \rangle$

$\langle N1_3 \ \text{sem} \rangle$ $=$ $\langle N1_1 \ \text{sem spec desc head} \rangle$

To simplify things in the present work, we instead include a lexical entry for *onion* as an adjective, and analyze *an onion ring* syntactically as we would *a mouldy carrot*.

4.4.4   Initial reference to simple masses

We now turn to the description of simple mass entities. Recall, from chapter 2, that masses can be of two kinds: an unspecified quantity of some substance, or a specified quantity of some substance. In each case, the **agr** features in the recoverable semantics are specified by the following mapping rule:

(4.38) $\langle \text{KB spec structure} \rangle$ $=$ mass

$\langle \text{RS sem spec agr countable} \rangle$ $=$ $-$

$\langle \text{RS sem spec agr number} \rangle$ $=$ sg

However, the construction of the remainder of the RS structure is different in each of the two cases. First, let us deal with masses of unspecified quantity.

Building the recoverable semantics   For simple masses, the KB structure corresponding to an ingredient described as *some salt* would look like that shown in figure 4.23. The algorithm for determining the content of initial references to simple masses is very simple:

If the **structure** of an entity x is *mass* and no **quantity** is specified,

- describe the **substance** of x, and

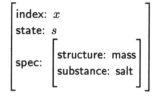

Figure 4.23
The KB structure corresponding to *some salt*.

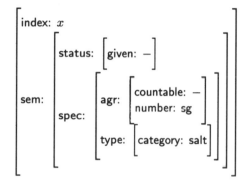

Figure 4.24
The RS structure corresponding to *some salt*.

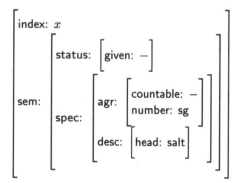

Figure 4.25
The AS structure corresponding to *some salt*.

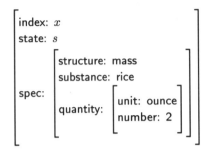

Figure 4.26
The KB entity corresponding to *two ounces of rice*.

- describe any other locally encoded properties of x.

We have a rule that picks up the substance:

(4.39)   ⟨KB spec structure⟩   =   mass
           ⟨RS sem spec type category⟩   =   ⟨KB spec substance⟩

In the current example, the resulting RS structure is then as shown in figure 4.24.

Building the abstract syntactic structure   The same mapping rules as are used for simple individuals apply here, resulting in the abstract syntactic structure shown in figure 4.25. The basic NP rules described in section 4.3 then apply, resulting in the generation of the noun phrase *some salt*.

4.4.5   Initial reference to masses specified by quantity

Describing a mass whose quantity is specified is slightly more complicated. Suppose we have a knowledge base structure that might be described as *two ounces of rice*, as shown in figure 4.26. The required recoverable semantic structure is of the general form shown in figure 4.27; the required KB→RS mapping rules are then as follows, where R is ⟨RS sem spec⟩:

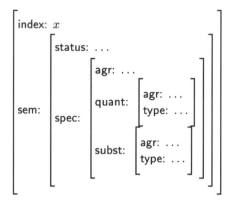

Figure 4.27
The general form of RS structures corresponding to quantities of mass.

(4.40)   ⟨R quant agr number⟩   =   ⟨KB spec quantity number⟩
          ⟨R quant agr countable⟩   =   +
          ⟨R quant type category⟩   =   ⟨KB spec quantity unit⟩
          ⟨R subst agr number⟩   =   sg
          ⟨R subst agr countable⟩   =   −
          ⟨R subst type category⟩   =   ⟨KB spec substance⟩

In the case of our example, the resulting recoverable semantic structure is shown in figure 4.28.

Building the abstract syntactic structure   The relevant RS→AS mapping rules are as follows, where A is ⟨AS sem spec⟩ and R is ⟨RS sem spec⟩. First, the various agreement features are determined by the rules given in (4.41).

(4.41)   ⟨A agr⟩   =   ⟨R quant agr⟩
          ⟨A desc spec₁ agr⟩   =   ⟨A agr⟩
          ⟨A desc spec₂ agr⟩   =   ⟨R subst agr⟩

Then, the basic algorithm described in section 4.3 for the embedding of properties is applied, first to build ⟨A desc spec₁ desc⟩ using the information specified in ⟨R quant type⟩, and then to build ⟨A desc spec₂ desc⟩ using the information specified in ⟨R subst type⟩.

This results in the abstract syntactic structure shown in figure 4.29.

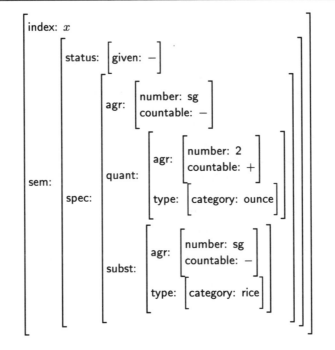

Figure 4.28
The RS structure corresponding to *two ounces of rice*.

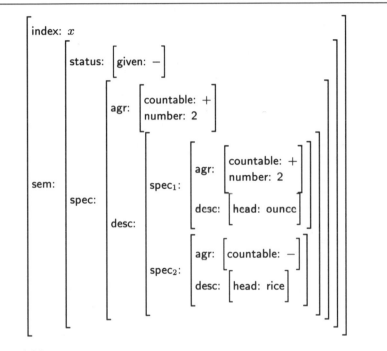

Figure 4.29
The AS structure corresponding to *two ounces of rice*.

Building the surface syntactic structure   There are interesting
differences between the linguistic behavior of measure phrases, such as
our present example, and the pseudo-partitives discussed above. First,
compare the number agreements in (4.42)–(4.44).

(4.42)   a. one ring of onion is ...
         b. two rings of onion are ...

(4.43)   a. a house of stone is ...
         b. two houses of stone are ...

(4.44)   a. one ounce of cheese is ...
         b. four ounces of cheese is ...

In the case of pseudo-partitives, the embedded NP appears to control
the number of the whole NP, but in measure phrases this does not seem
to be the case. Another difference between the two is exemplified by
(4.45) and (4.46).

(4.45)   a. a ring of onion
         b. an onion ring

(4.46)   a. an ounce of cheese
         b. *a cheese ounce

These differences might lead us to postulate different surface syntactic
structures for each. However, in the present work we accord measure
NPs the same analysis we presented for pseudo-partitives: we account
for the difference in behavior at the level of the semantic representation.
This is as it should be, for the two kinds of expressions are *semantically* different: pseudo-partitives describe individuals, whereas measure
phrases describe masses.

   The surface syntactic structure we assign to *two ounces of rice* is then
as shown in figure 4.30. The grammar rules required to construct this
from the abstract syntactic structure are just those we presented above
for pseudo-partitives. (The rule which introduces the category Q will be
introduced below.)

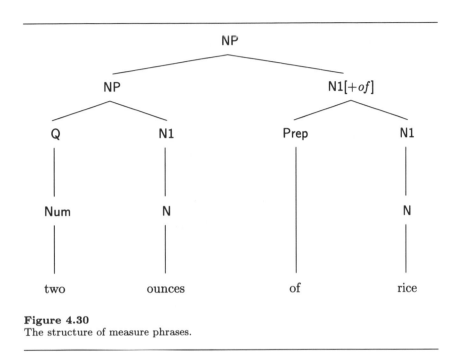

Figure 4.30
The structure of measure phrases.

4.4.6   Initial reference to sets of unspecified cardinality

We now turn to the process of making initial references to sets of entities. Recall from chapter 2 that there are various ways in which entities whose structure is **set** may be represented:

- as sets of unspecified cardinality, as in *some carrots*;

- as sets of specified cardinality, as in *six aubergines*;

- as sets specified by quantity, as in *three pounds of courgettes*; or

- as sets specified by explicit listing of constituents, as in *200 g of rice and peas*.

Different mapping rules are used in each case. We begin by considering sets of unspecified cardinality, as described by noun phrases like *some carrots*. The knowledge base structure corresponding to this entity is as shown in figure 4.31. If a set does not have a specified cardinality, then the rule in (4.47) is used to determine the **agr** features.

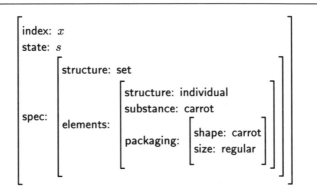

Figure 4.31
The KB entity corresponding to *some carrots*.

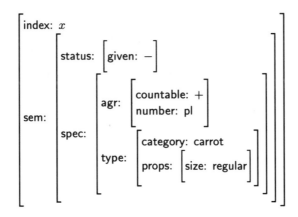

Figure 4.32
The RS structure corresponding to *some carrots*.

(4.47)   ⟨KB spec structure⟩   =   set
          ⟨RS sem spec agr countable⟩   =   +
          ⟨RS sem spec agr number⟩   =   pl

Much of the content of the corresponding recoverable semantic structure
is determined by the **elements** feature. The mapping rules used here are
just like those used for other kinds of **structure**, except that they make
use of ⟨KB spec elements⟩ instead of ⟨KB spec⟩; thus, corresponding to
the rule for simple individuals, (4.48), we have the rule (4.49).

(4.48)   ⟨KB spec substance⟩   =   ⟨KB spec packaging shape⟩
          ⟨RS sem spec type category⟩   =   ⟨KB spec substance⟩
          ⟨RS sem spec type props size⟩ =   ⟨KB spec packaging size⟩

(4.49)   ⟨KB spec elements substance⟩
                     = ⟨KB spec elements packaging shape⟩
         ⟨RS sem spec type category⟩ = ⟨KB spec elements substance⟩
         ⟨RS sem spec type props size⟩
                     = ⟨KB spec elements packaging size⟩

In the case of *some carrots*, the resulting recoverable semantic structure
is then as shown in figure 4.32.

The abstract syntactic and surface syntactic structures are then derived in the same way as for entities whose **structure** is individual, so we
will not repeat the details here.

4.4.7   Sets of specified cardinality

We next consider sets of specified cardinality, as in *three carrots*. Recall
that the corresponding KB structure is as shown in figure 4.33; the rules
used to construct an initial reference to sets of this kind are essentially
the same as those presented for sets of unspecified cardinality, except for
a number of minor differences. First, the KB→RS mapping rule which
determines the **agr** features includes the following:

(4.50)   ⟨RS sem spec agr number⟩   =   ⟨KB spec cardinality⟩

The RS→AS rules are as before. To deal with explicit number, we have
the following additional rules in the grammar:

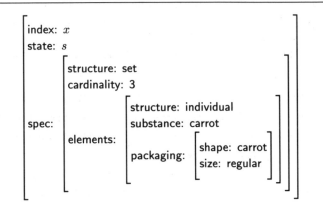

Figure 4.33
The KB entity corresponding to *three carrots*.

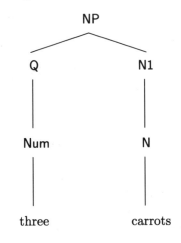

Figure 4.34
Sets specified by cardinality.

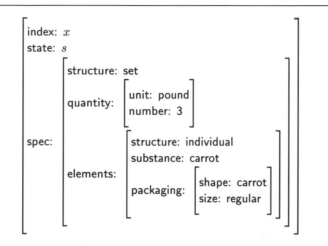

Figure 4.35
The KB entity corresponding to *three pounds of carrots*.

(4.51)   NP   →   Q N1
⟨Q sem status⟩   =   ⟨NP sem status⟩
⟨NP syn agr⟩   =   ⟨NP sem spec agr⟩
⟨N1 syn agr⟩   =   ⟨NP syn agr⟩
⟨Q syn agr⟩   =   ⟨N1 syn agr⟩
⟨Q sem number⟩   =   ⟨NP sem spec agr number⟩
⟨N1 sem⟩   =   ⟨NP sem spec desc⟩

Q   →   Num
⟨Num sem⟩   =   ⟨Q sem⟩

Thus, we analyze the surface syntactic structure of *three carrots* as shown
in figure 4.34.

4.4.8   Sets specified by quantity

Recall from chapter 2 that we can also specify sets in terms of a quantity,
as in *three pounds of carrots*. The knowledge base structure corresponding to this entity is as shown in figure 4.35. Structures of this kind are
dealt with in a manner essentially similar to that used for quantities of
mass such as *two ounces of rice* and individuals such as *a ring of onion*;
as ever, the differences are contained in the KB→RS rules. In this case,

we use the following mapping rules (these are, in fact, a combination of rules that we have seen already). First, the quant feature in the recoverable semantics structure is determined as in (4.52), where R is ⟨RS sem spec⟩:

(4.52)   ⟨R quant agr number⟩   =   ⟨KB spec quantity number⟩
         ⟨R quant agr countable⟩   =   +
         ⟨R quant type category⟩   =   ⟨KB spec quantity unit⟩

The subst feature is then built by the rules in (4.53), along with the standard rules for describing individuals, applied to the construction of ⟨RS sem spec type subst type⟩ instead of ⟨RS sem spec type⟩.

(4.53)   ⟨R subst agr number⟩   =   pl
         ⟨R subst agr countable⟩   =   +

The resulting RS structure is shown in figure 4.36.

The normal rules for constructing the abstract syntactic and surface syntactic structures apply, resulting in the surface syntactic structure shown in figure 4.37.

4.4.9   Sets specified by explicit listing of elements

Finally, we have to deal with those sets specified by an explicit listing of their elements, as in *salt and pepper* and *350 g of raisins and sultanas*. Recall that the corresponding knowledge base structure looks like that in figure 4.38, where the constituent entities are described by distinct knowledge base structures shown in figure 4.39.

The corresponding semantic structure includes specifications of the constituents of the set, derived in the normal way; these are collected together to provide a list as the value of the subst feature in the recoverable semantic structure, with this list structure being maintained in the abstract syntactic structure. This is then realized by means of the grammar rule in (4.54),[10] where first, second, and nth are shorthand for a mechanism that extracts the appropriate structure from a list of structures.

---

10. The rule is not actually implemented as shown here; a different representation is used that unpacks the list recursively, using the basic list operations *first* and *rest*.

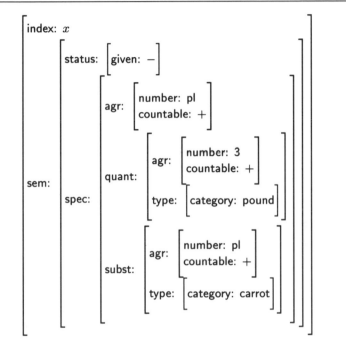

Figure 4.36
The RS structure corresponding to *three pounds of carrots*.

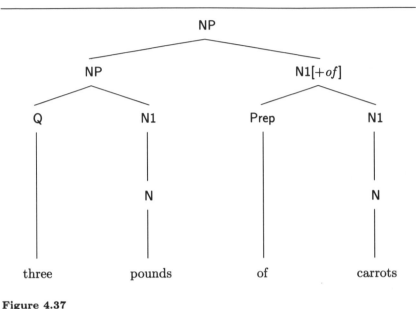

Figure 4.37
Sets specified by quantity.

(4.54) N1 → N1$_1$, N1$_2$, ..., Conj N1$_n$
                 $\langle$N1$_1$ sem$\rangle$ = $\langle$N1 sem first$\rangle$
                 $\langle$N1$_2$ sem$\rangle$ = $\langle$N1 sem second$\rangle$
                 ...
                 $\langle$N1$_n$ sem$\rangle$ = $\langle$N1 sem nth$\rangle$

The resulting surface syntactic structure is then as in figure 4.40.

4.4.10   Generating initial references

We can now summarize the processes involved in constructing an initial
reference to an entity. Initial reference is performed when the intended
referent x is not present in the discourse model, is not mutually known,
and is not inferrable from a mutually known entity. The steps in the
generation algorithm are as follows.

Building the recoverable semantic structure   First, we find the
knowledge base structure K corresponding to the intended referent x in
state s, where s is the current state.

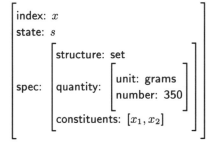

$$\left[\begin{array}{l} \text{index: } x \\ \text{state: } s \\[1em] \text{spec:} \quad \left[\begin{array}{l} \text{structure: set} \\[0.5em] \text{quantity:} \quad \left[\begin{array}{l} \text{unit: grams} \\ \text{number: 350} \end{array}\right] \\[1.5em] \text{constituents: } [x_1, x_2] \end{array}\right] \end{array}\right]$$

Figure 4.38
The KB entity corresponding to *350 g of raisins and sultanas*.

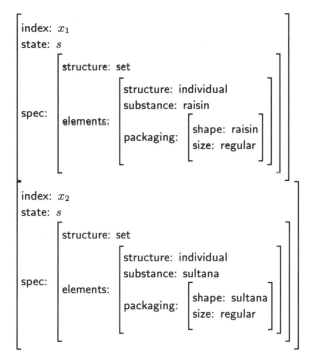

$$\left[\begin{array}{l} \text{index: } x_1 \\ \text{state: } s \\[1em] \text{spec:} \quad \left[\begin{array}{l} \text{structure: set} \\[0.5em] \text{elements:} \quad \left[\begin{array}{l} \text{structure: individual} \\ \text{substance: raisin} \\[0.5em] \text{packaging:} \quad \left[\begin{array}{l} \text{shape: raisin} \\ \text{size: regular} \end{array}\right] \end{array}\right] \end{array}\right] \\[4em] \text{index: } x_2 \\ \text{state: } s \\[1em] \text{spec:} \quad \left[\begin{array}{l} \text{structure: set} \\[0.5em] \text{elements:} \quad \left[\begin{array}{l} \text{structure: individual} \\ \text{substance: sultana} \\[0.5em] \text{packaging:} \quad \left[\begin{array}{l} \text{shape: sultana} \\ \text{size: regular} \end{array}\right] \end{array}\right] \end{array}\right] \end{array}\right]$$

Figure 4.39
The KB entities corresponding to the constituents of *350 g of raisins and sultanas*.

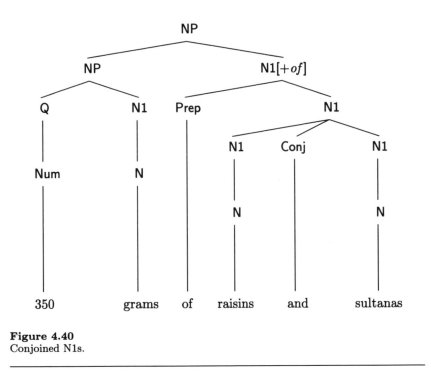

Figure 4.40
Conjoined N1s.

We then construct an empty recoverable semantic structure R. To this, we add the features ⟨index⟩ and ⟨status given⟩. The ⟨index⟩ is just the value of ⟨K index⟩, and the value of ⟨status given⟩ is always '−' for initial reference.

The semantic content of the recoverable semantic structure, i.e., the value of ⟨R sem⟩, is then constructed. How this is done depends on the value of ⟨K spec structure⟩, as follows.

First, we have to construct the appropriate values for ⟨R sem spec agr⟩ (i.e., the agreement features for the noun phrase that will result). The agreement features are determined by the following path equations, where the first equation in each case serves as a condition on the application of those following.

(4.55)
$$
\begin{aligned}
\langle \text{KB spec structure} \rangle &= \text{individual} \\
\langle \text{RS sem spec agr countable} \rangle &= + \\
\langle \text{RS sem spec agr number} \rangle &= \text{sg}
\end{aligned}
$$

$$
\begin{aligned}
\langle \text{KB spec structure} \rangle &= \text{mass} \\
\langle \text{RS sem spec agr countable} \rangle &= - \\
\langle \text{RS sem spec agr number} \rangle &= \text{sg}
\end{aligned}
$$

$$
\begin{aligned}
\langle \text{KB spec structure} \rangle &= \text{set} \\
\langle \text{RS sem spec agr countable} \rangle &= + \\
\langle \text{RS sem spec agr number} \rangle &= \text{pl}
\end{aligned}
$$

Next, we can fill out the semantic content of the recoverable semantic structure using the information in K. Again, how this is done depends on the value of ⟨K structure⟩:

- If K has structure individual, or it has structure mass and does not have a specified quantity, then we build up the contents of ⟨R sem spec type⟩ using the information in ⟨K spec⟩.

- If K has structure mass and has a value for ⟨spec quantity⟩, then the value of ⟨R sem spec quant⟩ is determined using the information in ⟨K spec quantity⟩, and the value of ⟨R sem spec subst⟩ is determined using the other information in ⟨K spec⟩ as for unspecified quantities of mass.

- If K has structure set and neither has any quantity specified, nor is specified in terms of particular constituents, then ⟨R sem spec type⟩

is constructed as for individuals and masses above, but using the information in ⟨K spec element⟩ instead of ⟨K spec⟩, In addition, if ⟨K spec cardinality⟩ is specified, this information is added to ⟨R sem spec agr⟩.

- If K has structure set and has a specified quantity, then ⟨R sem spec quant⟩ is constructed using the information in ⟨K spec quantity⟩, and ⟨R sem spec subst⟩ is constructed as using the information specified in ⟨K spec element⟩.

- If K has structure set and has an explicit list of constituents, then ⟨R sem spec subst⟩ is constructed as a list of structures, where each is constructed in accordance with the current algorithm. In addition, if K has a specified quantity, this is used to construct ⟨R sem spec quant⟩.

At the end of this process, we have a recoverable semantic structure that represents the semantic content of the noun phrase to be generated. Note that there are two basic types of RS structures: those which have a substructure addressed as ⟨sem spec type⟩, and those which have two sister substructures addressed as ⟨sem spec quant subst⟩. A third basic type, not covered here, has two sister substructures addressed as ⟨sem spec part⟩ and ⟨sem spec set⟩: we will consider these structures in section 5.2.

Building the abstract syntactic structure   Given a recoverable semantic structure R, we construct an abstract syntactic structure A according to the following algorithm. Note that the same mapping rules are used to build abstract syntactic structures: it is only at the level of constructing recoverable semantic structures that different mapping rules are required for initial and subsequent reference respectively.

First we construct an empty abstract syntactic structure A. To this, we copy across the structures ⟨index⟩, ⟨sem status⟩, and ⟨sem spec agr⟩ from R. We then construct the semantic content of the structure, i.e., the value of ⟨A sem⟩, using the information in ⟨R sem spec⟩. There are three parts to this algorithm, depending on the type of the recoverable semantic structure; two of these are described below, the procedures used for RS structures which have substructures ⟨sem spec part⟩ and ⟨sem spec set⟩ being described in section 5.2.

- If ⟨R sem spec type⟩ exists, then ⟨A sem spec desc⟩ is constructed from the information it contains. This basically involves structuring the semantic elements in such a way that they match the structure of the syntactic construction that will ultimately be generated.

- If $\langle$R sem spec quant$\rangle$ exists, then the two structures addressed as $\langle$A sem spec desc $spec_1\rangle$ and $\langle$A sem spec desc $spec_2\rangle$ are constructed, the former using the information in $\langle$R sem spec quant$\rangle$ and the latter using the information in $\langle$R sem spec subst$\rangle$. In each case, the construction process is really a recursive application of this algorithm.

The complete noun-phrase grammar used to build the surface string from this abstract syntactic structure is presented at the end of chapter 5.

5 Generating Anaphoric References

5.1 The Pronominalization Decision

The problem of pronominal reference resolution has always been of central importance in work on natural language interpretation. The corresponding problem in natural language generation is referred to as the **pronominalization decision**: When is it appropriate to use a pronoun to refer to an entity?

As was noted in chapter 4, in order to adhere to the principle of adequacy, an anaphoric definite noun phrase must distinguish the intended referent from any other entities with which it might be confused. In order to achieve this goal, the noun phrase in question must provide sufficient semantic content to uniquely identify the intended referent. Pronouns are, apart from gender information, essentially free of semantic content; intuitively, therefore, the use of the pronominal form suggests that the intended referent is so salient in the discourse that it is considered as an antecedent before any other entities are considered.

It is generally recognized that syntactic constraints may provide some assistance with respect to the resolution of intra-sentential pronominal anaphora. However, for intersentential pronominal anaphora, things are much less clear cut. Many existing generation systems make use of, or suggest making use of, Sidner's (1979) notion of focus in the generation of pronouns (see, for example, McDonald 1980: 220; Appelt 1982: 129; McKeown 1982: 127). The approach taken in the present work is closer to that of Grosz, Joshi, and Weinstein's (1983) notion of **centering**. Below, we draw a distinction between **immediate pronominalization** and **long-distance pronominalization**, and present the algorithm used in EPICURE for deciding on immediate pronominalization. We then suggest how long-distance pronominalization might be explained in terms of the effects of discourse structure.

5.1.1 Immediate pronominalization

Examination of English discourse shows that pronouns that refer to entities not mentioned in the current or the previous sentence or utterance are extremely rare.[1] Noting this fact, we can classify occurrences of anaphoric third-person pronouns in English as belonging to two categories, which we will call **immediate** and **long-distance** pronominalizations, respectively. We focus here on immediate pronominalization, and return to consider long-distance pronominalization later.

We define immediate pronominalization to be the use of a pronoun to refer to an entity to be found in the the **immediate context** of the discourse. Within EPICURE, the immediate context is represented by that part of the discourse model referred to as cache memory, as described in chapter 3. Because the computational model we have described deals only with single-clause sentences, this means we take the view that the immediate context consists of the preceding and current clauses of the discourse. As already suggested, this notion of immediate context is very close to what psycholinguists call syntactic memory. That pronominalization is, by and large, restricted to entities currently in syntactic memory is a view that has often been put forward in work on psycholinguistics. For example, Clark and Marshall (1981: 44) claim that "when the referents are recallable, or locatable, within immediate as opposed to long-term memory, the speaker can use a pronoun; otherwise, he cannot." Similarly, Johnson-Laird (1983: 129) reports work by Wykes (1981) in which children were shown to assume that pronouns are co-referential with the subjects of previous clauses.

5.1.2   The pronominalization algorithm

Within EPICURE, the pronominalization decision is effectively distributed across two levels of processing. It is at the point when the recoverable semantic content is to be determined that the possibility of pronominalization is first considered. However, when the abstract syntactic structure is constructed, EPICURE may decide that a pronominalizable reference to an entity may be omitted altogether. This works as follows.

As in chapter 3, we use the term **center** to refer to that entity which is the **result** of the previously described operation. Thus, by the time the KB→RS rules begin construction of the recoverable semantics corresponding to the participants in an event to be described, one of these participants may already be marked as the center. For example, in (5.1)

---

1. In a large sample of pronouns considered by Hobbs (1978: 322–323), 98% of antecedents were found to be either in the same or the previous sentence.

the recoverable semantic structure corresponding to the object of the second utterance before the semantic content for the participants has been decided will look like that shown in figure 5.1.[2]

(5.1)   a. Soak the beans.
        b. Drain <u>them</u>.

The fact that the x is the center means that no semantic content is required in order to identify it; thus, a null **type** feature is added, as in figure 5.2. Nothing more is decided about producing a reference to this entity until the RS→AS mapping rules come into effect. Then, the following algorithm is applied:

- If a participant has the feature [**center**, +] then:

    - If that participant has the feature [**oblig**, +], copy the recoverable semantic structure corresponding to the participant across to the abstract syntactic structure, and add **agr** features consistent with the gender and number of x.
    - Otherwise, omit it from the abstract syntactic structure.

Thus, in the present example, the abstract syntactic structure corresponding to the pronominalized reference will be as shown in figure 5.3. The grammar rule in (5.2) then produces the required surface string; the case of the pronoun will be determined by the sentence rule.

(5.2)   NP → Pronoun
                  ⟨Pronoun sem status⟩   =   ⟨NP sem status⟩
                  ⟨Pronoun sem spec⟩   =   ⟨NP sem spec desc⟩
                  ⟨Pronoun syn agr⟩   =   ⟨NP sem spec agr⟩

The lexical entry for the pronominal form used here is shown in figure 5.4.

Now consider the case where the participant does not have the feature [**oblig**, +], as determined by the verb case frame used in building the recoverable semantic structure. This leads to the participant's being omitted entirely from the abstract syntactic structure, resulting in utterances like (5.3b), where ϕ marks the omission of the participant, including the case-marking preposition.

---

2. Recall from chapter 3 that the **oblig** feature is determined by the case frame of the particular verb to be used.

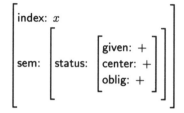

Figure 5.1
The RS structure corresponding to the object of *Drain them*.

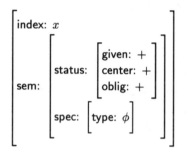

Figure 5.2
The effect of centerhood on the RS structure.

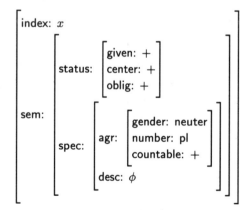

Figure 5.3
The AS structure corresponding to the object of *Drain them*.

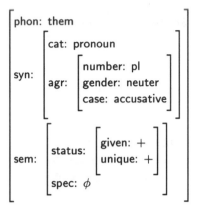

Figure 5.4
The lexical entity for *them*.

(5.3)   a. Fry the onions.

b. Add the carrots ϕ.

In addition, EPICURE will use pronominal reference to refer to an entity if that entity was last mentioned in the previous sentence; thus, it is not only the center that is pronominalizable (in other words, the algorithm used here is very close to the basic pronominalization algorithm proposed by Grosz, Joshi, and Weinstein 1983). This is still a very simplistic approach to pronominalization; however, in the current domain, the algorithm works satisfactorily.

A possible extension of the algorithm not considered here would be one that permits pronominal reference to events (Webber 1988; Schuster 1988; Oberlander and Dale 1991). Since events are entities just as physobjs are, there is no reason why they should not serve as the referents of pronouns; the only problem is determining which events should be available as candidates for pronominal reference.

5.1.3   Local and global focus

Grosz (1977), and subsequently Grosz and Sidner (1985, 1986), suggested a two-level approach to the modeling of discourse status that intuitively corresponds to the distinction between short-term (or syntactic) and long-term (or semantic) memory.

The basic ideas here were expounded in Grosz 1977. In that work, Grosz distinguished **global focus** and **local focus** (also referred to as **immediate focus**). The general claim was that a distinction can be drawn between the hearer's memory for concepts and the hearer's memory for linguistic form. Grosz claimed that local focus is more relevant to pronominal reference, since the syntactic form of the preceding utterance will still be available, whereas global focus is more relevant to definite noun-phrase reference. This distinction can be likened to Chafe's distinction between **givenness** and **definiteness**. In another attempt to get at the intuitions involved, Sidner (1979) suggested that local focus is, essentially, "what is being talked about." Global focus, in Grosz's view, could further be decomposed into a collection of **focus spaces**, organized in a hierarchy that matched the hierarchical structure of the task-oriented dialogues she was dealing with.

As was noted above, work in psycholinguistics lends support to the view that the hearer's memory for text consists of two parts, referred to as syntactic and semantic memory respectively.

The structures of discourse structures   Grosz's early work (1977, 1981) was concerned solely with task-oriented dialogues. In more recent work (Grosz and Sidner 1986), the theory has been developed to apply to discourse in general. The basic ideas of the theory are as follows.

A discourse consists of hierarchically arranged **discourse segments**. Each discourse segment may itself consist of a number of discourse segments, and so on. A series of utterances constitute a discourse segment if they together serve to realize a particular **discourse purpose**. As yet, no algorithm has been developed for determining the structure of a discourse in terms of this segmentation. However, clue words and phrases such as *however*, *in any case*, and *finally* are generally agreed to be surface indicators of discourse structure (see, for example, Cohen 1984).

Grosz and Sidner suggest that three different structures can be identified within a discourse. First, there is the **linguistic structure** of the discourse, as just described. Underlying this is the **intentional structure**. A discourse, as a whole, has a principal purpose or intention, which corresponds to the top-level discourse as a whole. However, communicating this intention may require that a number of lower-level discourse purposes be realized. Corresponding to each of these purposes, there will be an embedded discourse segment. This decomposition may continue to an arbitrary depth.

The third structure of a discourse is **attentional state**. This defines the focus of attention in a discourse. Unlike the intentional structure, this does not mirror the linguistic structure of the discourse, but changes as a discourse proceeds, and is stack-like in nature. Corresponding to each discourse segment is a focus space, which contains the salient entities and relations introduced in that discourse segment. When a discourse segment is initiated, a new focus space is placed on the focus stack. When a discourse segment is completed, its focus space is removed from the stack. This mechanism attempts to capture the intuition that once some subdiscourse is complete, its contents are no longer relevant to the ongoing discourse.

Note that the theory is concerned only with the *structure* of a discourse: the implication is that the principles are applicable across a wide range of discourse types, irrespective of the particular *semantic* relations holding between the discourse segments (e.g., whether a subdiscourse is an elaboration of some point or provides support for an argument). This is in opposition to the work of Reichman (1981, 1985), who suggests that the different semantic or rhetorical relations that can hold between **context spaces** affect the focus of the discourse in different ways.

The interaction of reference and discourse structure   Grosz and Sidner (1986: 178) make the following claim (emphases added):

> Just as linguistic devices affect structure, so the discourse segmentation affects the interpretation of linguistic expressions in a discourse. *Referring expressions provide the primary example of this effect.* The segmentation of discourse constrains the use of referring expressions by delineating certain points at which there is a significant change in what entities (objects, properties, or relations) are being discussed. For example, *there are different constraints on the use of pronouns and reduced definite noun phrases within a segment than across segment boundaries.* While discourse segmentation is obviously not the only factor governing the use of referring expressions, it is an important one.

DS0   1.   A: I'm going camping next weekend. Do you have a two-person
                  tent I could borrow?

       2.   B: Sure. I have a two-person backpacking tent.

DS1   3.   A: The last trip I was on there was a huge storm.

       4.   It poured for two hours.

       5.   I had a tent, but I got soaked anyway.

       6.   B: What kind of a tent was it?

       7.   A: A tube tent.

       8.   B: Tube tents don't stand up well in a real storm.

       9.   A: True.

       10.   B: Where are you going on this trip?

       11.   A: Up in the Minarets.

       12.   B: Do you need any other equipment?

       13.   A: No.

       14.   B: Okay. I'll bring the tent in tomorrow.

Figure 5.5
The tent example (from Grosz 1977: 2).

This claim, if true, obviously has considerable significance for the modeling of discourse. Grosz and Sidner do not state any explicit rules derived
from their general claim; however, they draw attention to some reference
phenomena that they interpret as lending it support. We will consider
two examples from Grosz's earlier work on focusing in discourse (Grosz
1977), and two from the more recent work (Grosz and Sidner 1986). In
each case, we will assume that the structural analysis assigned to these
discourses by the authors is correct. The structure assigned is indicated
by means of the annotations on the left-hand side of the examples.

The tent example   In the discourse shown in figure 5.5, we have a
conversation between two individuals. Grosz suggests that the discourse
contains two discourse segments, DS0 and DS1, where DS1 is embedded within DS0. Notice that the reference to *the tent* in utterance 14
refers back to the tent last mentioned in utterance 2—not the more recently mentioned tube tent, which was introduced in utterance 5 and

---

1. The "movies" are so attractive to the great American public,

2. especially to young people,

3. that it is time to take careful thought about their effect on mind and morale.

4. Ought any parent to permit his children to attend a moving picture show often or without being quite certain of the show he permits them to see? ...

Figure 5.6
The movies example (from Grosz and Sidner 1986:183).

---

last mentioned explicitly in utterance 7.

Although an explanation could be given in terms of pragmatic factors (the speaker is unlikely to be offering to bring the other person's tent), Grosz offers an alternative explanation: because of the structure of the discourse, she suggests that the tube tent is no longer a potential referent by the time we reach utterance 14, since the focus space in which it was introduced (i.e., the focus space corresponding to DS1) has since been popped from the focus stack.

The movies example   In the text in figure 5.6, Grosz and Sidner suggest that the full noun phrase *a moving picture show* is used to refer back to *the "movies"* even though the antecedent was mentioned in the previous utterance; thus, a full noun phrase is used in a situation where we might have expected a pronoun to be used. Grosz and Sidner suggest that this is because the anaphor and its antecedent are in two different (sister) discourse segments.

There is something a little odd about the anaphoric relation being postulated in this example, since the supposed anaphor is an *indefinite* noun phrase. For this example to count as evidence for Grosz and Sidner's claim, it would be better if the supposed anaphor was unambiguously an anaphor in the normal sense. Fortunately for the theory, however, the use of full noun phrases in preference to pronouns for subsequent reference has been noted by others (notably Reichman [1981]). The text in (5.4), extracted from a letter of reference (slightly modified to protect the innocent), exemplifies the same phenomenon:

18. A: The two screws are loose, but I'm having trouble getting the wheel off.

19. E: Use the wheelpuller. Do you know how to use it?

20. A: No.

21. E: Do you know what it looks like?

22. A: Yes.

23. E: Show it to me please.

24. A: OK.

25. E: Good. Loosen <u>the screw in the center</u> and place the jaws around the hub of the wheel, then tighten the screw onto the center of the shaft ...

Figure 5.7
The screw example (from Grosz and Sidner 1986:186).

(5.4)   I first met Dr. Smythe-Jones in 1979, while he was on leave from the University of the Yucatan. He spent some time as a visiting lecturer in Hamburg.... During his time here, he proved to be a very innovative thinker.

<u>Smythe-Jones's</u> academic career may not have started very early, but he....

If we take the paragraph break as a plausible indication of discourse structure, then the use of the proper name *Smythe-Jones* instead of a pronoun can be interpreted as emphasizing that a new discourse segment has begun. As a corollary, use of a pronoun would then be interpreted as an indication that the current discourse segment remains open.

The screw example   In the discourse shown in figure 5.7, we have a dialogue between an apprentice (A) and an expert (E). Here, neither of the screws mentioned in utterance 18 is interpreted as the intended referent of *the screw in the center* in utterance 25; instead, the intended referent is part of the wheelpuller introduced in utterance 19 (thus the referent is never actually introduced into the discourse explicitly, but only implicitly). The claim here seems to be that, since the intended referent is (by association with the explicitly mentioned wheelpuller) in the current focus space, potential distractors in focus spaces further

E: Good morning. I would like for you to re-assemble the compressor.

. . .

E: I suggest you begin by attaching the pump to the platform.

[. . . other subtasks]

E: Good. All that remains then is to attach the belt housing cover to the belt housing frame.

A: All right. I assume the hole in the housing cover opens to the pump pulley rather than to the motor pulley.

E: Yes, that is correct. The pump pulley also acts as a fan to cool the pump.

A: All right, the belt housing cover is on and tightened down.

[30 minutes and 60 utterances after beginning]

E: Fine. Now let's see if it works.

Figure 5.8
The compressor example (from Grosz 1977: 23).

down the stack are not considered. Note, however, that we do not need to appeal to discourse structure here: straightforward recency of mention of an associated entity would provide an equally plausible explanation.

The compressor example Finally, we have another example from Grosz's earlier work, shown in figure 5.8. Here the pronoun *it* in the final sentence of the discourse refers to the compressor, which was last mentioned back at the beginning of the discourse. The implication here is that the entities introduced in the intervening discourse are no longer considered as "potential distractors", because the focus spaces in which they were introduced are no longer on the focus stack. This is then essentially the same claim that was made for the tent example discussed above.

Note, however, that this example can also be explained as deixis, since the compressor is present when the pronominal reference is made.

Summary so far As should be obvious from the above examples, the general claim is that the *structure* of a discourse—irrespective of its content—determines, in our terms, the context with respect to which an intended referent must be distinguished.

However, as we noted, in three of the four examples there are alternative explanations for the referential behavior observed: pragmatics in the case of the tent example, recency in the case of the screw example, and deixis in the case of the compressor example. Also, as noted above, there is something odd about the anaphor/antecedent relation postulated in the movies example. The tent example is perhaps the most convincing; however, whereas the others are drawn from real discourses, this particular example is hand-constructed (Grosz 1978: 230).

Thus, the evidence offered by Grosz and Sidner for the claim they make is not as strong as we might wish. There are other problems: for example, little is said about the constraints upon subsequent reference to entities that have appeared only in focus spaces that are now closed. Grosz and Sidner claim only that the entities in the popped focus space are no longer referrable to "in the same way," but it is not clear what this really means.

Nonetheless, the notion that the universe of referents in a discourse can be partitioned in some way is a popular one. The same underlying ideas surface in several recent approaches to discourse structure within computational linguistics: Reichman's context space theory (1978, 1981, 1985) makes similar claims for the effect of discourse structure on reference, as does the linguistic discourse model (LDM) due to Polanyi and Scha (Polanyi and Scha 1984; Polanyi 1985, 1986). [3] Within linguistics, Grimes (1982) has made use of a notion of reference spaces that is essentially the same as Grosz and Sidner's approach; and Linde (1979) demonstrated how the use of referring expressions within discourses describing an apartment suggests that discourse structure has an important role to play. Other work has focused on what we might call logical structure rather than rhetorical structure in discourse; thus, Karttunen's (1976) suggestions for dealing with hypothetical entities, Kamp's (1981) discourse representation theory (DRT), and Fauconnier's (1985) work on mental spaces are broadly compatible in that they view structural concerns as important in restricting the context of interpretation of re-

---

3. The theories developed by these researchers vary in their emphasis and complexity. Grosz and Sidner's is the simplest of the three, since it attempts to abstract away from any particular semantic or rhetorical relations in discourse. Apart from a claim about pronominalization made by Reichman, the three theories do not make substantially different claims about the effects of discourse structure on reference.

ferring expressions. From a more psychological perspective, Sanford and Garrod (1981) suggest that memory consists of four independently addressable components: explicit focus, implicit focus, long term semantic memory, and long term text memory. Reichgelt (1986) suggests a model of the human language processor that involves embedding of models within models. Chafe (1977, 1979) suggests a hierarchical model of memory whose units are the memory (corresponding to a story), the episode (corresponding to a paragraph), the thought (corresponding to a sentence), and the focus (corresponding to a phrase or a clause).

5.1.4   Long-distance pronominalization

The algorithm above does not deal with instances of pronominalization where the antecedent is not in the immediate context; that is, it does not deal with long-distance pronominalization as that term was defined earlier. In this section, we make some observations about long-distance pronominalization, and suggest how it might be incorporated in the current framework.[4]

Grimes (1979) points out that some languages, such as Bacairi of Brazil, have two different third-person pronominal forms. In such languages, one form is used to refer to what Grimes calls the **local topic** and the other form is used to refer to what he calls the **global topic**. This distinction seems to correspond to the two kinds of pronominalization suggested here. Thus, although English has only one pronominal form, this single surface form may perform both functions. There then arises the question of how the hearer is to determine which function is being performed by a particular instance of the pronominal form. In what follows, it will be suggested that uses of the pronominal form where it is not clear which function is being performed are **inconsiderate uses**, and those where the function being performed is clear are **considerate uses** (this terminology is adopted from Kantor [1977]). The claim will be made that, if the pronoun is being used in a considerate fashion, the discourse structure itself provides a means of determining which function is being performed.

In the foregoing discussion of discourse structure, it was noted that

---

4. Although compatible with the approach taken to pronominalization in the work described here, the solution proposed in this section is not implemented, since it requires a formal means of determining the global topic of a discourse—something that has so far escaped researchers in the area.

full definite noun phrases are sometimes used in situations where the
antecedent noun phrase is in the previous sentence. As an explanation
for this phenomenon, it was suggested that, if the hearer is presented
with a pronoun to resolve, then this serves as an indication that the discourse segment containing the previous utterance has *not* been closed;
thus, using a definite noun phrase is a way of indicating that a segment
has closed. We also saw, however, a case which appeared to show use
of a pronoun where a segment had just been closed (the compressor example in figure 5.8). This may give a clue as to the situations in which
long-distance pronominalization can be used. However, since this particular example might be explained as deixis, we will consider some other
occurrences of long-distance pronominalization before putting forward a
hypothesis.

Examples of long-distance pronominalization   As noted above,
examples of long-distance pronominalization are rare. Two examples
will be presented here. One of these examples I consider to be an unac-
ceptable use of pronominal reference, and the other I view as acceptable. [5]
Unfortunately, intuitions on matters of this sort are far from clear. We
are not concerned here with relatively clear-cut grammaticality judgments; the acceptability judgments required are much more subtle. In
each case below, the pronominal references are all resolvable; the claim
here, however, is that some are more easily resolved than others. That is,
some instances of long-distance pronominalization are considerate and
some are inconsiderate, and the aim here is to define the circumstances
required for considerate use.

   In (5.5), we have a pronoun separated from its antecedent by two
complete sentences.

(5.5)   The first years of Henry's reign, as recorded by the admiring
        Hall, were given over to sport and gaiety, though there was little
        of the licentiousness which characterized the French Court. The
        athletic contests were serious but very popular. Masques, jousts
        and spectacles followed one another in endless pageantry. He

---

5. I have informally questioned various individuals as to their judgments on the
examples that follow, but I have not carried out a strictly controlled experiment:
thus, it might be viewed as misleading if I were to talk of "informant's judgements".
However, most people I have asked do share my judgments on the examples discussed,
and so, although I will refer to the judgments as my own, it should be made clear
that this does not imply that they are therefore idiosyncratic. I will address specific
objections to the judgments as they arise in what follows.

R: Except, however, John and I just saw this two hour TV show.

M: Uh hum,

R: where they showed—it was an excellent French TV documentary—and they showed that, in fact, *the aggressive nature of the child* is not really that much influenced by his environment.

M: How did they show that?

R: They showed that by filming kids in kindergarten ...

M: Uh hum,

R: showing his behavior among other children,

M: And then?

R: and showed him ten years later acting the same way, towards, um,

D: Well, of course, that's where he learns his behavior, in kindergarten.

M: Oh, sure.

R: Now, another thing, it wasn't that he didn't have

J: What? What's that? What'd you say?

R: The aggressive child in kindergarten who acted the same way later on.

J: Yeah, he did.

R: Oh, and it was twins. The important thing was that there were two children from the same environment, whereas only one of the brothers acted that way. So you couldn't blame it on the child's home.

Figure 5.9
(from Reichman 1981: 5)

brought to Greenwich a tremendously vital court life, a central importance in the country's affairs and, above all, a great naval connection. (Halliday and Hasan 1976: 14)

Here, Halliday and Hasan suggest, the pronoun *he* in the fourth sentence refers back to *Henry*, last mentioned in the first sentence.[6]

In the final sentence of the discourse shown in figure 5.9, the pronoun *it* is used to refer to *the aggressive nature of the child*, last mentioned at the beginning of this section of the discourse.[7]

---

6. To be more precise, an entity—the first years of Henry's reign—to which Henry is explicitly associated is mentioned. We will ignore this complication, since the point remains if we replace the first sentence by a similar sentence which mentions Henry himself.

7. At least, Reichman (1981: 6) maintains that this is the antecedent of the pronoun. An alternative reading is that the antecedent is *acted that way* in the preceding clause.

The first years of Henry's reign, as recorded by the admiring Hall, were given over to sport and gaiety, though there was little of the licentiousness which characterized the French Court.

The athletic contests were serious but very popular. Masques, jousts and spectacles followed one another in endless pageantry.

<u>He</u> brought to Greenwich a tremendously vital court life, a central importance in the country's affairs and, above all, a great naval connection.

Figure 5.10
A possible discourse structure for the "Henry's reign" example.

The effect of discourse structure on pronominalization   The relative rarity of long-distance pronominalizations might lead us to postulate one of two reasons for their occurrence. On the one hand, we might suggest that all instances of long-distance pronominalization are merely sloppy and inconsiderate language use—that in such instances the speaker mistakenly assumes some entity to be the focus of attention for the hearer only because the speaker has been thinking about it, and thus uses a pronominal reference. Alternatively, we might suggest that long-distance pronominalization is legitimate, but that it is rare because it may occur only under special circumstances.

As suggested earlier, pronoun use may indicate that the current discourse segment has not been closed. However, in both the compressor example and the nature/nurture example there are what we might take to be explicit indications of discourse segment closure immediately before the use of the "long distance" pronoun in each case: in the compressor example, we have the clue word *now* in *Now let's see if it works*, and in the nature/nurture example we have the clue word *so* in *So you couldn't blame it on the child*.

One of the claims made by Grosz and Sidner's (1986) theory of discourse structure is that it is not possible to use a pronoun to refer to an entity in a closed focus space. If this is correct, then, in conjunction with the assumption about the availability of antecedents for immediate pronominalization we adopted above, this means that the only place a pronoun *cannot* be used to refer to an entity in the preceding clause is in the first utterance immediately following the closure of a discourse segment.

We might hypothesize, then, that the only place it is legitimate to use long-distance pronominalization, precisely because it cannot be mistaken for immediate pronominalization, is in this location.

This claim could be generalized to also cover the deictic reading of Grosz's compressor example if we suggest that the relevant distinction is not between immediate and long-distance pronominalization, but between pronominal reference to entities in cache memory and pronominal reference to entities that are in some sense globally salient (perhaps because of their relevance to the discourse, or perhaps because of their physical presence).

If the closing of the segment is clearly indicated by some other means, then the hearer will not look in cache memory for the antecedent, but instead will consider the most globally salient entities first. Of course, before this notion can be computationally useful, we require a clear notion of what may be a global topic. However, it looks as though discourse structure may at least provide a way of explaining the few instances of long-distance pronominalization that do occur. [8]

What about Henry's Reign? Without further argumentation, the above hypothesis does not explain the instance of long-distance pronominalization in the "Henry's reign" example. However, we might suggest that the text contains an embedded discourse segment, as shown in figure 5.10. If we then assume that the referent of *Henry* is the global topic of the discourse, then, under this analysis, the use of the pronoun *he* can be viewed as legitimate, since it is used to refer to the global topic in exactly those circumstances where this is permitted—except that the speaker has failed to provide any other clues as to the structure of the discourse. The plausibility of this explanation is increased if we add some "clue words" to indicate the structure of the discourse, as shown in figure 5.11.

---

8. A computationally feasible alternative would be to suggest that, when a discourse segment is closed, cache memory is reloaded with whatever it contained immediately prior to that discourse segment being opened, much as a procedure call stack frame has any "shadowing" of its variable names removed when control is returned to it. This would be taking the programming language metaphor too far, however, since there is no guarantee that the entities last mentioned in a discourse segment are necessarily the most salient or important entities in that discourse segment.

The first years of Henry's reign, as recorded by the admiring Hall, were given over to sport and gaiety, though there was little of the licentiousness which characterized the French Court.

For example, the athletic contests were serious but very popular; and masques, jousts and spectacles followed one another in endless pageantry.

All in all, he brought to Greenwich a tremendously vital court life, a central importance in the country's affairs and, above all, a great naval connection.

Figure 5.11
Clue words added to the "Henry's reign" example.

5.2   Subsequent Reference

We have now covered the mechanisms EPICURE uses to construct initial references to entities, and pronominal references to entities. In this section, we consider forms of subsequent reference other than pronominalization. In this category we include the following:

- simple definite noun phrase reference to individual, mass, and set discourse entities, as in *the carrot*, *the salt*, and *the butterbeans*,

- subsequent references to sets by means of enumeration of the elements of the set, as in *the carrots, potatoes and broad beans*, and by means of superordinate terms, as in *the vegetables*,

- references to entities by means of their participation in events, as in *the eggs you boiled*, and

- references to entities which are introduced as being derived from other entities which have not been previously mentioned, as in *the kernels of a fresh ear of corn*.

We present the mechanisms required to generate each kind of reference given the appropriate knowledge base structures as input. In addition, we examine the processes required for each of the following kinds of reference:

- references to entities whose existence is inferrable from existing discourse entities, as in *the skin* when, for example, *a tomato* has just been mentioned,

- references to the complements of sets, as in *the rest of the vegetables*, and

- references to entities which are associated with, or part of, existing discourse entities, as in *one of the eggs*.

Limitations of the underlying knowledge representation used here prevent us from being able to generate the latter kinds of referring expressions directly from knowledge base structures; however, we show the RS→AS rules required in each case. Not all of the above are subsequent references in the normal understanding of that term; however, each of these forms of reference involves processing that has something to do with subsequent reference, as we will see.

Before we go on to examine each kind of reference in detail, we first discuss the general mechanism by means of which EPICURE decides on the semantic content of a description. We view the generation of subsequent referring expressions as, in essence, distinguishing an entity from that set of entities with which it might be confused. We call this set of potential distractors the **context**. This approach then leads to two questions:

- How do we go about distinguishing an entity from a set of other entities?

- How do we determine the constituency of this set of other entities?

Below, we address both of these questions. First we consider how an entity can be distinguished from other entities, by introducing a notion of **discriminatory power**. We then consider the question of how the relevant context is determined.

5.2.1   Telling objects apart

The principle of adequacy introduced in chapter 4 requires that a subsequent reference contains sufficient information to distinguish an entity from all its potential distractors. At the same time, the principle of efficiency requires that we say no more than we have to.

We describe here an abstract mechanism that, given an arbitrary set of entities, determines which properties of an entity are required in order to distinguish that entity from the set. We then describe the application of this mechanism in the generation of noun phrase referring expressions.

Kinds of adjectives   Linguists and formal semanticists have long recognized that adjectives and the nouns they modify fit together in various
ways. Different writers propose different categorizations, but most agree
on the two following broad categories (although not always under the
names used here):

- **Relative** adjectives are those whose meaning depends upon the
  head noun which they modify: thus, for example, someone who
  might be described as *a small wrestler* is not necessarily describable as *a small jockey*. These adjectives are sometimes referred
  to as measure adjectives, since they perform a measuring function
  with respect to some comparison class that is determined (sometimes indirectly) by the noun which the adjective modifies.

- **Absolute** adjectives, sometimes referred to as intersective adjectives or predicative adjectives, denote a set of objects in much the
  same way as head nouns do: thus, the denotation of a noun phrase
  containing a head noun and a single intersective adjective is the
  intersection of the set denoted by the adjective and the set denoted
  by the head noun.

It can be argued that the only absolute adjectives in English are **derived** adjectives, like *four-legged*: all four-legged things have four legs.
Adjectives like *red* are often taken to be absolute, but on closer inspection it is not clear if this is correct: the notion of *red* in the expression
red wine, for example, appears to be quite different from that in *red
telephone box*, and different again from that in *red hair*.

There are, of course, many adjectives that fall into neither of the above
categories. Some adjectives seem to negate the normal content of the
noun they modify: for example, *fake* and *false* (an entity describable
as *a fake gun* is not altogether a gun). There are also adjectives, like
alleged and *possible* (as in *an alleged criminal* and *a possible solution*),
that do not commit the speaker to asserting that the head noun with
which they are used is true of entity referred to. Several authors have
proposed formal treatments to distinguish different kinds of adjectives:
see, for example, Kamp 1975, Bartsch 1975, and Keenan and Faltz 1978.

The mechanism described below applies, in the first instance, only
to absolute adjectives, although we will use some relative adjectives as
examples. In the current domain, this restriction is acceptable, since
many of the adjectives used to describe ingredients are in fact derived

adjectives, being derived from the verbs that describe processes that have been applied to those ingredients. The mechanism could perhaps be extended to cover relative adjectives by making use of the observation that many relative adjectives could be modeled using the notion of a perspective discussed at the end of chapter 2; such properties would then be relative to a perspective.

Discriminatory power   Suppose that we have a set of entities U such that

$$(5.6) \quad U = \{x_1, x_2, \ldots, x_n\}$$

and that we wish to distinguish one of these entities, x_i, from all the others. Suppose, also, that the domain includes a number of attributes (a_1, a_2, and so on), and that each attribute has a number of permissible values (v_1, v_2, and so on); and that each entity is described by a set of attribute-value pairs. In a simple blocks world, for example, *basic category* and *color* might be attributes; permissible values of these attributes are, respectively, *cube, pyramid,* and *sphere* and *red, green,* and *blue.*

In order to distinguish x_i from the other entities in U, we need to find some set of attribute-value pairs that are together true of x_i but of no other entity in U. This set of attribute-value pairs constitutes a **distinguishing description** of x_i with respect to the context U. A **minimal distinguishing description** is then a set of such attribute-value pairs, where the cardinality of that set is such that there exist no other sets of attribute-value pairs of lesser cardinality that are sufficient to distinguish the intended referent.

We find a minimal distinguishing description by observing that different attribute-value pairs differ in the effectiveness with which they distinguish an entity from a set of entities. Suppose U has N elements, where $N > 1$. Then, any attribute-value pair true of the intended referent x_i will be true of n entities in this set, where $n \geq 1$. For any attribute-value pair $\langle a, v \rangle$ that is true of the intended referent, we can compute the discriminatory power (notated here as F) of that attribute-value pair with respect to U by means of the function in (5.7).

$$(5.7) \quad F(\langle a,v \rangle, U) = \frac{N - n}{N - 1}, \qquad 1 \leq n \leq N$$

More generally, sometimes we want to distinguish some proper subset S of entities in U, where that subset contains more than one element (as in *the red blocks*). Discriminatory power is then calculated as in (5.8), where m is the cardinality of S.

$$(5.8) \quad F(\langle a,v \rangle, U) = \frac{N - n}{N - m}, \qquad\qquad m \leq n \leq N$$

F thus has as its range the real-number interval [0,1], where a value of 1 for a given attribute-value pair indicates that the attribute-value pair singles out the intended referent from the context, and a value of 0 indicates that the attribute-value pair is of no assistance in singling out the intended referent; an intermediate value indicates that the attribute-value pair is useful, but not sufficient to distinguish the intended referent.

As an example, suppose we have a context that contains five blocks, and two of these, including our intended referent, have the color red: then,

$$(5.9) \quad F(\langle color,\ red \rangle, U) = 3/4.$$

Thus, the property of redness may help to distinguish our intended referent, but it does not do uniquely.

On the other hand, if all the blocks are red, then

$$(5.10) \quad F(\langle color,\ red \rangle, U) = 0.$$

Thus, in such a situation, the property of redness is of no value in distinguishing our intended referent.

If none of the other blocks are red, then

$$(5.11) \quad F(\langle color,\ red \rangle, U) = 1.$$

Thus, redness is the only property required in order to distinguish the intended referent.

Determining a distinguishing description using discriminatory power   In order to produce a referring expression that adheres as much as possible to the principles of adequacy and efficiency, we have to make use of the properties with the greatest discriminatory power. Suppose we have a set P of attribute-value pairs which are true of the intended referent: the algorithm for selecting a minimal distinguishing description D, if one exists, for an entity x_i in a context U is then as follows. We accumulate the required attribute value pairs in D, which is initially an empty list, according to the the following procedure.

- If $P = \emptyset$, then a unique description cannot be constructed; return D.

- Otherwise, for each $\langle a_i, v_i \rangle \in P$, calculate $F(\langle a_i, v_i \rangle, U)$.

- Select the attribute-value pair with the highest F, and provided $F > 0$, add this attribute-value pair to D.

- If $F = 1$, then return D, which now contains a minimal distinguishing description.

- If $F > 0$, then let U be the set of $x_i \in U$ such that $\langle a_i, v_i \rangle$ is true of x_i, and repeat the process with this new context.

- If $F = 0$, then no unique description can be constructed: return D.

The resulting description, if it exists, will satisfy the principles of efficiency and adequacy. Note that there may be more than one such description. This gives rise to the question of how we choose among different, equally minimal, distinguishing descriptions. There are a number of possible factors:

- The purpose for which the description is being constructed will determine which properties are most useful.

- There may be a conventional order in which properties are selected (this is borne out, at least to some extent, by the psychological evidence: see, for example, Herrmann and Laucht 1976).

- Properties may be selected according to some ordering which is context-dependent (this might include both global factors such as the particular domain of discourse and local factors such as properties previously used in the current discourse).

This problem does not arise in the current domain, and so the present work makes no particular claims in this respect.

Using discriminatory power in constructing noun phrases   The abstract process described above requires some slight modifications before it can be used effectively for noun phrase generation. In particular, we should note that, in noun phrases, the head noun typically appears even in cases where it does not add any discriminatory power. For example, suppose there are six entities on a table, all of which are cups although only one is red: I am then likely to describe that particular cup as as *the red cup* rather than simply *the red*. There are exceptions to this general rule, of course. For example, most days I buy my lunch at a local baker's, where I often ask for *two brown cheese and tomatoes*; the sales assistant knows that I mean *two brown cheese and tomato rolls*.

The head noun in a noun phrase usually denotes the **basic category** (after Rosch et al. 1976) or **basic-level descriptor** of an entity: this is the "level of abstraction at which the organism can obtain the most information with the least cognitive effort." The algorithm described above for calculating discriminatory power assumes that there is a sense in which all properties are equal: that is, it is only the relative discriminatory power, and nothing else, that causes a particular property to be selected. However, in real language use, there are other factors that play a role in the choice of which properties should be used in describing an entity. That some properties are more useful than other properties which have the same discriminatory power is certainly true where *epistemic* identification is required: suppose there are three cups on the table, and it is mutually known that only one is red, and that the red cup is the only one that has a green sticker on its base. The discriminatory power of these two properties (being red, and having a green sticker on the base) is the same, but—if you have to actually identify the cup in question—the property of being red is, in most circumstances, more useful than the property of having a green sticker on its base.

Thus, in order to implement the above algorithm, we always first add to D (the description being constructed) that property of the entity denoted by its **category** feature. In many cases, this means that no further properties need be added.

Using discourse structure to reduce the context   We are not yet in the clear. Although we now have a mechanism that, given a context of entities U, permits us to determine how best to distinguish an entity in this context from the other elements of the context, we have not yet said anything about how the context set itself is determined.

The simplest solution would be to take the entire contents of the discourse model (i.e., every entity that has been mentioned in the discourse) to be the relevant context. However, the larger the context with respect to which an entity must be distinguished, the more computationally expensive the process of distinguishing the intended referent will be, and so it is sensible to look for some way of cutting down the size of the context. An intuitively appealing solution would be to order the entities that have been mentioned in the previous discourse in terms of salience; however, it is not at all clear what metric of saliency should be used. One candidate sometimes suggested in the literature is *recency of mention*: in constructing a referring expression, the intended referent need only be distinguished from those entities which have been mentioned since the intended referent was last mentioned. Given that our discourse model is already partitioned into separate focus spaces, we might suggest that entities last mentioned in focus spaces near the top of the focus stack are more salient than those last mentioned in focus spaces further down the focus stack. That is, taking FS_n to be the set of entities introduced in focus space n (where n is the ordinal position of the focus space on the stack, with the 0th space being the space on the bottom of the stack), and taking s to be a function that determines the salience of a set of entities; then, if FS_T is the focus space on the top of the focus stack, the following holds:

(5.12) $s(FS_T) > s(FS_{T-1}) > \ldots > s(FS_0)$.

In fact, this is a stronger claim than is supported by the evidence of Grosz and Sidner's examples discussed earlier; as it stands, the evidence supports only the claim that

(5.13) $s(FS_T) > s(FS_{T-1})$.

Thus, an alternative generalization consistent with the data would be

(5.14) $[s(FS_T) > s(FS_{T-1})] \wedge [s(FS_T) > s(FS_{T-2})] \wedge \ldots$
$$[s(FS_T) > s(FS_0)].$$

That is, only the topmost focus space is more salient than any other, and nothing is known of the relative salience of the others.

Determining the correct answer to this question (if, indeed, discourse structure has any real effect on this at all) is beyond the scope of the present work. In the present domain, since the number of entities we are dealing with is relatively small, it is adequate to take the global working set to be the context.

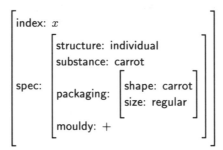

Figure 5.12
The KB entity corresponding to *a mouldy carrot*.

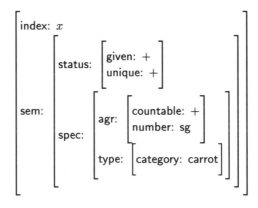

Figure 5.13
The RS structure corresponding to *the carrot*.

5.2.2   Subsequent reference to individuals

We are now in a position to describe the processes EPICURE uses in constructing subsequent references to entities. We begin by considering the simpler forms of subsequent reference.

Suppose we wish to generate a subsequent reference to an entity x, which has already been mentioned in the discourse. The discourse model will include a knowledge base structure which specifies all the information that has been provided about that entity in the discourse so far. So, for example, we might have the KB structure in figure 5.12 as the representation within the discourse model for an entity that was introduced as *a mouldy carrot.*

In order to make a subsequent reference to this entity, we have to construct a minimal distinguishing description, as described in the previous section. The basic algorithm is as follows:

To refer to an entity x where that entity is already present in the discourse model:

- Build the basic RS structure with the appropriate **agr** features and a value of "+" for **given**.

- Locate the context U within which x is to be distinguished.

- Determine the set of properties L to be used to identify x, and add these to the RS structure.

- If L provides a distinguishing description, then set **unique** to have a value of "+"; otherwise, set **unique** to have a value of "−".

Recall that we first consider the property denoted by the head noun (in this case, the **substance**, since this is the same as the **shape** of the **packaging**) for its discriminatory power. If this is the only carrot that has been mentioned in the discourse, then

(5.15) $F(\langle \text{substance, carrot} \rangle, U) = 1$

and so the only information that needs to be specified in the recoverable semantic structure is the **substance**. The resulting recoverable semantic structure is then as shown in figure 5.13. The mapping to abstract syntactic structure and the subsequent realization by means of the grammar are as before.

In the case where there is another carrot in the context, then

(5.16) $F(\langle \text{substance, carrot} \rangle, U) < 1$

(The exact value of F depends on the number of entities in the context.) If this other carrot is not mouldy, then adding the property **mouldy** to the recoverable semantic structure will result in a distinguishing description.

However, if both carrots are mouldy, and there are no other properties that can be used to distinguish the intended referent, then we cannot use a definite referring expression to pick out the intended referent. Suppose there are no other carrots in the context than the two mouldy ones: then the **mouldy** property will not have been added to the set of properties to

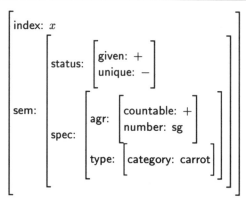

Figure 5.14
The RS structure corresponding to *a carrot*.

be realized, since it does nothing to cut down the set of possible referents. Note that if there is no way to distinguish one of these carrots from the other, then it does not matter which of the two the hearer believes the intended referent to be. If it did matter, then this would be on the basis of some property that one carrot possessed while the other did not; and if this was the case, then that property could be used in the description. [9] Thus, the intended referent can be safely described either as *a carrot* or as *one of the carrots*. The algorithm used is then as follows:

- Try to build a unique description.
- If this is not possible, then either

    - describe the entity as nonunique; or
    - describe the entity as one of the set picked out by the description.

In the present system, we generate the first of these. The recoverable semantic structure is then as shown in figure 5.14 and the resulting noun phrase generated is *a carrot*. Currently, EPICURE will not generate the second alternative, since this requires the intended referent and the set of

---

9. More precisely, the referring expression is **nonspecific**: the speaker is unlikely to have a particular carrot in mind in a situation like this. However, since we do not provide mechanisms for dealing with nonspecific reference, we assume that the speaker does have a specific carrot in mind.

which it is part to both be available as elements of the working set: this is not possible, given the current restriction on the constituency of the working set that all the elements are disjoint. This means that we are unable to specify the appropriate KB→RS rules; however, we can specify the rest of the processing that would be used. The recoverable semantic structure is then as shown in figure 5.15, and the recoverable semantic structure of the embedded set is as shown in figure 5.16. The **status** and **agr** features in the surface semantic structure are then determined in the normal way, as in (5.17).

(5.17) $\langle$AS index$\rangle$ $=$ $\langle$RS index$\rangle$
       $\langle$AS sem status$\rangle$ $=$ $\langle$RS sem status$\rangle$
       $\langle$AS sem spec agr$\rangle$ $=$ $\langle$RS sem spec agr$\rangle$
       $\langle$AS sem spec desc spec agr$\rangle$ $=$ $\langle$AS sem spec agr$\rangle$

The recoverable semantic structure above can be glossed as describing *a carrot of the carrots*. To remove the obvious redundancy here, the following rule applies:

(5.18) $\langle$RS sem spec part type$\rangle = \langle$RS sem spec set sem spec type$\rangle$
       $\langle$AS sem spec desc spec desc head$\rangle = \phi$

The structure $\langle$AS sem spec desc set$\rangle$ is constructed from $\langle$RS sem spec set$\rangle$ in the normal way. The resulting abstract syntactic structure appears in figure 5.17, with the embedded structure shown in figure 5.18. This structure is then unified with the following grammar rule:

(5.19) NP_1 $\rightarrow$ NP_2 PP[$+of$]
                $\langle NP_2$ sem status$\rangle$ $=$ $\langle NP_1$ sem status$\rangle$
                $\langle NP_2$ sem$\rangle$ $=$ $\langle NP_1$ sem spec desc spec$\rangle$
                $\langle PP$ sem$\rangle$ $=$ $\langle NP_1$ sem spec desc set$\rangle$

The word *one* is defined in the dictionary as an indefinite pronoun, with the lexical entry shown in figure 5.19. The resulting surface syntactic structure is then as in figure 5.20.

Subsequent references to masses and sets are performed in essentially the same fashion. References to sets can specify the cardinality explicitly, as in *the three carrots*. This noun phrase is assigned the surface syntactic structure in figure 5.21.

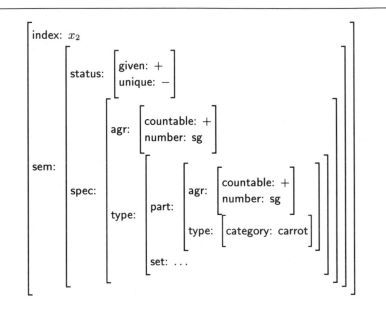

Figure 5.15
The RS structure corresponding to *one of the carrots*.

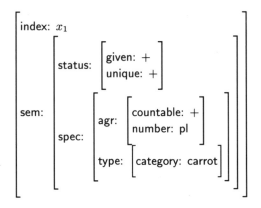

Figure 5.16
The RS structure corresponding to the embedded set in *one of the carrots*.

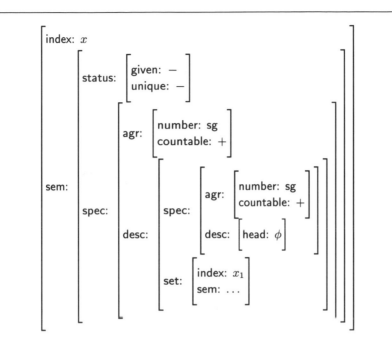

Figure 5.17
The AS structure corresponding to *one of the carrots.*

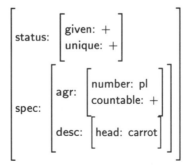

Figure 5.18
The AS structure corresponding to the embedded set in *one of the carrots.*

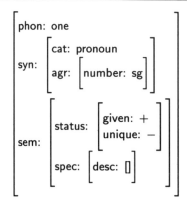

Figure 5.19
The lexical entry for *one*.

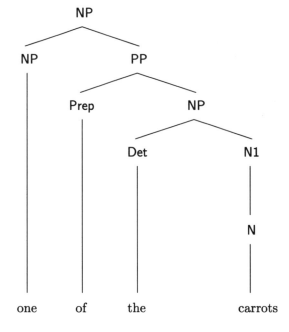

Figure 5.20
Nonunique descriptions.

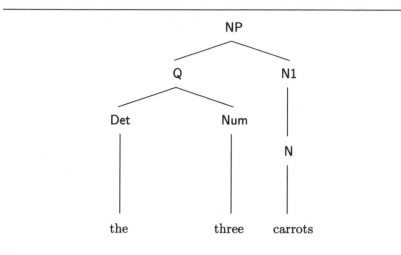

Figure 5.21
Definite sets specified by cardinality.

5.2.3   Referring to sets and complements

Sometimes EPICURE needs to make a subsequent reference to a set of entities, where the constituents of that set are made of different basic substances. In such cases, a superordinate term can often be used. Suppose, for example, the following ingredient has been introduced into the discourse:

(5.20)   2 lbs of carrots and parsnips

Recall, from chapter 2, that the knowledge base also encodes the hierarchical relationships that hold between substances; thus, we have, for example:

(5.21)   a. ako(carrot, vegetable)
         b. ako(parsnip, vegetable)

Whenever a subsequent reference to a set x of explicitly listed elements is required, the following holds:

- If $\exists m \exists s \forall x_i \in x$ substance$(x_i, s) \wedge$ ako(s, m) then the elements of the set can be described as having **substance** m.

Before this property can be used to describe the set, we have to ensure that there are no other entities in the relevant context which can
be described by the superordinate; thus, the superordinate substance is
treated just like any other property by the discriminatory power mechanism.

In the present example, the resulting subsequent reference would then
be *the vegetables*. If we were to use a superordinate term to describe *2 lbs
apples and pears*, the resulting subsequent reference might be *the fruit*.
Note that this expression is mass, rather than count, although it really
describes a set. The current mechanisms cannot deal with this; however,
since what we have here is basically a mismatch between semantic and
syntactic countability, this would be dealt with by the RS→AS mapping
rules, in the same way as disagreements between semantic and syntactic
number would be handled, as discussed earlier.

The mechanisms here could be extended to deal with the generation
of referring expressions like *the remainder of the vegetables* by means
of the following algorithm, where x is the intended referent (a set of
vegetables in the current example)[10]:

- Find a superordinate term to describe the elements of x;

- If there are other ingredients in the recipe which can also be described by this superordinate term, but each such ingredient has
  already been used in the recipe, then the expression *the remainder
  of* ... can be used to describe x.

This could be implemented by giving each ingredient a **used** attribute,
whose initial value is '−'. The basic discriminatory power algorithm
would then identify x in the example above as *the unused vegetables*.

5.2.4   References to containing inferrables

Some entities are referred to in terms of their associations with other
entities, as in (5.22).

(5.22)   a. a half of the cucumber

b. the skin of the avocado

---

10. The basic approach here is similar to that used in Davey's PROTEUS to construct
noun phrases of the form *the other* ....

Note that the entity with which the intended referent is associated need not be already present in the discourse model: thus, we find ingredients specified at the start of a recipe in the same way, except that an indefinite noun phrase, rather than a definite noun phrase, is used to refer to the "containing" entity:

(5.23)   a. the juice of a lemon

        b. the kernels of a fresh ear of corn

We handle both kinds of references in essentially the same way. The basic algorithm is as follows.

To refer to an entity which has an ancestor, where the entity itself has not been mentioned before:

- If the ancestor has already been mentioned, build a recoverable semantic structure as for any other already mentioned entity.

- If the ancestor is new to the discourse, build a recoverable semantic structure as for initial reference.

- Describe the intended referent as being part of the ancestor.

- Set the intended referent's ⟨status given⟩ attribute to '+'.

Suppose, for example, we have an ingredient which is to be introduced as *the juice of a lemon*. This will be represented by the KB structure shown in figure 5.22, where the ancestor x_1 is represented by the KB structure shown in figure 5.23. The algorithm used is then as follows:

- If the intended referent has a substance, then describe the entity in terms of this.

- Otherwise, build a RS structure where ⟨RS sem spec part⟩ is derived from the KB that represents the intended referent, and ⟨RS sem spec set⟩ is derived from the KB that represents the ancestor.

The resulting recoverable semantic structure is then as shown in figure 5.24, where the embedded structure is as shown in figure 5.25. Entities introduced by reference to their ancestors are always assumed given. The same basic mechanisms are also used when the ancestor itself has already been mentioned in the discourse; thus, we treat examples like *the skin of the avocado* in the same way.

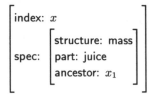

$$\begin{bmatrix} \text{index: } x \\[2pt] \text{spec:} \begin{bmatrix} \text{structure: mass} \\ \text{part: juice} \\ \text{ancestor: } x_1 \end{bmatrix} \end{bmatrix}$$

Figure 5.22
The KB entity corresponding to *the juice of a lemon*.

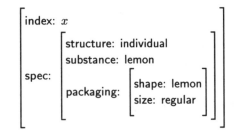

$$\begin{bmatrix} \text{index: } x \\[2pt] \text{spec:} \begin{bmatrix} \text{structure: individual} \\ \text{substance: lemon} \\ \text{packaging:} \begin{bmatrix} \text{shape: lemon} \\ \text{size: regular} \end{bmatrix} \end{bmatrix} \end{bmatrix}$$

Figure 5.23
The KB entity corresponding to the ancestor lemon.

The RS→AS rules and grammar rules used here have already been described. The resulting noun phrases are analyzed syntactically as in figure 5.26.

Sets specified as subsets of other sets are analyzed syntactically in the same way: thus, *four ounces of the lentils* has the structure shown in figure 5.27.

5.2.5   Referring to inferrable entities

In the previous section, we saw that entities introduced by reference to their ancestors, as in (5.24), are assumed given.

(5.24)   a. the juice of a lemon

       b. the skin of the avocado

In this section, we consider references to **inferrable entities**, i.e., entities whose existence can be inferred from the known existence of other entities, in such a way that not only are they assumed given, but there

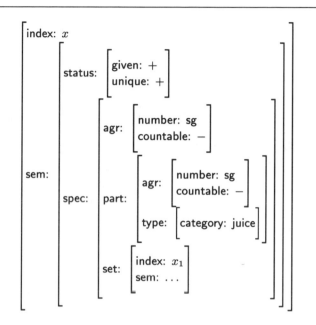

Figure 5.24
The RS structure corresponding to *the juice of a lemon*.

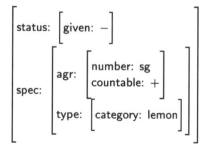

Figure 5.25
The RS structure corresponding to the lemon itself.

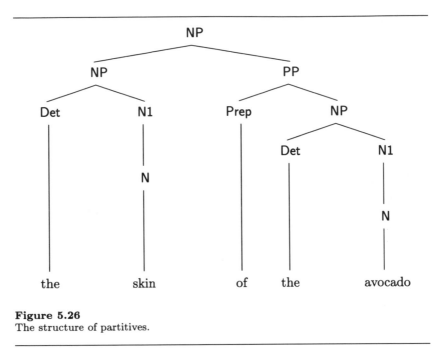

Figure 5.26
The structure of partitives.

is also no requirement to mention the ancestor.[11] So, for example, we find things like

(5.25)   a. Boil the egg.
         b. Remove <u>the shell</u>.

Examples of this kind appear, at first glance, relatively easy to explain: eggs typically have shells. Similarly, every orange has a number of segments, permitting the use of the referring expression in (5.26b).

(5.26)   a. Take an orange.
         b. Coat <u>one of the segments</u> with sugar.

We might suppose, then, that the generation of expressions like these simply requires us to add a rule along the following lines:

(5.27)   To refer to x_1, where x_1 is a part of x_2, if the hearer can be assumed to infer that the ancestor of x_1 is x_2, then it is sufficient to describe x_1 simply by its part name.

---

11. The material described here does not figure in the version of EPICURE described in chapter 6.

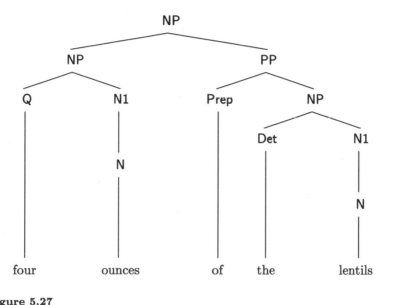

Figure 5.27
Sets derived from other sets.

Notice that any implementation of this rule has to take account of the following data. First, if the ancestor has more than one part of the kind in question, then a definite determiner is not appropriate:

(5.28)   a. Take an orange.

        b. *Coat <u>the segment</u> with sugar.

Second, if there is more than one possible ancestor, a more detailed description may be required:

(5.29)   a. Take an avocado and a peach.

        b. *Remove <u>the skin</u>.

(5.30)   a. Take an avocado and a peach.

        b. Remove <u>the skin of the avocado</u>.

We begin by first considering the simplest case:

(5.31)   a. Boil the egg.

        b. Remove <u>the shell</u>.

Our general rule for referring to associated entities can be glossed as follows, where **associated-with** is a generalization of **part-of**:

- if **associated-with**(x, y) where y is some entity already mentioned in the discourse, then this is a property that can be used in the description.

At its simplest, this would give us the information in (5.32), which, if realized, would result in any of the forms showin in (5.33).

(5.32)   **shell**$(x) \land$ **associated-with**$(x, y) \land$ **egg**(y)

(5.33)   a. the shell of the egg

        b. the egg shell

        c. the egg's shell

However, the hearer can be assumed to have the general knowledge in (5.34).

(5.34) $\forall x\ \textbf{egg}(x) \supset [\exists y\ \textbf{shell}(y) \land \textbf{associated-with}(y, x)]$

The system must first then ask. Can the hearer infer the existence of the intended referent? Given that the hearer has the relevant general knowledge, and the fact that the egg in question is already in the discourse model, we add associated entities to the discourse model. Thus, we add the information in (5.35).

(5.35) $\exists x$ shell$(x) \wedge$ associated-with(x, y)

In order to satisfy the principle of efficiency, EPICURE tries to obey the following rule:

- If the hearer already knows of the existence of an entity, do not bother to describe any properties of it except those required to identify it.

As we saw earlier in this section, we generally identify an entity by means of its basic category, plus any properties required to distinguish it from other entities it might be confused with. So, in the present case, all we have to say is *the shell*. The basic point is this: if we want to refer to an associate of an entity x that is already present in the discourse model, we add all the associates of x whose existence the hearer is able to infer to the discourse model (but not to cache memory, since this might license pronominalization). Once this has been done, the standard subsequent reference algorithms described earlier apply. In the present example, it is as if the discourse had included (5.36a).

(5.36)   a. There is a shell.
         b. Boil the egg.
         c. Remove the shell.

In the case of the (5.37), we might have the general rule in (5.38).

(5.37)   a. Take an orange.
         b. Coat one of the segments with sugar.

(5.38) $\forall x$ orange$(x) \supset$
         $[\exists y$ set$(y) \wedge [\forall z\ z \in y \supset$ segment$(y)] \wedge$ associated-with$(y, x)]$

That is, every orange has a set of segments. Since EPICURE wants to refer to a particular segment here, we have the following information:

(5.39)   segment$(x) \wedge x \in z \wedge$ set$(z) \wedge$ associated-with$(z, y) \wedge$ orange(y)

Thus, we must also search for associations other than direct ones:

(5.40) $\forall x, z \; x \in z \land \exists y$ associated-with$(z, y) \supset$
            associated-with(x, y)

In order to generate the referring expression in question, we add to the discourse model an entity representing the set of segments:

(5.41) $\exists z$ set$(z) \land \forall y \; y \in z \supset$ segment(y)

Thus, the set of segments can be assumed known to the hearer, but no single element of this set is known uniquely. Since we know that

(5.42)   segment$(x) \land x \in z$

we can make use of a reference strategy which suggests, wherever possible, referring to newly introduced entities as members of already-mentioned sets. This would result in the generation of the noun phrase *one of the segments*.

Finally, consider (5.43).

(5.43)   a. Take an avocado and a peach.

          b. Remove the skin of the avocado.

This example shows that, if we add any associates to the discourse model, we also have to add the associates of other equally salient entities. The referring expression construction algorithms then have to take these other associates into account.

5.2.6   Referring to participation in events

The fact that an entity x has participated in an event e is just another property that is available for incorporation in a description. [12]

To enable this information to be used, each entity in the knowledge base is augmented with a participates-in attribute, which lists the events in which the entity has participated. The property of having participated in a specific event can then be used to describe that entity. So, for example, if a particular carrot has participated in a number of events, we would have the knowledge base structure shown in figure 5.28. Suppose the event e_3 was described as (5.44).

---

12. Again, the mechanisms described in this section do not figure in the version of EPICURE described in chapter 6.

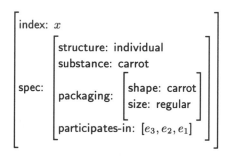

$$\begin{bmatrix} \text{index: } x \\ \text{spec: } \begin{bmatrix} \text{structure: individual} \\ \text{substance: carrot} \\ \text{packaging: } \begin{bmatrix} \text{shape: carrot} \\ \text{size: regular} \end{bmatrix} \\ \text{participates-in: } [e_3, e_2, e_1] \end{bmatrix} \end{bmatrix}$$

Figure 5.28
A carrot with a history.

(5.44)   Grate the carrot.

Then, the carrot x might be described in the following ways:

(5.45)   a. the carrot you grated
         b. the carrot that was grated

Thus, the event in which it participated can be described with a number of different degrees of specificity.

From this, we might build the recoverable semantic structure shown in figure 5.29, where the embedded **participated**-in structure is shown in figure 5.30. When the abstract syntactic structure is constructed, the embedded object here would be elided, with the resulting structure being as shown in figure 5.31. The full detail of the mechanisms required to implement this remain to be worked out, but the basic idea should be clear.

5.2.7   Generating subsequent reference

Here the procedures used for the generation of subsequent reference, not including pronominal reference, will be summarised. Only the process of building a recoverable semantic structure is described here; the construction of the corresponding abstract syntactic structures is as described at the end of section 4.4.

Given an input knowledge base structure K corresponding to the intended referent x, the processes used to build a recoverable semantic structure for subsequent reference are as follows.

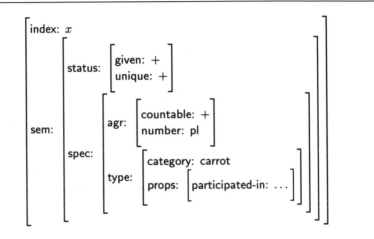

Figure 5.29
The RS structure corresponding to a carrot that has participated in an event.

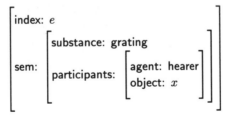

Figure 5.30
The RS structure corresponding to the event participated in.

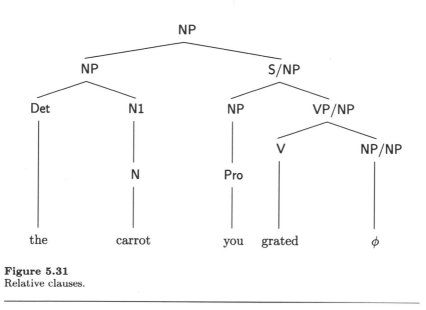

Figure 5.31
Relative clauses.

First, we build a recoverable semantic structure whose ⟨index⟩ is the index of the intended referent, and whose ⟨sem status given⟩ attribute has the value '+'.

What we do next depends on the structure of the intended referent.

If x has an ancestor, we build the substructure addressed as ⟨R sem spec part⟩ using the information contained in ⟨K spec⟩, and we build the substructure addressed as ⟨R sem spec set⟩ by applying this algorithm recursively to the the knowledge base entity corresponding to the ancestor of x.

If ⟨K structure⟩ is individual and the entity's substance is the same as its packaging, we build the substructure addressed as ⟨R sem spec type⟩ using the minimum amount of information from ⟨K spec⟩ required to distinguish x from the other entities in the context. The attribute ⟨R sem spec agr countable⟩ is set to +, and ⟨R sem spec agr number⟩ is set to sg.

If ⟨K structure⟩ is individual and the entity's substance is different from the entity's packaging, we build the substructure addressed as ⟨R sem spec type⟩ using the minimum amount of information from ⟨K spec⟩ required to distinguish x from the other entities in the context, using the entity's substance as the value for ⟨R sem spec type category⟩; the attribute ⟨R sem spec agr countable⟩ is set to '−', and ⟨R sem spec agr number⟩ is set to sg. Thus, subsequent references to entities introduced as *a ring of onion* are of the form *the onion* where this is a mass, rather than a count, noun phrase.

If the ⟨K structure⟩ is mass, we build the substructure addressed as ⟨R sem spec type⟩ using the minimum amount of information from ⟨K spec⟩ required to distinguish x from the other entities in the context, using the entity's substance as the value for ⟨R sem spec type category⟩; the attribute ⟨R sem spec agr countable⟩ is set to '−', and ⟨R sem spec agr number⟩ is set to sg. Thus, even if quantity information is contained within the knowledge base structure, this is ignored when generating subsequent references.

If the ⟨K structure⟩ is set, and the constituents of the set are not explicitly listed, we build the substructure addressed as ⟨R sem spec type⟩ using the minimum amount of information from ⟨K spec element⟩ required to distinguish x from the other entities in the context, using the substance of the entity's elements as the value for ⟨R sem spec type category⟩; the attribute ⟨R sem spec agr countable⟩ is set to '+', and ⟨R sem spec agr number⟩ is set to pl. Thus, even if quantity or cardinality information is contained within the knowledge base structure, this is ignored when generating subsequent references.

If the ⟨K structure⟩ is set, and the constituents of the set are explicitly listed, we first try build the substructure addressed as ⟨R sem spec type⟩ using a superordinate term which describes all the elements of the set. If this is not possible, then the current algorithm is applied to each the knowledge base structure corresponding to each element of ⟨K spec constituents⟩, with the results being accumulated in as a list in ⟨R sem spec type⟩.

In each case above, if a unique description can be constructed, then ⟨R sem status unique⟩ is set to '+'; otherwise it is set to '−'.

5.3   *One*-**Anaphora**

In this section, we turn to the generation of *one*-anaphoric expressions. First, we consider the scope for viewing *one*-anaphora as being purely a matter of syntactic substitution, before going on to present the approach taken in EPICURE, where *one*-anaphora takes place in the mapping from recoverable semantic structure to abstract syntactic structure.

5.3.1   The syntactic analysis of *one*-anaphora

There are two kinds of what we might call *one*-anaphora. First, we have the words *one* and *some*, which seem to function as pro-forms for complete noun phrases, as in the following examples:

(5.46)   a. Do you have any green peppers?

      b. Yes, I have <u>one</u>.

(5.47)   a. Do you have any green peppers?

      b. Yes, I have <u>some</u>.

However, *one* can also, along with *ones*, function as a pro-form for a nominal expression or N1 category. Thus, we have (5.48) and (5.49).

(5.48)   a. Do you have any green peppers?

      b. No, but I have <u>a red one</u>.

(5.49)   a. Do you have any green peppers?

      b. No, but I have <u>some red ones</u>.

In the case of the *one/some* pair, it seems most plausible to suggest that the forms are not actually substituting for complete NPs, but rather are functioning as determiners in situations where the remainder of the containing noun phrase has been elided in each case. Such an analysis would then also explain instances like (5.50b) without the need to postulate that all the cardinal numbers are pro-NPs:

(5.50)   a. Do you have any green peppers?

      b. Yes, I have sixteen ϕ.

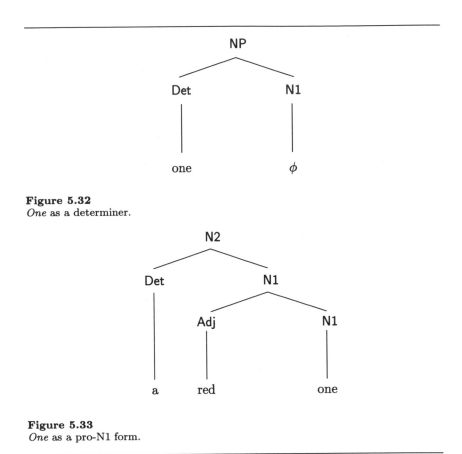

Figure 5.32
One as a determiner.

Figure 5.33
One as a pro-N1 form.

Accordingly, then, we suppose the surface syntactic structure of the *one* in (5.46) to be that shown in figure 5.32,[13] and the surface syntactic structure of the noun phrase *a red one* in (5.48) to be that shown in figure 5.33.

5.3.2   *One*-anaphora as syntactic substitution

Focusing first on the *one/ones* pair, we might take the view that the word *one* literally substitutes for N1 syntactic constituents. Suppose the preceding context contains the noun phrase *a green pepper* and we are

---

13. Strictly speaking, to be consistent with the analyses presented earlier in this chapter, *one* here would be of category Q rather than Det, but we ignore this for the purposes of the present exposition.

about to generate a reference to an entity where the semantic content of that reference is to be the same as that in the noun phrase *a red pepper*. In order to generate an instance of *one*-anaphora here, we could use the following algorithm, where NP_1 is the noun phrase in the preceding context:

- Construct the complete syntactic structure for the required semantic content.

- Compare this structure with that of NP_1. If they have any N1 constituents in common, find the largest and replace this by the pro-N1 form *one*.

Thus, in the present example, we would first construct the surface syntactic structure corresponding to *the red pepper*, then recognize that the N1 constituent *pepper* occurs in both, and replace it with *one* in the noun phrase being generated, resulting in the noun phrase *a red one*.

Because of the recursive structure of N1 constituents, this simple algorithm deals straightforwardly with examples like (5.51).

(5.51)   a. Jeremy bought a large old Germanic manuscript.

b. Shona could only afford <u>a small one</u>.

Some augmentation of the simple algorithm would be required to make it work properly. For example, number would have to be factored out of the comparison of N1 structures, to cover the following data:

(5.52)   a. Do you have any green peppers?

b. No, but I have some red <u>ones</u>.

(5.53)   a. Do you have any green peppers?

b. No, but I have a red <u>one</u>.

(5.54)   a. Do you have a green pepper?

b. No, but I have some red <u>ones</u>.

Similarly, the algorithm would have to be restricted to count noun phrases, to rule out the following:

(5.55)   a. Do you have some white rice?

b. *No, but I have <u>a brown one</u>.

However, there are other problems. First, it is not clear how the rule can be elegantly integrated with a rule for the use of *one/some*: given the syntactic analyses used here, the resulting rule would be something like the following (again, modulo appropriate augmentations to deal with the issues of number and countability just mentioned):

- Construct the complete syntactic structure for the required semantic content.

- Compare this structure with that of NP_1. If they have any N1 constituents in common, find the largest and replace this by the pro-N1 form *one*, unless the largest common N1 is immediately dominated by the NP node in the new noun phrase, in which case elide the N1 altogether.

Even this is not enough, since we then require some mechanism to ensure that the determiner *a* is replaced by *one*.

Although a little inelegant, a rule with the above behaviour could be specified. Other problems, however, make this approach increasingly less appealing. First, it does not rule out (5.56), since, *syntactically*, *one* can stand in for *wine bottle*.

(5.56)   a.   Do you have any wine bottles?

         b.   No, but I have a red one.

This suggests that the substitution should be semantically constrained. In fact, this is essentially the approach taken in the most sophisticated approach to the generation of *one*-anaphora to be found in the literature: in the HAM-ANS system (Jameson and Wahlster 1982), the possibilities for *one*-anaphora are determined by considering a structure which corresponds to our abstract syntactic structure; successively smaller subtrees in this structure are considered for ellipsis until one is found that can be elided without information loss. Since the structures being compared are essentially semantic in nature,[14] it is reasonable to suppose that examples like (5.56b) could be ruled out relatively straightforwardly.

Apart from this benefit, carrying out the substitution at the level of semantics has other advantages: the idea of generating an entire parse

---

14. As alluded to earlier, our abstract syntactic structure also encodes information of a semantic nature; in this respect, it is very similar to the structure used by Jameson and Wahlster.

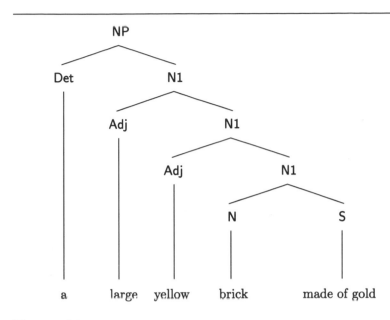

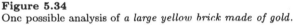

Figure 5.34
One possible analysis of *a large yellow brick made of gold.*

tree and then replacing parts of it seems both computationally inefficient and psychologically unreal. However, the approach just described suffers from another problem, precisely because the semantic representation in question is so close to the surface syntactic representation. This only becomes apparent when we consider noun phrases which have postmodifiers as well as premodifiers. Consider the following example:

(5.57)   a. Do you have a large yellow brick made of gold?
         b. No, but I have a small *one*.

Here, *one* appears to be standing in for *yellow brick made of gold*; and so, we might assume the surface syntactic structure of *a large yellow brick made of gold* to be as in figure 5.34 (this has been simplified a little to omit detail irrelevant for the current purposes).

  However, note that we can also have the following:

(5.58)   a. Do you have a large yellow brick made of gold?
         b. No, but I have a small *one* made of silver.

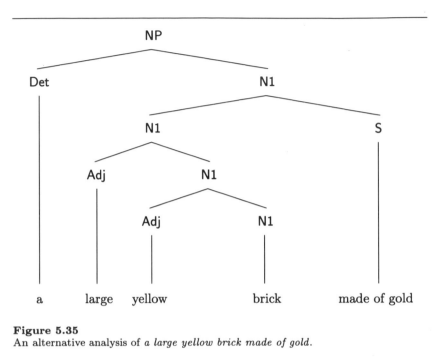

Figure 5.35
An alternative analysis of *a large yellow brick made of gold*.

Now, in order to be able to generate this instance of *one*-anaphora by means of the approaches described above, we would need to attribute a *different* surface syntactic structure to the noun phrase *a large yellow brick made of gold*, as shown in figure 5.35.

There is no single structural analysis of the original noun phrase makes available all the possible antecedents for *one*-anaphors as syntactic constituents; and this is true no matter what syntactic analysis we use. In fact, the only way to make the possible antecedents available structurally would be to assign the noun phrase some kind of lattice-like structure.

This problem arises because the representations suggested match the surface syntax too closely. In the next section, we consider an alternative approach to *one*-anaphora which does not suffer from this restriction.

5.3.3 *One*-anaphora and recoverable semantic structure

We view *one*-anaphora as being an operation applied at the level of recoverable semantics. Recall that, for a noun phrase like *a large ripe banana*, the corresponding recoverable semantic structure would be as shown in figure 5.36. Thus, all the properties of the entity other than that which is to be realized by the head noun are maintained by means of what is essentially a flat list. In this respect, our approach is very close to that of Webber (1979).[15] This contrasts with the abstract syntactic structure, which has the form shown in figure 5.37. Below, we show how the use of the recoverable semantic structure allows us to avoid the problems we discussed in the previous section.

One-**anaphora and the discourse model**   First, it is important to note how the use of *one*-anaphora integrates with the use of the discourse model in EPICURE. The important point here is that it is the recoverable semantic structure of an utterance which is put in cache memory, and not the abstract syntactic structure. To see why this is so, consider the sequence of utterances in (5.59).

(5.59)   a. Claire bought a red t-shirt.

       b. Joe bought a blue <u>one</u>.

       c. Richard bought a red <u>one</u>.

One-anaphora appears to obey the same kind of locality constraint as does verb phrase ellipsis and most pronominalization; thus, we assume that the antecedent for a *one*-anaphor will always be found in cache memory. However, this means that, for the (5.59c) to be possible, the cache memory contents resulting from (5.59b) must include the semantic element corresponding to the noun *t-shirt*. This is not part of the abstract syntactic structure of the noun phrase *a blue one*, but it is part of the recoverable semantic structure corresponding to this noun phrase. For this reason, it is the recoverable semantic structure of an utterance that is saved in cache memory.

Generating *one*-**anaphora**   To see how the generation of *one*-anaphora works in EPICURE, consider the following short discourse:

(5.60)   a. Slice the green pepper.

       b. Now remove the top of the red <u>one</u>.

Just before generation of (5.60b) commences, that part of the cache memory structure corresponding to the noun phrase in (5.60a) will be

---

15. Webber uses restricted quantification as a means of isolating the semantic content of the head noun of a noun phrase.

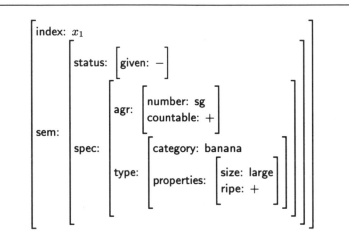

Figure 5.36
The RS structure corresponding to *a large ripe banana*.

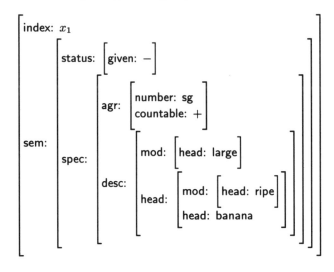

Figure 5.37
The AS structure corresponding to *a large ripe banana*.

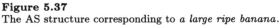

as shown in figure 5.38. As the semantic content of (5.60b) is determined, the current clause work space will contain the RS structure corresponding to the noun phrase, as shown in figure 5.39. For simplicity, we rule out *one*-anaphora if the clause in cache memory contains more than one participant (other than the agent). This removes the need to provide a more sophisticated mechanism for dealing with examples like those in (5.61).

(5.61)   a. Do you have a green pepper or a carrot?

         b. *Yes, I have <u>one</u>.

The possibilities for the use of *one*-anaphora are then determined by RS→AS mapping rules. In the following, RS_1 is the recoverable semantic structure corresponding to the noun phrase in the previous utterance, and RS_2 is the recoverable semantic structure corresponding to the current noun phrase semantics being constructed.

First, we have a rule that checks for the case where an entity has exactly the same type as an entity mentioned in the previous sentence (i.e, that situation where the *one/some* pair can be used):

(5.62)   **if** $\langle RS_1$ sem spec type$\rangle = \langle RS_2$ sem spec type$\rangle$
         then $\langle AS_2$ sem spec desc head$\rangle = \phi$

The resulting abstract syntactic structure would then be as shown in figure 5.40. The grammar realizes this structure as the word *one*.

However, if the two type structures are not the same, then the second *one*-anaphora mapping rule may apply:

(5.63)   **if** $\langle RS_1$ sem spec type category$\rangle = \langle RS_2$ sem spec type category$\rangle$
         then build the appropriate N1 substitution

If this second rule triggers, then a little more work needs to be done to construct the appropriate abstract syntactic structure. The procedure here is essentially similar to that used in the construction of the abstract syntactic structure for a noun phrase which does not involve *one*-anaphora: a list L of the properties to be realized has to be constructed, mirroring the embedding of the adjectives in the resulting noun phrase. In addition, however, those attribute-value pairs which appear in $\langle RS_1$ spec type properties$\rangle$ are omitted from L, and the element corresponding to the head noun is set to ϕ. The abstract syntactic structure

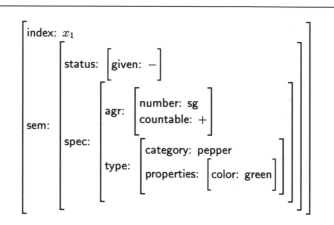

Figure 5.38
The cache memory structure corresponding to *the green pepper*.

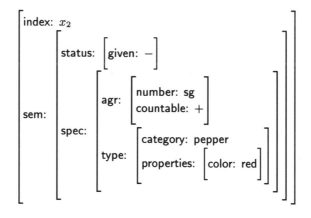

Figure 5.39
The contents of the current clause work space.

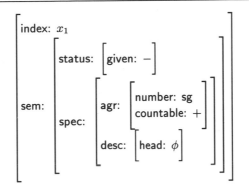

Figure 5.40
The AS structure corresponding to the indefinite *one*.

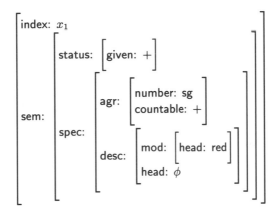

Figure 5.41
The AS structure corresponding to *the red one*.

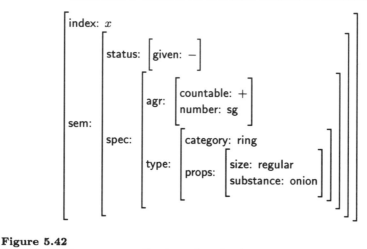

Figure 5.42
The RS structure corresponding to *a ring of onion*.

in the case of our present example is then as shown in figure 5.41. This results in the generation of the noun phrase *the red one*.

Although the appropriate grammar rules are not implemented in the current version of EPICURE, the above mechanisms will also work for cases where the *one*-anaphor substitutes for both premodifiers and post-modifiers, as discussed in the previous section.

More complex *one*-anaphora   Although the above rules work satis-factorily where references to straightforward individuals are concerned, there are some other cases where an additional mechanism is required. We note below some of the relevant details for incorporating more com-plex instances of *one*-anaphora into the present framework.

Suppose, for example, we have an ingredient which is packaged in a non-default way, as might be described by the noun phrase *a ring of onion*. The recoverable semantic structure corresponding to this will be as shown in figure 5.42. Now, consider the following data:

(5.64)   a. a ring of onion
         b. one of potato
         c. two of potato

(5.65)   a. a ring of onion

b. ?a cube of it

(5.66)   a. an onion ring

b. a potato one

Thus, the **packaging** of the ingredient is available as an antecedent for
one-anaphora, but the **substance** is not.

Similarly, where entities are described as quantities of individuals,
note that we have the following *one*-anaphoric possibilities:

(5.67)   a. 4 lbs of green peppers

b. 2 lbs of red ones

c. 4 lbs of green peppers and 2 lbs of red [ones]

(5.68)   a. two ounces of salt

b. one of pepper

Thus, in the structure shown in figure 5.43, both **types** are *one*-anaphoric-
ally accessible.

The full details of the mechanisms required here, and their interactions
with the other aspects of *one*-anaphora, remain to be worked out.

5.3.4   Summary

Ultimately, *one*-anaphora is possible whenever an entity is of the same
type as an entity mentioned in the local context, although the notion of
type required here is very broad: basically, any collection of attribute-
value pairs which includes an attribute-value pair that can be realized
by means of a head noun constitutes a type. This also means that there
is an ordering on types: some are underspecified with respect to others,
and less specified types subsume those which are more fully specified.

In the mechanism described above, these types are implicit: that is,
whether or not two entities share the same type is calculated from the
information known about those entities. Another approach, suggested
by McDonald (1980), would be to actually maintain a lattice-like structure of types. This approach seems intuitively more appealing than the
approach described above: rather than building a recoverable semantic
structure which is subsequently pared down to produce the required abstract syntactic structure, we could then work outwards from the shared
type of the two entities, adding the distinguishing properties. The problem is, of course, the computational expense of maintaining such an

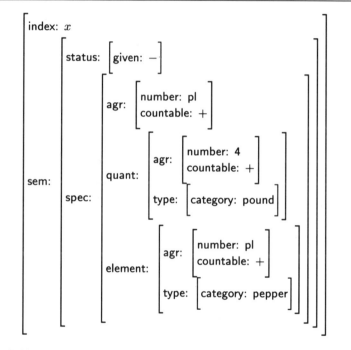

Figure 5.43
The RS structure corresponding to *four pounds of peppers*.

elaborate structure of types: given n attributes, there could be as many as 2^{n-1} types. The issues involved in the implementation of such a scheme are beyond the scope of the present work.

In summary, the view taken in this section has been to suggest that *one*-anaphora is best dealt with at some level of semantic representation. However, evidence from other languages may suggest that this is not correct, and that a more "surfacey" approach may be necessary.[16] To see this, consider the Dutch words *huis* and *woning*: both words correspond to the English word *house*, but *huis* is neuter whereas *woning* is gendered. When these words serve as the linguistic antecedents of *one*-anaphoric forms, any adjectives that modify the *one*-anaphors adopt the gender information of the antecedent: thus, in (5.69b), the adjective *kleine* is gendered because *woning* is gendered, and in (5.69c), the adjective *klein* is neuter because *huis* is neuter.

(5.69) a. Jan has a big house and Mary a small one.

   b. Jan heeft een grote woning en Marie een kleine.

   c. Jan heeft een groot huis en Marie een klein.

Thus, the process of generating *one*-anaphoric expressions requires access to syntactic information about gender which we would not expect to be present at the level of semantics: this suggests that an account of *one*-anaphora which operates purely at the level of semantics will ultimately fail.

5.4   The Referring Expression Algorithm Summarized

The preceding sections of this chapter have presented in detail the mechanisms used to generate both initial and subsequent references to various kinds of individuals, masses and sets, including the use of pronominal anaphora and one-anaphora.

5.4.1   The basic algorithm

For each intended referent x, the clause generation process will have constructed a semantic structure R which specifies the index of the entity, and optionally some information regarding its status (i.e., whether or not

---

16. This was pointed out to me by Gerard Kempen.

it is specified as obligatory by the case frame used in the current clause
being constructed).

Given this structure R, the the basic referring expression algorithm is
as follows. First, we build the recoverable semantic structure.

- If x is the current center, then add this information to $\langle$R sem
  status$\rangle$ and set $\langle$R sem spec type$\rangle$ to be ϕ.

- Otherwise, if x is present in the discourse model, build the recoverable semantics of a subsequent reference.

- Otherwise, construct the recoverable semantics for an initial reference.

The abstract syntactic structure A can then be constructed as follows.

- If x is both the center and non-obligatory, then omit it from the
  abstract syntactic structure corresponding to the clause.

- If x is the center but is obligatory then do nothing: this will be
  realized as a pronoun.

- Otherwise, see if *one*-anaphora is possible, and construct the abstract syntactic structure appropriately.

- If *one*-anaphora is not possible, then construct the abstract syntactic structure in the normal way.

5.4.2   The noun phrase grammar

The complete noun phrase grammar as presented in this chapter is as
shown in figures 5.44 and 5.45.

NP	→	Det N1		
		⟨Det sem⟩	=	⟨NP sem status⟩
		⟨NP syn agr⟩	=	⟨NP sem spec agr⟩
		⟨N1 syn agr⟩	=	⟨NP syn agr⟩
		⟨Det syn agr⟩	=	⟨N1 syn agr⟩
		⟨N1 sem⟩	=	⟨NP sem spec desc⟩
NP	→	Pronoun		
		⟨Pronoun sem status⟩	=	⟨NP sem status ⟩
		⟨Pronoun sem spec⟩	=	⟨NP sem spec desc⟩
		⟨Pronoun syn agr⟩	=	⟨NP sem spec agr⟩
NP_1	→	NP_2 PP[$+of$]		
		⟨NP_2 sem status⟩	=	⟨NP_1 sem status⟩
		⟨NP_2 sem⟩	=	⟨NP_1 sem spec desc spec⟩
		⟨PP sem⟩	=	⟨NP_1 sem spec desc set⟩
NP_1	→	NP_2 N1[$+of$]		
		⟨NP_2 sem⟩	=	⟨NP_1 sem spec desc $spec_1$⟩
		⟨N1 sem⟩	=	⟨NP_1 sem spec desc $spec_2$⟩
		⟨N1 syn agr⟩	=	⟨NP_1 sem spec agr⟩
		⟨NP_2 sem status⟩	=	⟨NP_1 sem status⟩
NP	→	Q N1		
		⟨Q sem status⟩	=	⟨NP sem status⟩
		⟨NP syn agr⟩	=	⟨NP sem spec agr⟩
		⟨N1 syn agr⟩	=	⟨NP syn agr⟩
		⟨Q syn agr⟩	=	⟨N1 syn agr⟩
		⟨Q sem number⟩	=	⟨NP sem spec agr number⟩
		⟨N1 sem⟩	=	⟨NP sem spec desc⟩

Figure 5.44
The grammar rules for noun phrases.

| N1 | $\rightarrow$ | N | | |
| | | $\langle$N sem$\rangle$ | $=$ | $\langle$N1 sem head$\rangle$ |

N1$_1$	$\rightarrow$	AP N1$_2$		
		$\langle$AP sem$\rangle$	$=$	$\langle$N1$_1$ sem mod$\rangle$
		$\langle$N1$_2$ sem head$\rangle$	$=$	$\langle$N1$_1$ sem head$\rangle$

N1$_1$	$\rightarrow$	N1$_2$ N1$_3$		
		$\langle$N1$_2$ sem$\rangle$	$=$	$\langle$N1$_1$ sem spec desc mod$\rangle$
		$\langle$N1$_3$ sem$\rangle$	$=$	$\langle$N1$_1$ sem spec desc head$\rangle$

N1	$\rightarrow$	N1$_1$, N1$_2$, ..., Conj N1$_n$		
		$\langle$N1$_1$ sem$\rangle$	$=$	$\langle$N1 sem first$\rangle$
		$\langle$N1$_2$ sem$\rangle$	$=$	$\langle$N1 sem second$\rangle$
		...		
		$\langle$N1$_n$ sem$\rangle$	$=$	$\langle$N1 sem nth$\rangle$

| Q | $\rightarrow$ | Num | | |
| | | $\langle$Num sem$\rangle$ | $=$ | $\langle$Q sem$\rangle$ |

AP$_1$	$\rightarrow$	Adv AP$_2$		
		$\langle$Adv sem$\rangle$	$=$	$\langle$AP$_1$ sem mod$\rangle$
		$\langle$AP$_2$ sem head$\rangle$	$=$	$\langle$AP$_1$ sem head$\rangle$

| AP | $\rightarrow$ | Adj | | |
| | | $\langle$Adj sem$\rangle$ | $=$ | $\langle$AP sem head$\rangle$ |

Figure 5.45
The rest of the noun phrase grammar.

6 A Worked Example

6.1 The Target Recipe

As a basis for the target recipe to be described in this chapter, we will use the recipe for butterbean soup shown in figure 6.1, from Rose Elliot's *Bean Book*. There are various aspects of this recipe that are not directly relevant to the issues discussed in this book. Below, we make a number of simplifications to the recipe that permit us to focus on the particular phenomena of interest in the context of the present work.

6.1.1 Simplifying the recipe

We categorize here the simplifications made to the target recipe. This categorization provides us with a systematic way of reintroducing the complexity of the original recipe if we should choose to do so at some later point. In general, the simplifications are necessary because of inadequacies in the underlying representation of objects and events, rather than inherent limitations in the approach taken to syntax.

Reduction to single clauses Since this book is primarily concerned with the generation of referring expressions, little emphasis has been placed on the construction of anything other than simple sentence structures. Thus, we expand each multi-clause sentence in the original recipe to a series of single clause sentences. This requires the removal of some conjunctions from the text, and results in slight lessening of discourse coherence: where the conjunction is *and*, such a transformation seems to be meaning preserving, but removal of *but*, for example, could be construed as resulting in some loss of meaning. For the present purposes, this is of no great significance.

Removal of conditions on actions Some actions specified in the recipe have conditions of various sorts associated with them: for example, *reheat the soup, but don't let it boil*. Representation of the information in such clauses is a needless complication from our point of view, so we will remove these from the recipe.[1]

---

1. Indeed, the incorporation of the planning constructs that would be necessary in order to model conditions of this kind is nontrivial, and an area of active research; see Tate 1985.

CREAM OF BUTTER BEAN SOUP

4 oz butter beans
1 large onion
1 medium-sized potato
2 carrots
2 sticks celery
1 oz butter
$1\frac{1}{2}$ pints water or unsalted stock
$\frac{1}{2}$ pint milk
a bouquet garni: a couple of sprigs of parsley, a sprig of thyme and a
bayleaf, tied together
4–6 tablespoons of cream
sea salt
freshly ground black pepper
grated nutmeg

Soak the butter beans, then drain and rinse them. Peel and chop the
onion and potato; scrape and chop the carrots; slice the celery. Melt the
butter in a large saucepan and add the vegetables; saute them for 7–8
minutes, but don't let them brown, then add the butter beans, water or
stock, the milk and the bouquet garni. Simmer gently, with a lid half on
the saucepan, for about $1\frac{1}{4}$ hours, or until the butter beans are tender.
Remove the herbs, then liquidise the soup, stir in the cream and add the
sea salt, freshly ground black pepper and nutmeg to taste. Reheat the
soup, but don't let it boil. Serve each bowl sprinkled with croutons.

Figure 6.1
Butter bean soup.

Removal of temporal expressions We are not particularly interested in expressions which indicate the durations of actions (e.g., *for 7–8 minutes*), nor with the use of words which indicate temporal ordering (e.g., *then*).

Other minor changes There are a number of other changes we make to simplify the generation process. Some of these are of little significance, while others are due to the limitations of the theory embodied in the present work.

1. Although there are numerous *ad hoc* possibilities, it is not immediately clear how we might represent the expression *to taste*, in *add the sea salt ... to taste* in an elegant manner; we therefore remove it from the recipe. This is not significant given the concerns of the present work.

2. We are asked to melt the butter *in a large saucepan*. Since we have been focusing on the generation of references to the ingredients in recipes, we ignore this referring expression. Similarly, we simplify the simmering instruction, *simmer gently, with a lid half on the saucepan* by removing the *with* prepositional phrase. Such entities are essentially functionally defined: as discussed in chapter 2, the representation of functional perspectives is beyond the scope of the present work.

3. The adverb of manner is also removed from the simmering instruction, since it cannot be accommodated in the representation currently used for events.

4. We remove the final command regarding the serving of the soup, since this would require the representation of another object which is not an ingredient (i.e., the referent of *each bowl*).

5. The recipe allows for either *stock* or *water* to be used. As discussed at the end of chapter 2, the representation of disjunction is a difficult problem, and one that has not been addressed in the present work; thus, we remove both the disjunction in the ingredients list, and the reference to it in the body of the instructions.

6. The currently implemented domain modeling mechanism is not capable of handling the removal of parts from entities: thus, we remove the instruction to remove the bouquet garni from the soup.

We also remove all references to this ingredient. Again, this is not crucial to the issue of referring expression generation, but is rather a limitation inherent in the simple planning framework adopted in the present work.

7. The grammar used by EPICURE does not currently cater for the generation of expressions of range, and so we replace the ingredient specified as *4–6 tablespoons of cream* by *4 tablespoons of cream*. A relatively simple extension to the current noun phrase generation mechanism would permit generation of ranges like these.

6.1.2 Target output and actual output

The result of the above simplifications is the target recipe shown in figure 6.2; figure 6.3 shows EPICURE's version of the target recipe. Line numbers have been added to both to aid comparison. EPICURE's output differs from the target recipe in a number of ways. We will examine these in detail in the remainder of this chapter, where we walk through the generation process.

6.2 The Ingredients of Recipe Generation

In order to generate a given recipe, EPICURE requires three basic sets of data structures:

- a set of knowledge base entities corresponding to the ingredients in the recipe to be described;

- a set of planning operators that describe the effects of carrying out the required actions, and that (where appropriate) stipulate how actions may be decomposed; and

- some specification of the hearer's capabilities.

In this section, we describe the Prolog representation of each of these. Some understanding of Prolog will be necessary for much of what follows.

6.2.1 The representation of feature structures in Prolog

Various aspects of the generation process described in the preceding chapters make crucial use of unification. This makes Prolog a natural choice for implementation; however, Prolog provides primarily for

1   4 oz butter beans
2   1 large onion
3   1 medium-sized potato
4   2 carrots
5   2 sticks celery
6   1 oz butter
7   $1\frac{1}{2}$ pints unsalted stock
8   $\frac{1}{2}$ pint milk
9   4 tablespoons of cream
10 sea salt
11 freshly ground black pepper
12 grated nutmeg

13 Soak the butter beans.
14 Drain and rinse them.
15 Peel and chop the onion and potato.
16 Scrape and chop the carrots.
17 Slice the celery.
18 Melt the butter.
19 Add the vegetables.
20 Saute them.
21 Add the butter beans, stock and milk.
22 Simmer.
23 Liquidise the soup.
24 Stir in the cream.
25 Add the sea salt, freshly ground black pepper and nutmeg.
26 Reheat the soup.

Figure 6.2
A simplified target.

1   four ounces of butter beans
2   a large onion
3   a medium potato
4   two carrots
5   two sticks of celery
6   one ounce of butter
7   1.5 pints of unsalted stock
8   0.5 pints of milk
9   four tablespoons of cream
10   some sea salt
11   some freshly ground black pepper
12   some grated nutmeg

13   Soak, drain and rinse the butter beans.
14   Peel and chop the onion.
15   Peel and chop the potato.
16   Scrape and chop the carrots.
17   Slice the celery.
18   Melt the butter.
19   Add the vegetables.
20   Saute them.
21   Add the butter beans, the stock and the milk.
22   Simmer.
23   Liquidise the soup.
24   Stir in the cream.
25   Add the seasonings.
26   Reheat.

Figure 6.3
The output produced by EPICURE.

term unification, where the number of arguments of a given predicate is fixed, with each being identified by its position in the structure in question. For our purposes, **graph unification** would be more appropriate, since this permits values to be identified by their labels (i.e., by attribute), and, most importantly from our point of view, permits structures to be extended as desired. Thus, following Eisele and Dörre (1986: 551), we represent feature structures by open-ended lists of pairs:

(6.1)   `[A1 = V1, A2 = V2, ..., An = Vn|_]`

where each A_i is an atomic attribute, and each V_i is the value associated with that attribute. A value may either be an atomic symbol, a term denoting a feature structure, or a list of values (notated by means of a '+' preceding the list of values).

Unification of two feature structures is then achieved by the following Prolog predicates:

(6.2)
```
merge(X, X):- !.
merge([A = V|Rest1], F2):-
      delete(A = V2, F2, Rest2),
      merge(V1, V2),
      merge(Rest1, Rest2).

delete(F, [F|X], X):- !.
delete(F, [A|X], [A|Y]):-
      delete(F, X, Y).
```

Thus, unification of two structures amounts to inserting into each of the two structures those that are present in the other; where both structures have a complex value for an attribute, these values must be recursively unified.

6.2.2   The ingredients

The ingredients in a recipe are represented by a set of knowledge base structures. As discussed in chapter 2, although a state is essentially a set of propositions that describe what is true in that state, it is more convenient to model the behavior of the ingredients in a recipe using a more object-centered approach: thus, each knowledge base structure describes a particular entity in a particular state. In the context of our target recipe, suppose our initial state is s_0: the knowledge base structure corresponding to the working set is then as shown in figure 6.4. The corresponding Prolog structure is shown in figure 6.5. [2]

$$\begin{bmatrix} \text{index: } x \\ \text{state: } s_0 \\ \text{spec: } \begin{bmatrix} \text{structure: set} \\ \text{constituents: } [x_1, x_2, x_3, x_4, x_5, x_6, x_7, x_8, x_9, x_{10}, x_{11}, x_{12}] \end{bmatrix} \end{bmatrix}$$

Figure 6.4
The KB entity corresponding to the working set.

```
kb([index = x1,
    state = s0,
    spec  = [structure    = set,
             constituents = +[x1,x2,x3,x4,x5,x6,
                              x7,x8,x9,x10,x11,x12]
            |_]
   |_]).
```

Figure 6.5
The Prolog structure corresponding to the working set.

Each constituent of the working set is then represented by a distinct knowledge base structure. So, for example, *a large onion* is represented as shown in figure 6.6, with the corresponding Prolog structure in figure 6.7. For completeness, we provide the Prolog representations some other kinds of knowledge base entities. A set such as that described by the noun phrase *two sticks of celery* is represented as shown in figure 6.8; *4 oz of butter beans* is represented as in figure 6.9; the mass *1 oz of butter* is represented as in figure 6.10; and and the simple mass *grated nutmeg* as in figure 6.11.

6.2.3 The plan operators

As discussed in chapters 2 and 3, a planning operator specifies the effects of an action, and the possible decomposition of an action. Within EPICURE, a planning operator is basically an underspecified event, such that when the participants in the event and the **begin** and **end** states of the event are instantiated, the result is a more fully specified event. In

---

2. The "+" symbol at the head of the value of the constituents attribute is used to indicate to the system that this is a list-valued feature.

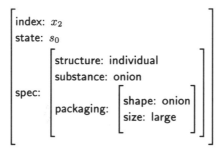

Figure 6.6
The KB entity corresponding to *a large onion*.

```
kb([index = x2,
    state = s0,
    spec  = [structure = individual,
             substance = onion,
             packaging = [shape = onion,
                          size  = large
                          |_]
             |_]
    |_]).
```

Figure 6.7
The Prolog structure corresponding to *a large onion*.

```
kb([index = x5,
    state = s0,
    spec  = [structure   = set,
             cardinality = 2,
             element     = [structure = individual,
                            packaging = [shape = stick,
                                         size  = regular
                                         |_],
                            substance = celery
                            |_]
             |_]
    |_]).
```

Figure 6.8
The Prolog structure corresponding to *two sticks of celery*.

```
kb([index = x1,
    state = s0,
    spec  = [structure = set,
             quantity  = [number = 4,
                          unit   = ounce
                          |_],
             element   = [structure = individual,
                          packaging = [shape = butter_bean,
                                       size  = regular],
                          substance = butter_bean
                          |_]
             |_]
    |_]).
```

Figure 6.9
The Prolog structure corresponding to *4 oz of butter beans*.

```
kb([index = x6,
    state = s0,
    spec  = [structure = mass,
             substance = butter,
             quantity  = [number = 1,
                          unit   = ounce
                          |_]
             |_]
    |_]).
```

Figure 6.10
The Prolog structure corresponding to *1 oz of butter*.

```
kb([index = x12,
    state = s0,
    spec  = [structure = mass,
             substance = nutmeg,
             grated    = +
             |_]
    |_]).
```

Figure 6.11
The Prolog structure corresponding to *grated nutmeg*.

```
effects([index  = E,
    occurs = [begin = S0,
              end   = S1
              |_],
    spec = [substance    = adding,
            participants = [in  = [base     = X1,
                                   addendum = X2
                                   |_],
                            out = [result   = X3
                                   |_]
            effects =
            [add = +[:X3:spec:structure  = set,
                     :X3:spec:constituents = +[X1,X2]],
             delete = +[]
             |_]
            |_]
   |_]).
```

Figure 6.12
The effects clause for the **adding** operator.

principle, the various kinds of information associated with a planning operator could be maintained within a single structure; however, for implementational reasons, the representation of operators is distributed, so that corresponding to each operator there are up to three distinct clauses:

- an **opschema** clause, which specifies the number and nature of the participants in the event;

- an **effects** clause, which specifies the effects of the operator; and

- an optional **constituents** clause, which specifies the decomposition of the action corresponding to the operator.

As an example, the **adding** operator has the **effects** clause shown in figure 6.12. No possible decompositions are specified for the **adding** operator, since it is considered a primitive in the present system. The **bean_preparing** operator, however, has the decomposition shown in figure 6.13.

When an event is decomposed into a number of subevents, the planning mechanism ensures that the appropriate ordering relations are main-

```
constituents([index  = E,
   occurs = [begin = S0,
             end    = Sn|_],
   spec   = [substance    = bean_preparing,
             participants = [in  = [object = X|_],
                             out = [result = X|_]
                             |_],
             constituents =
                   +[[index  = E1,
                      occurs = [begin = S0,
                                end    = S1|_],
                      spec = [substance    = soaking,
                              participants = [in  = [object = X
                                                     |_],
                                              out = [result = X
                                                     |_]
                                              |_]|_]|_],
                     [index  = E2,
                      occurs = [begin = S1,
                                end    = S2|_],
                      spec = [substance    = draining,
                              participants = [in =  [object = X
                                                     |_],
                                              out = [result = X
                                                     |_]
                                              |_]|_]|_],
                     [index  = E3,
                      occurs = [begin = S2,
                                end    = Sn|_],
                      spec = [substance    = rinsing,
                              participants = [in =  [object = X
                                                     |_],
                                              out = [result = X
                                                     |_]
                                              |_]|_]
                      |_]]
                    |_]
   |_]).
```

Figure 6.13
Preparing beans.

tained between the states. In the case of the `bean_preparing` operator, for example, when this structure is instantiated, the particular instantiations used for the **begin** and **end** states are asserted in the Prolog database as being ordered appropriately: i.e.,

(6.3)   S0 < S1 < S2 < Sn

6.2.4   The hearer's knowledge

The final kind of information EPICURE requires in order to be able to construct an appropriate discourse is some indication of the hearer's capabilities. In the context of the current recipe, we have (6.4).

(6.4)
```
physically_capable(user, adding).
physically_capable(user, chopping).
physically_capable(user, draining).
physically_capable(user, peeling).
physically_capable(user, liquidising).
physically_capable(user, melting).
physically_capable(user, reheating).
physically_capable(user, rinsing).
physically_capable(user, sauteing).
physically_capable(user, scraping).
physically_capable(user, simmering).
physically_capable(user, slicing).
physically_capable(user, soaking).
physically_capable(user, stirring_in).

physically_capable(epicure, requesting).
```

Note that changing each of these data structures will have different effects on the output generated by EPICURE. Of course, the particular ingredients and plan operators provided determine the particular recipe that EPICURE will generate. However, changing the system's knowledge of what the hearer is "physically capable" of determines how that particular recipe will be described; also, as we will see, making different assumptions about the underlying structure of the recipe plan can have quite noticeable effects on the eventual output.

6.3   Generating the Discourse Specification

6.3.1   The top-level goal

In conjunction with the data structures described in the previous section, EPICURE is given a top-level goal corresponding to the recipe to be generated. In a full-blown planning system, we would present the planner with an initial state and a goal state, and have the system work out a plan to perform the transition between the two. Currently, EPICURE does not incorporate a planner appropriate to this task, and so, instead, we present EPICURE with a top-level goal for which it already knows an appropriate decomposition. The planning axioms are then used to determine to what extent the event corresponding to this goal should be decomposed to accommodate the hearer's particular capabilities.

In the case of the target recipe, the top-level goal is a making-butterbean-soup event, whose decomposition is defined by the **constituents** clause shown in figure 6.14.

6.3.2   The planning axioms

The planning axioms are essentially identical to those specified in chapter 3, except that they also return a suitable plan. The first clause determines whether an agent is capable of an action and, if he or she is, instantiates the agent slot of that event appropriately:

(6.5)   can_guarantee(Agent, Eventuality):-
                path_value(spec:substance, Eventuality, Action),
                physically_capable(Agent, Action),
                effects(Eventuality),
                makedag([:spec:participants:agent = Agent],
                        Eventuality, Eventuality).

The **path_value** predicate used here determines the value of the specified path in the specified feature structure, and the **makedag** predicate instantiates a feature structure in accordance with a list of one or more constraints.

The delegation strategy is implemented very straightforwardly:

(6.6)   can_guarantee(epicure, Eventuality):-
                physically_capable(epicure, requesting),
                can_guarantee(user, Eventuality).

Finally, we have the action decomposition strategy:

```
constituents([index   = Index,
   occurs = [begin = S0,
              end   = Sn|_],
   spec    = [substance     = butter_bean_soup_making,
              participants = [in  = [object =
                                          +[A,B,C,D,E,F,G,H,I,J,K,L]
                                          |_],
                              out = [result = X
                                          |_]
                              |_],
              constituents =
                 +[[index   = I1,
                    occurs = [begin = S0,
                               end   = S1
                               |_],
                    spec    =
                      [substance     = preparing_bb_ingredients,
                       participants = [in  = [object = +[A,B,C,D,E]
                                                  |_],
                                       out = [result = +[A,B,C,D,E]
                                                  |_]
                                       |_]
                      |_]
                    |_],
                   [index   = I2,
                    occurs = [begin = S1,
                               end   = Sn
                               |_],
                    spec    =
                      [substance     = cooking_bb_soup,
                       participants =
                          [in  = [object =
                                       +[A,B,C,D,E,F,G,H,I,J,K,L]
                                       |_],
                           out = [result = X
                                       |_]
                           |_]
                      |_]
                    |_]]
              |_]
   |_]).
```

Figure 6.14
The top-level decomposition.

(6.7)   can_guarantee(Agent, Eventuality):-
              constituents(Eventuality),
              path_value(spec:constituents, Eventuality, +SubEvents),
              can_guarantee1(Agent, SubEvents).

The `can_guarantee1` predicate checks that each element of the list of
`SubEvents` can be guaranteed. The recursion here terminates when a
level of decomposition is reached where the hearer is believed to be
capable of carrying out the actions required. The resulting plan structure
is then returned as the value of `Eventuality`.

Given the hearer's capabilities specified in the previous section, applying this mechanism to the top-level goal results in the plan structure
shown in figure 6.15; the key provides an English gloss of each node
in the plan, with those nodes which are not explicitly described in the
output surrounded by brackets.

6.3.3 Optimization

The optimization mechanisms are then applied to this plan, and as a
result some events are folded together. As discussed in chapter 3, the
only optimizations implemented in the current version of the system are
the collapsing together of those events which have the same arguments or
the same operator. The resulting structure is that shown in figure 6.16.

6.3.4 Discourse generation

The plan is then passed to the discourse generator, which walks over it
as specified in chapter 3, using a depth-first recursive descent strategy.
The discourse model is maintained appropriately during this process,
with new focus spaces being opened as each subsequent level in the plan
is reached, and being closed as the corresponding discourse segment
ends.

The eventuality specifications at the leaves of the structure are first
passed to the domain modeler, and then to the clause generator, again
as described in chapter 3.

6.4 Generating the Text

EPICURE's output differs from the target recipe in a number of ways.
Below, we highlight various steps in the process of generating the target,

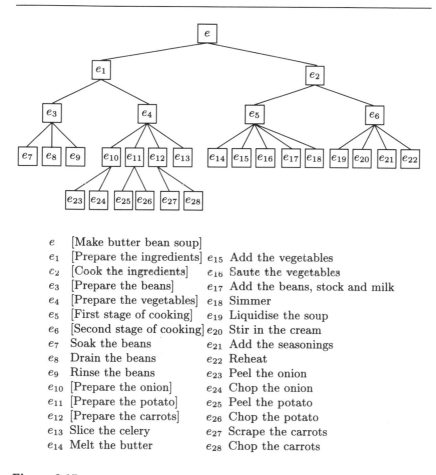

e	[Make butter bean soup]
e_1	[Prepare the ingredients]
e_2	[Cook the ingredients]
e_3	[Prepare the beans]
e_4	[Prepare the vegetables]
e_5	[First stage of cooking]
e_6	[Second stage of cooking]
e_7	Soak the beans
e_8	Drain the beans
e_9	Rinse the beans
e_{10}	[Prepare the onion]
e_{11}	[Prepare the potato]
e_{12}	[Prepare the carrots]
e_{13}	Slice the celery
e_{14}	Melt the butter
e_{15}	Add the vegetables
e_{16}	Saute the vegetables
e_{17}	Add the beans, stock and milk
e_{18}	Simmer
e_{19}	Liquidise the soup
e_{20}	Stir in the cream
e_{21}	Add the seasonings
e_{22}	Reheat
e_{23}	Peel the onion
e_{24}	Chop the onion
e_{25}	Peel the potato
e_{26}	Chop the potato
e_{27}	Scrape the carrots
e_{28}	Chop the carrots

Figure 6.15
The butter bean soup plan.

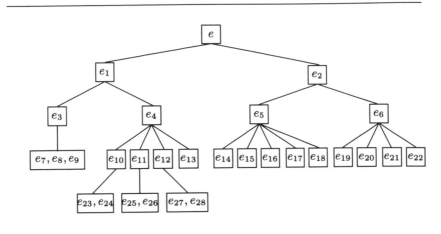

Figure 6.16
The optimized butter bean soup plan.

commenting upon some points of interest.

6.4.1 Describing the ingredients

Describing the ingredients involves applying the initial reference mechanism described in chapter 4 to each ingredient in the working set. In each case we build a recoverable semantic structure, and then an abstract syntactic structure which is passed to the grammar. The results achieved here are essentially identical to the ingredients list in the target recipe, apart from a number of minor cosmetic differences:

- We insert *of* in noun phrases that describe quantities.
- We use the determiner *some* for unspecified quantities of mass.
- The orthographic form of numbers is different: we use words rather than digits.

The first two differences could be removed by adding to the system a parameter that specifies whether or not a "telegraphic form" is used when building a noun phrase; note that, in general, we *do* want to include words like *of* and *some* when ingredients are referred to in the body of the recipe.

6.4.2 Describing the recipe

More noteworthy differences occur in the body of the recipe.

Describing more than one operation in a sentence First, consider line 13 in the actual output, which corresponds to lines 13 and 14 in the target output. In the actual output, the the operations of *soaking*, *draining*, and *rinsing* are collected together by the optimization phase:

(6.8)   Soak, drain and rinse the butter beans.

This is possible because all three actions are subactions in the decomposition of the *bean-preparing* operator: recall from chapter 3 that the optimization routines operate across daughters that have the same mother node in the plan (where those daughters are atomic events). In the target recipe, however, only the second and third actions are collected together:

(6.9)   Soak the butter beans.
         Drain and rinse them.

Note that, by modifying the plan decomposition and therefore the discourse structure, we can produce the same configuration as that found in the target. We can add a further intermediate level of decomposition, such that bean preparation has two stages, where the first stage consists only of a *soaking* action, and the second stage consists of the two subactions of *draining* and *rinsing*. Since the optimization routines *only* operate across daughters that have the same mother node, we would then generate exactly the description found in the target.

The operation of the optimization routines gives rise to a related difference found in lines 13 and 14 of the actual output, which corresponds to line 14 of the target: whereas we generate (6.10a), in the target these operations are collected together to produce (6.10b).

(6.10)   a. Peel and chop the onion.
             Peel and chop the potato.
         b. Peel and chop the onion and potato.

One way we could produce this output would be to modify the optimization routines so that they operate on elements which are not atomic;

however, notice that this then produces the wrong results in the case of the *soaking, draining, and rinsing* discussed above. An alternative solution would be to modify the plan structure so that, instead of there being a level of structure intermediate between the plan node corresponding to *preparing the vegetables* and the more specific actions described, these specific actions would be daughters of the *preparing the vegetables* node.

What both these differences emphasize, however, is the arbitrariness involved in proposing that a particular structure underlies a piece of text. This is related, as we saw in chapter 2, to the question of the individuation of events. Finding satisfactory answers to these questions is, of course, beyond the remit of the present work.

Eliding NPs Note that, in many cases, a participant in an event is omitted from the description of that event. This occurs in lines 19, 21, 22, 24, and 26 in both the target and the actual output; these are repeated in (6.11), with the omitted participant added in brackets.

(6.11) a. Add the vegetables [to the butter].
        b. Add the butter beans, the stock and the milk [to the sautéed vegetables].
        c. Simmer [the vegetables, butter beans, stock and milk].
        d. Stir in the cream [to the soup].
        e. Add the seasonings [to the soup].

In addition, note that in the actual output, line 26 is generated as (6.12a) whereas the target recipe contains (6.12b).

(6.12) a. Reheat.
        b. Reheat the soup.

Recall that, within EPICURE, a participant can be omitted from the description of an event if that participant is marked as being nonobligatory and also as being the current center. Whether or not the description of a participant is obligatory is determined by the case frame of the associated verb; and the center of an utterance is, in the current domain, the result of the preceding operation.

This mechanism generates (with the exception of line 26) the desired output, but at best it is a gross simplification of what is really going on. In particular, consider lines 19 and 20:

(6.13)   Add the vegetables.
         Sauté them.

Just as in the target recipe, we generate the appropriate pronoun. Note
that the result of the adding operation here is, strictly speaking, butter
and vegetables combined; thus, we generate a pronoun because we apply
the sautéing operation not to the result of the previous operation, but
to one of its inputs.[3] Although we get the correct results, the method
is a little dubious: there ought to be a more principled way to make
the butter "disappear". One solution would be to distinguish "central"
ingredients from ingredients that play an "in-service" role. The details
of how this might work are left for future work.

Returning to the case of *reheat the soup*, here EPICURE elides the reference to the soup although the target recipe does not. In fact, a simple
modification to the plan structure will produce the desired result. First,
note why EPICURE elides the reference to the soup. The *reheating* event
is a sister event to the preceding *add* event: since the *reheating* event
is applied to the result of the *adding* event, the soup is the center, and
since the case frame for the verb *reheat* marks its object as nonobligatory, the mechanisms that build the abstract syntactic structure can
omit the reference to the soup. However, recall that centers are retained
across discourse segment closures: thus, if we restructure the plan so
that the *reheating* action is not a sister of the preceding *liquidising*, *stir-
ring*, and *adding* actions, but is in a separate discourse segment, then
the object of the reheating action must be described by a definite noun
phrase. This is exactly what happens in line 23:

(6.14)   Liquidize the soup.

where the soup is explicitly mentioned even though it is the result of the
previous operation, because this action is in a distinct discourse segment
to that which contains the previous operation.

Describing mixtures   One problem for which EPICURE does not provide an elegant solution is that of describing the results of collecting
different ingredients together (as distinct from describing a collection of
similar ingredients: see below). In the context of the present recipe, the

---

3. Recall that our pronominalization algorithm permits a pronominal reference to
be used to any entity mentioned in the previous sentence.

question is this: at which point in the recipe do we have *soup* rather than just a collection of ingredients?

Notice that the first mention of the soup is in line 23:

(6.15)   Liquidize the soup.

In fact, however, the entity referred to as the soup is actually introduced previous to this, in line 21:

(6.16)   Add the butter beans, the stock and the milk.

Although not mentioned in this or in the following sentence (because it is then elided as discussed above), a distinct entity corresponding to the soup, with the butter beans, stock, milk and vegetables as constituent objects, is introduced as the result of this *adding* operation. In order to enable this to be described as *the soup*, however, we make use of a special form of the *adding* operator, which has the effect that the object which is the result of the *adding* operation has as its substance *soup*. This is far from elegant, but it is difficult to see how this could be done in a more principled way without a sizeable increase in the complexity of modeling the execution of the recipe.[4]

Using superordinate terms   Finally, we should note the use of superordinate terms in both lines 19 and 25:

(6.17)   a. Add the vegetables.
         b. Add the seasonings.

The first of these is as in the target recipe; however, the target does not use a superordinate in line 25. EPICURE uses a superordinate here by virtue of the following information in the knowledge base

(6.18)   ako(pepper, seasoning).
         ako(salt, seasoning).
         ako(nutmeg, seasoning).

and by virtue of the assumption that the hearer knows these facts. Thus, we could generate the target text here by abandoning this assumption; or, perhaps more plausibly, by not looking upon nutmeg as being the same kind of thing as salt and pepper.

---

4. Ideally, we would want to reason from what is known about the constituent ingredients at the time the *adding* event takes place: so, for example, the fact that the ingredients are hot and that they include an appropriate quantity of liquid warrants the use of the name *soup*.

6.5 Conclusions

6.5.1 The Aims Revisited

At the beginning, we set out to present a collection of algorithms and
data structures for the generation of pronouns, anaphoric definite noun
phrases, and *one*-anaphoric phrases by consolidating and advancing upon
what has been done in this area by earlier researchers. In the course of
working toward this goal, we analyzed closely the particular kinds of
referring expressions that appear in a particular domain, and presented
a knowledge representation language that embodied all the relevant distinctions required by the ontology we adopted (chapter 2). We incorporated this ontology into a wider framework for language generation
as a whole (chapter 3), and showed how the knowledge representation
could be successfully used to produce appropriate referring expressions
for a range of complex object types (chapter 4). In so doing, we also
elaborated algorithms for the generation of various kinds of subsequent
reference that paid heed to the complexity of the objects to be described
(chapter 5).

Although there are obviously gaps in the coverage of the work presented, and limitations to the mechanisms proposed, the originally stated
aim of the work has been met. In the course of doing so, we have touched
on a number of different areas. Among the various ideas explored in the
present work, the following are the most important.

- We introduced the the notion of a generalized physical object as
  a way of representing singular entities, mass entities, and entities
  that are sets. The representation also allows parallels to be drawn
  between objects and events, although these parallels are not explored in the present work.

- We adopted the view that planning operators are essentially underspecified events, and used this, in conjunction with a simple
  model of the hearer, to allow us to determine the appropriate level
  of detail at which a given plan should be described.

- We made use of a discourse model that distinguished local and
  global focus; the model adopted was closely tied to a notion of
  discourse structure, which allowed us to make specific claims about
  long-distance pronominalization. There is considerable scope for

further work in testing some of the claims made for the effects of discourse structure on the form of referring expressions.

- We presented a model of the generation of referring expressions that made use of two intermediate levels of representation. Apart from simplifying the processing conceptually, this allowed us to suggest an approach to the generation of *one*-anaphora that overcomes the deficiencies of previous attempts.

Of course, there is much more to be done in all these areas.

6.5.2 Some Possible Extensions

At the beginning of this book, the view was expressed that the way forward for work in language generation required research to be focused on particular issues. We have focused on the generation of referring expressions as a particular issue, but in so doing we have found it necessary to touch on many other issues that arise in the generation task. This section mentions some avenues of possible research for which the present work might serve as a basis.

Generating referring expressions   Although various aspects of the generation of referring expressions have been covered in detail, the problems are by no means solved. The mechanisms we have described possess a number of particular limitations which could fruitfully be addressed. Among the more interesting of these are the following.

- Although the ontology developed in the course of the present work is fairly sophisticated, it has its limitations. In particular, as discussed at the end of chapter 2, the ontology described here is perhaps best viewed as the bottom layer of a multi-layer knowledge representation formalism, where subsequent layers allow for the representation of different perspectives on objects. This would then permit the representation of the kinds of objects (such as blocks and boxes) found in systems which make use of simpler ontologies, but would allow us to do so with much stronger underpinnings. It remains to be seen what the ramifications of this would be for the generation of referring expressions.

- A major limitation of the present work is its avoidance of any complexity of quantification. This limitation is acceptable in the domain of application used in the book, but should be removed to permit wider application of the knowledge representation formalism.

- Related to the above is the potential for further expansion of the grammatical coverage of the system, particularly with respect to determination.

- Another direction in which the mechanisms could be extended is with respect to other kinds of reference: in particular, the representation language could be extended to deal with attributive, non-specific and generic reference. The work of Kronfeld (1990) would be of relevance in this respect.

- Finally, the mechanisms for anaphora generation could be extended to deal with other kinds of anaphora, particularly verb-phrase ellipsis.

Generating connected discourse   Apart from these extensions, there are also a number of other areas which have been touched upon in the present work, and which could be pursued further. Two of particular interest are as follows:

- There is a wealth of issues to be explored in the relationship between discourse structure and discourse generation. To name but a few: what is the most suitable notion of discourse structure for use in discourse generation? How adequate is an account based purely on the *structural* aspects of a discourse? Do the *semantics* of the particular relations between the discourse segments have no effect? What size are discourse segments? Can all forms of reference be explained in structural terms, or do we still require a notion of linear distance? What is the relationship between speech-act theory and discourse intention?

- The system described here involves generating natural language from plans. There are many other back ends one might use to supply input to the generation process, but even within this single area there are many unresolved questions. In particular, the mechanisms could be extended to deal with nonlinear planners, and to deal with more complex planning systems which permit iteration and the use of conditionals.

The present work has demonstrated at least a few of the ingredients necessary for fluent natural language generation. However, as with all research, we have found many more questions than answers: there are plenty of leftovers waiting to be consumed.

Bibliography

A. Akmajian and A. Lehrer 1976. NP-like quantifiers and the problem of determining the head of an NP. *Linguistic Analysis* 2: 395–414.

J. F. Allen 1983. Recognizing intentions from natural language utterances. In M. Brady and R. C. Berwick (eds.) *Computational Models of Discourse.* MIT Press.

J. F. Allen and C. R. Perrault 1978. Participating in dialogues: Understanding via plan deduction. In Proceedings of the Second National Conference of the Canadian Society for the Study of Computational Intelligence, Toronto.

J. F. Allen and C. R. Perrault 1980. Analyzing intention in dialogues. *Artificial Intelligence* 15: 143–178.

D. E. Appelt 1982. Planning Natural-Language Utterances to Satisfy Multiple Goals. Technical note 259, SRI International, Menlo Park, California.

D. E. Appelt 1985. *Planning English Sentences.* Cambridge University Press.

D. E. Appelt and A. Kronfeld 1987. A computational model of referring. In Proceedings of the Tenth International Joint Conference on Artificial Intelligence, Milan.

J. L. Austin 1962. *How To Do Things With Words.* Clarendon Press.

E. Bach 1986. The algebra of events. *Linguistics and Philosophy* 9: 5–16.

R. Bartsch 1975. Subcategorization of adnominal and adverbial modifiers. In E. L. Keenan (ed.) *Formal Semantics of Natural Language.* Cambridge University Press.

R. Bernardo 1977. The Cognitive Relevance of the Sentence. Master's thesis, University of California, Berkeley.

D. Bobrow and T. Winograd 1977. An overview of KRL-0, a knowledge representation language. *Cognitive Science* 1: 3–46.

R. J. Brachman 1979. Taxonomy, descriptions, and individuals in natural language understanding. In Proceedings of the 17th Annual Meeting of the Association for Computational Linguistics, University of California, San Diego.

D. S. Brée and R. A. Smit 1986. Linking propositions. In Proceedings of the 11th International Conference on Computational Linguistics, Bonn.

B. C. Bruce 1975a. Belief Systems and Language Understanding. Report 2973, Bolt, Beranek and Newman Inc., Cambridge, Mass.

B. C. Bruce 1975b. Case systems for natural language. *Artificial Intelligence* 6: 327–360.

B. Butterworth 1975. Hesitation and semantic planning in speech. *Journal of Psycholinguistic Research* 4: 75–87.

J. Calder, E. Klein and H. Zeevat 1988. Unification categorial grammar: A concise, extendable grammar for natural language processing. In Proceedings of the 12th International Conference on Computational Linguistics, Budapest.

L. Carlson 1981. Aspect and quantification. In P. Tedeschi and A. Zaenen (eds.) *Syntax and Semantics*, volume 14: *Tense and Aspect*. Academic Press.

D. Carter 1987. *Interpreting Anaphors in Natural Language Texts*. Ellis Horwood.

W. L. Chafe 1977. Creativity in verbalization and its implications for the nature of stored knowledge. In R. O. Freedle (ed.) *Discourse Production and Comprehension*, volume 1. Ablex.

W. L. Chafe 1979. The flow of thought and the flow of language. In T. Givon (ed.) *Syntax and Semantics*, volume 12: *Discourse and Syntax*. Academic Press.

E. Charniak and D. McDermott 1985. *Introduction to Artificial Intelligence*. Addison-Wesley.

H. H. Clark and C. R. Marshall 1981. Definite reference and mutual knowledge. In A. K. Joshi, B. L. Webber, and I. A. Sag (eds.) *Elements of Discourse Understanding*. Cambridge University Press.

W. F. Clocksin and C. S. Mellish 1981. *Programming in Prolog*. Springer-Verlag.

P. R. Cohen 1978. On Knowing What to Say: Planning Speech Acts. Technical report 118, University of Toronto.

P. R. Cohen 1981. The need for identification as a planned action. In Proceedings of the Seventh International Joint Conference on Artificial Intelligence, University of British Columbia, Vancouver, B.C.

P. R. Cohen 1984a. The pragmatics of referring and the modality of communication. *American Journal of Computational Linguistics* 10: 97–146.

P. R. Cohen and C. R. Perrault 1979. Elements of a plan-based theory of speech acts. *Cognitive Science* 3: 177–212.

P. R. Cohen and H. J. Levesque 1980. Speech acts and the recognition of shared plans. In Proceedings of the Third Conference of the Canadian Society for Computational Studies of Intelligence, Victoria, B.C.

R. Cohen 1984b. A computational theory of the function of clue words in argument understanding. In Proceedings of the 10th International Conference on Computational Linguistics and the 22nd Annual Meeting of the Association for Computational Linguistics, Stanford University.

J. H. Danks 1977. Producing ideas and sentences. In S. Rosenberg (ed.) *Sentence Production: Development in Research and Theory*. Erlbaum.

L. Danlos 1987. *The Linguistic Basis of Text Generation*. Cambridge University Press.

A. Davey 1978. *Discourse Production*. Edinburgh University Press.

K. De Smedt 1990. Incremental sentence generation: a computer model of grammatical encoding. Technical report 90-01, Nijmegen Institute of Cognitiou Research and Technology.

K. De Smedt and G. Kempen 1987. Incremental sentence production, self-correction and coordination. In G. Kempen (ed.) *Natural Language Generation: New Results in Artificial Intelligence, Psychology and Linguistics.* Martinus Nijhoff.

A. Eisele and J. Dörre 1986. A lexical functional grammar system in Prolog. In Proceedings of the 11th International Conference on Computational Linguistics, Bonn.

G. Fauconnier 1985. *Mental Spaces: Aspects of Meaning Construction in Natural Language.* MIT Press.

R. E. Fikes and N. J. Nilsson 1971. STRIPS: A new approach to the application of theorem proving to problem solving. *Artificial Intelligence* 2: 189–208.

C. Fillmore 1968. The case for case. In E. Bach and R. T. Harms (eds.) *Universals in Linguistic Theory.* Holt, Rinehart and Winston.

G. Gazdar, E. Klein, G. Pullum, and I. A. Sag 1985. *Generalized Phrase Structure Grammar.* Blackwell.

B. A. Goodman 1985. Repairing reference identification failures by relaxation. In Proceedings of the 23rd Annual Meeting of the Association for Computational Linguistics, University of Chicago.

B. A. Goodman 1986. Reference identification and reference identification failures. *Computational Linguistics* 12: 273–305.

H. P. Grice 1975. Logic and Conversation. In P. Cole and J. L. Morgan (eds.) *Syntax and Semantics*, volume 3: *Speech Acts*. Academic Press.

J. E. Grimes 1978. Topic levels. In Theoretical Issues in Natural Language Processing–2, University of Illinois.

J. E. Grimes 1982. Reference spaces in text. In Proceedings of the 51st Nobel Symposium, Stockholm.

B. J. Grosz 1977. The Representation and Use of Focus in Dialogue. Technical note 151, SRI International, Menlo Park, California.

B. J. Grosz and I. A. Sag 1981. Focusing and description in natural language dialogs. In A. K. Joshi, B. L. Webber, and I. A. Sag (eds.) *Elements of Discourse Understanding.* Cambridge University Press.

B. J. Grosz, A. K. Joshi, and S. Weinstein 1983. Providing a unified account of definite noun phrases in discourse. In Proceedings of the 21st Annual Meeting of the Association for Computational Linguistics, Massachusetts Institute of Technology.

B. J. Grosz and C. L. Sidner 1985. Discourse structure and the proper treatment of interruptions. In Proceedings of the Ninth International Joint Conference on Artificial Intelligence, University of California, Los Angeles.

B. J. Grosz and C. L. Sidner 1986. Attention, intentions, and the structure of discourse. *Computational Linguistics* 12: 175–204.

R. Guindon 1985. Anaphora resolution: Short-term memory and focusing. In Proceedings of the 23rd Annual Meeting of the Association for Computational Linguistics, University of Chicago.

M. A. K. Halliday 1973. *Explorations in the Functions of Language*. Edward Arnold.

M. A. K. Halliday 1985. *An Introduction to Functional Grammar*. Edward Arnold.

M. A. K. Halliday and R. Hasan 1976. *Cohesion in English*. Longman.

K. J. Hammond 1986. CHEF: A model of case-based planning. In Proceedings of the 5th Annual Meeting of the American Association for Artificial Intelligence, Philadelphia.

J. Hankamer and I. A. Sag 1976. Deep and surface anaphora. *Linguistic Inquiry* 7: 391–426.

P. J. Hayes 1974. Some problems and non-problems in representation theory. In Proceedings of the Summer Conference of the Society for the Study of Artificial Intelligence and the Simulation of Behaviour, University of Sussex.

P. J. Hayes 1978. The naive physics manifesto. In D. Michie and B. Meltzer (eds.) *Machine Intelligence 4*. Edinburgh University Press.

P. J. Hayes 1985. The second naive physics manifesto. In R. J. Brachman and H. J. Levesque (eds.) *Readings in Knowledge Representation*. Morgan Kaufmann.

P. Hellwig 1986. Dependency unification grammar. In Proceedings of the 11th International Conference on Computational Linguistics, Bonn.

T. Herrmann and M. Laucht 1976. On multiple verbal codability of objects. *Psychological Research* 38: 355–368.

G. Hirst 1981a. *Anaphora in Natural Language Understanding*. Springer-Verlag.

G. Hirst 1981b. Discourse-oriented anaphora resolution: A review. *American Journal of Computational Linguistics* 7: 85–98.

J. R. Hobbs 1978. Resolving pronoun references. *Lingua* 44: 311–338.

J. R. Hobbs and D. A. Evans 1979. Conversation as Planned Behavior. Technical note 203, SRI International, Menlo Park, California.

J. R. Hobbs 1985. Ontological promiscuity. In Proceedings of the 23rd Annual Meeting of the Association for Computational Linguistics, University of Chicago.

E. H. Hovy 1990. Unresolved issues in paragraph planning. In R. Dale, C. S. Mellish, and M. Zock (eds.) *Current Research in Natural Language Generation*. Academic Press.

A. Jameson and W. Wahlster 1982. User modelling in anaphora generation: ellipsis and definite description. In Proceedings of the Fifth European Conference on Artificial Intelligence, Pisa.

P. N. Johnson-Laird 1983. *Mental Models*. Cambridge University Press.

A. K. Joshi 1983. Factoring recursion and dependencies: An aspect of tree-adjoining grammars (TAG) and a comparison of some formal properties of TAGs, GPSGs, PLGs, and LFGs. In Proceedings of the 21st Annual Meeting of the Association for Computational Linguistics, Massachusetts Institute of Technology.

A. K. Joshi and K. Vijay-Shankar 1985. Some computational properties of tree adjoining grammars. In Proceedings of the 23rd Annual Meeting of the Association for Computational Linguistics, University of Chicago.

C. Jullien and J. Marty 1989. Plan revision in person-machine dialogue. In Proceedings of the 4th Conference of the European Chapter of the Association for Computational Linguistics, Manchester.

J. A. W. Kamp 1975. Two theories about adjectives. In E. L. Keenan (ed.) *Formal Semantics of Natural Language*. Cambridge University Press.

J. A. W. Kamp 1981. A theory of truth and semantic representation. *Formal Methods in the Study of Language* 136: 277–322.

R. N. Kantor 1977. The Management and Comprehension of Discourse Connection by Pronouns in English. Ph.D. Thesis, Ohio State University.

R. F. Karlin 1988. Defining the semantics of verbal modifiers in the domain of cooking tasks. In Proceedings of the 26th Annual Meeting of the Association for Computational Linguistics, State University of New York.

L. Karttunen 1976. Discourse referents. In J. McCawley (ed.) *Syntax and Semantics*, Volume 7. Academic Press.

L. Karttunen 1986. D-PATR: A development environment for unification-based grammars. In Proceedings of the 11th International Conference on Computational Linguistics, Bonn.

M. Kay 1975. Syntactic processing and functional sentence perspective. In Theoretical Issues in Natural Language Processing, Massachusetts Institute of Technology.

E. L. Keenan and L. M. Faltz 1978. *Logical Types for Natural Language*. UCLA Occasional Papers in Linguistics.

G. Kempen and E. Hoenkamp 1987. An incremental procedural grammar for sentence formulation. *Cognitive Science* 11: 201–258.

A. Kobsa, J. Allgayer, C. Reddig, N. Reithinger, D. Schmauks, K. Harbusch, and W. Wahlster 1986. Combining deictic gestures and natural language for referent identification. In Proceedings of the 11th International Conference on Computational Linguistics, Bonn.

A. Kronfeld 1990. *Reference and Computation: An Essay in Applied Philosophy of Language*. Cambridge University Press.

G. Leech and J. Svartvik 1975. *A Communicative Grammar of English*. Longman.

A. Lehrer 1969. Semantic cuisine. *Journal of Linguistics* 5: 39–55.

A. Lehrer 1972. Cooking vocabularies and the culinary triangle of Levi-Strauss. *Anthropological Linguistics* 14: 155–171.

W. J. M. Levelt 1989. *Speaking: From Intention to Articulation*. MIT Press.

C. Linde 1979. Focus of attention and the choice of pronouns in discourse. In T. Givon (ed.) *Syntax and Semantics*, Volume 12: *Discourse and Syntax*. Academic Press.

J. R. Lindsley 1975. Producing simple utterances: How far ahead do we plan? *Cognitive Psychology* 7: 1–19.

J. R. Lindsley 1976. Producing simple utterances: Details of the planning process. *Journal of Psycholinguistic Research* 5: 331–354.

G. Link 1983. The logical analysis of plurals and mass terms: A lattice-theoretical approach. In R. Bauerle, C. Schwarze, and A. von Stechow (eds.) *Meaning, Use and Interpretation of Language*. Walter de Gruyter.

J. Lyons 1968. *Introduction to Theoretical Linguistics*. Cambridge University Press.

P. MacNeilage 1973. Linguistic units and speech production. Presented at the 85th Meeting of the Acoustical Society of America, Boston.

W. C. Mann 1983. An overview of the Nigel text generation grammar. In Proceedings of the 21st Annual Meeting of the Association for Computational Linguistics, Massachusetts Institute of Technology.

W. C. Mann, M. Bates, B. J. Grosz, D. D. McDonald, K. R. McKeown, and W. Swartout 1982. Text generation. *American Journal of Computational Linguistics* 8: 62–69.

W. C. Mann and J. Moore 1982. Computer generation of multiparagraph English text. *American Journal of Computational Linguistics* 7: 17–29.

W. C. Mann and S. Thompson 1986. Rhetorical Structure Theory: Descripton and Construction of Text. Reprint 86-174, USC Information Sciences Institute, Marina Del Rey, California.

W. C. Mann and S. A. Thompson 1988. Rhetorical structure theory: Toward a functional theory of text organization. *Text* 8: 243–281.

C. M. I. M. Matthiessen 1981. A grammar and a lexicon for a text-production system. In Proceedings of the 19th Annual Meeting of the Association for Computational Linguistics, Stanford University.

C. M. I. M. Matthiessen 1984. How to Make Grammatical Choices in Text Generation. Reprint 83-120, USC Information Sciences Institute, Marina Del

Rey, California.

C. M. I. M. Matthiessen and R. Kasper 1987. Systemic Grammar and Functional Unification Grammar and Representational Issues in Systemic Functional Grammar. Reprint 87-179, USC Information Sciences Institute, Marina Del Rey, California.

B. Mayo 1961. Objects, events, and complementarity. *Philosophical Review* 70: 340–361.

K. F. McCoy 1985. Correcting object-related misconceptions. Ph.D. thesis, University of Pennsylvania.

D. D. McDonald 1977. Linguistic Reasoning During Language Generation. Technical report 404, MIT Artificial Intelligence Laboratory.

D. D. McDonald 1979. Steps Towards a Psycholinguistic Model of Language Production. Working paper 193, MIT Artificial Intelligence Laboratory.

D. D. McDonald 1980a. A linear-time model of language production: Some psycholinguistic implications. In Proceedings of the 18th Annual Meeting of the Association for Computational Linguistics, University of Pennsylvania.

D. D. McDonald 1980b. Natural Language Generation as a Process of Decision-Making under Constraints. Ph.D. thesis, Department of Computer Science and Electrical Engineering, MIT.

D. D. McDonald and J. D. Pustejovsky 1985. TAGs as a grammatical formalism for generation. In Proceedings of the 23rd Annual Meeting of the Association for Computational Linguistics, University of Chicago.

K. R. McKeown 1982. Generating Natural Language Text in Response to Questions about Database Structure. Ph.D. thesis, University of Pennsylvania.

K. R. McKeown 1985. *Text Generation: Using Discourse Strategies and Focus Constraints to Generate Natural Language Text.* Cambridge University Press.

C. S. Mellish 1987. Implementing Systemic Classification by Unification. Presented at Workshop on Natural Language Processing, Unification and Grammatical Formalisms, Stirling.

C. S. Mellish 1988. Natural language generation from plans. In M. Zock and G. Sabah (eds.) *Advances in Natural Language Generation*, volume 1: *An Interdisciplinary Perspective.* Pinter.

C. S. Mellish and R. Evans 1989. Natural language generation from plans. *Computational Linguistics* 15: 233–249.

M. W. Meteer 1990. Abstract linguistic resources for text planning. In Proceedings of the Fifth International Natural Language Generation Workshop, Dawson, Pennsylvania.

J. A. Moore and W. C. Mann 1979. A snapshot of KDS, a knowledge delivery system. In Proceedings of the 17th Annual Meeting of the Association for

Computational Linguistics, University of California, San Diego.

J. W. Ney 1983. Optionality and choice in the selection of order of adjectives in English. *General Linguistics* 23: 94–128.

J. Oberlander and R. Dale 1991. Generating expressions referring to eventualities. In Proceedings of the 13th Annual Conference of the Cognitve Science Society, University of Chicago.

E. Ochs 1979. Planned and unplanned discourse. In T. Givon (ed.) *Syntax and Semantics*, Volume 12: *Discourse and Syntax*. Academic Press.

C. L. Paris 1988. Planning a text: Can we and how should we modularize this process? In Proceedings of the AAAI Workshop on Text Planning and Realization, St. Paul, Minnesota.

F. J. Pelletier (ed.) 1979. *Mass Terms: Some Philosophical Problems*. Reidel.

L. Polanyi and R. Scha 1984. A syntactic approach to discourse semantics. In Proceedings of the 10th International Conference on Computational Linguistics and the 22nd Annual Meeting of the Association for Computational Linguistics, Stanford University.

L. Polanyi 1985. A theory of discourse structure and discourse coherence. In Papers from the General Session at the Twenty-First Regional Meeting of the Chicago Linguistics Society, Chicago.

L. Polanyi 1986. The Linguistic Discourse Model: Towards a Formal Theory of Discourse Structure. Report 6409, Bolt, Beranek and Newman Inc., Cambridge, Mass.

F. P. Popowich 1988. Reflexives and Tree Unification Grammar. Ph.D. thesis, Centre for Cognitive Science, University of Edinburgh.

E. Prince 1981. A taxonomy of given-new information. In P. Cole (ed.) *Radical Pragmatics*. Academic Press.

H. Reichenbach 1947. *Elements of Symbolic Logic*. Macmillan.

H. Reichgelt 1986. Reference and Quantification in the Cognitive View of Language. Ph.D. thesis, School of Epistemics, University of Edinburgh.

R. Reichman 1978. Conversational coherency. *Cognitive Science* 2: 283–327.

R. Reichman 1981. Plain Speaking: A Theory and Grammar of Spontaneous Discourse. Report 4681, Bolt, Beranek and Newman Inc., Cambridge, Mass.

R. Reichman 1985. *Getting Computers to Talk Like You and Me*. MIT Press.

E. B. Reiter 1990. Generating Appropriate Natural Language Object Descriptions. Ph.D. thesis, Harvard University.

N. Reithinger 1987. Generating referring expressions and pointing gestures. In G. Kempen (ed.) *Natural Language Generation: New Results in Artificial Intelligence, Psychology and Linguistics*. Martinus Nijhoff.

E. Rosch, C. Mervis, W. Gray, D. Johnson and P. Boyes-Braem 1976. Basic objects in natural categories. *Cognitive Psychology* 8: 382–439.

R. Rubinoff 1990. Natural Language Generation as an Intelligent Activity. Technical report MS-CIS-90-32, Department of Computer and Information Science, University of Pennsylvania.

E. D. Sacerdoti 1974. Planning in a hierarchy of abstraction spaces. *Artificial Intelligence* 5: 115–135.

E. D. Sacerdoti 1977. *A Structure for Plans and Behavior*. North-Holland.

A. J. Sanford and S. C. Garrod 1981. *Understanding Written Language*. Wiley.

E. Schuster 1988. Anaphoric reference to events and actions: a representation and its advantages. In Proceedings of the 12th International Conference on Computational Linguistics, Budapest.

D. R. Scott and C. S. Souza 1990. Getting the message across in RST-based text generation. In R. Dale, C. S. Mellish, and M. Zock (eds.) *Current Research in Natural Language Generation*. Academic Press.

J. Searle 1969. *Speech Acts: An Essay in the Philosophy of Language*. Cambridge University Press.

E. O. Selkirk 1977. Some remarks on noun phrase structure. In P. W. Culicover, T. Wasow, and A. Akmajian (eds.) *Formal Syntax*. Academic Press.

S. M. Shieber 1986. *An Introduction to Unification-Based Approaches to Grammar*. University of Chicago Press.

S. M. Shieber 1988. A Uniform Architecture for Parsing and Generation. Technical note 437, SRI International, Menlo Park, California.

P. Sibun 1990. The local organization of text. In Proceedings of the Fifth International Natural Language Generation Workshop, Dawson, Pennsylvania.

C. L. Sidner 1979. Towards a Computational Theory of Definite Anaphora Comprehension in English Discourse. Technical report 537, MIT Artificial Intelligence Laboratory.

W. R. Swartout 1983. XPLAIN: A System for Creating and Explaining Expert Consulting Programs. Reprint 83-4, USC Information Sciences Institute, Marina Del Rey, California.

A. Tate 1976. Project Planning Using a Hierarchic Non-Linear Planner. Research report 245, Department of Artificial Intelligence, University of Edinburgh.

A. Tate 1985. A review of knowledge-based planning techniques. *Knowledge Engineering Review* 2: 4–16.

I. Taylor 1969. Content and structure in sentence production. *Journal of Verbal Learning and Verbal Behavior* 8: 170–175.

H. S. Thompson 1977. Strategy and tactics in language production. In Papers from the Thirteenth Regional Meeting of the Chicago Linguistics Society, Chicago.

E. P. K. Tsang 1986. Plan generation in a temporal frame. In Proceedings of the Seventh European Conference on Artificial Intelligence, Brighton.

H. Uszkoreit 1986. Categorial unification grammars. In Proceedings of the 11th International Conference on Computational Linguistics, Bonn.

Z. Vendler 1968. *Adjectives and Nominalization*. Mouton.

W. Wahlster, E. André, W. Graf and T. Rist 1991. Designing illustrated texts: How language production is influenced by graphics generation. In Proceedings of the 5th Conference of the European Chapter of the Association for Computational Linguistics, Berlin.

B. L. Webber 1979. *A Formal Approach to Discourse Anaphora*. Garland.

B. L. Webber 1988. Discourse deixis: Reference to discourse segments. In Proceedings of the 26th Annual Meeting of the Association for Computational Linguistics, State University of New York.

J. L. Weiner 1980. BLAH: A system which explains its reasoning. *Artificial Intelligence* 15: 19–48.

T. Winograd 1972. *Understanding Natural Language*. Academic Press.

T. Winograd 1983. *Language as a Cognitive Process*, volume 1: *Syntax*. Addison-Wesley.

T. Wykes 1981. Inference and children's comprehension of pronouns. *Journal of Experimental Child Psychology* 32: 264–278.

H. Zeevat, E. Klein and J. Calder 1987. An introduction to unification categorial grammar. In N. J. Haddock, E. Klein, and G. Morrill (eds.) *Edinburgh Working Papers in Cognitive Science*, volume 1: *Categorial Grammar, Unification Grammar, and Parsing*. Centre for Cognitive Science, University of Edinburgh.

E. Zemach 1979. Four ontologies. In F. J. Pelletier (ed.) *Mass Terms: Some Philosophical Problems*.

I. Zukerman 1986. Comprehension-driven generation of meta-technical utterances in math tutoring. In Proceedings of the 5th Annual Meeting of the American Association for Artificial Intelligence, Philadelphia.

Name Index

Subject Index